Dr. Richter's
Fresh
Produce Guide

©2000 Try-Foods International, Inc.
All rights reserved. No part of this book may be reproduced or transmitted in any form or by any means,
electronic or mechanical, including photocopying, recording or by any information storage and
retrieval system, without permission in writing from the Publisher.

Try-Foods International, Inc.
207 Semoran Commerce Place
Apopka, Florida 32703

Printed in the United States of America

To reorder call 1-800-421-8871 • Visit our website: www.tryfoods.com

We know that fresh fruits and vegetables taste great. Who doesn't look forward to luscious, ripe tomatoes in summer or pumpkin pie in the fall? It is no coincidence that people just love to eat such nutritious foods.

As a doctor, I recognize that medicines and treatments are just a small part of the battle for good health. Preventive medicine is the key – achieving a harmonious balance between your physical and mental health. Good nutrition and a healthy lifestyle are essential for personal well-being.

Fruits and vegetables provide fundamental roles in human health – nutrients, vitamins, minerals and medicinal benefits. Uniquely, they contain thousands of compounds that help our bodies function properly, including antioxidants that fight diseases...even cancer. Eating fresh fruits and vegetables is far better than taking supplements offering the same nutrients. Produce is easy to digest; so calories from fruits and vegetables "go easy" on the body. Many new, beautiful cookbooks are available, featuring the fruits and vegetables outlined in this guide. Keep it handy for reference.

In this book, we provide education in the wonderful variety of produce available in your market today – some tried and true, some newly available year-round in North American markets. Interest in different varieties of fruits and vegetables is skyrocketing. Mainstream and specialty grocers provide fresh produce of an ever-increasing variety for consumers. The produce pictures in this book help the adventurous shopper identify unfamiliar varieties with anticipation of trying something new.

Fresh produce has it all - great taste, never-ending variety, and health benefits beyond measure. Your doctor would agree – eat well and be healthy. Bon appetit!

Henry J Richter

Henry Richter, MD

Try-Foods International, Inc. expresses their gratitude to the following companies and organizations who contributed products, photographs and data for the production of this book.

Brooks Tropicals
California Tree Fruit Agreement
Florida Department of Citrus
Freida's, Inc.
Idaho-Eastern Oregon Onion Committee
Northwest Cherry Growers
Produce Marketing Association
Petoseed Company, Inc.
Washington State Fruit Commission

To order additional copies of this book, call 1-800-421-8871.

Table of contents

Fruits & Vegetables

A World of Choices for Busy Lifestyles

This handy guide will help you make smart selections from the almost endless variety of produce available in your supermarket today. The in-store produce experts will also be happy to answer your questions about selecting and preparing fruits and vegetables—just ask!

Read on for some helpful hints and nutrition information to make choosing fruits and vegetables for you and your family quick and easy. Fruits and vegetables are naturally delicious, nutritious and simple to prepare, so here's to your health!

Experience the difference

Experimenting with exotic fruits and vegetables is an easy way to add color, interest and excitement to your family's meals.

Tastes from around the world

You can enjoy a taste of the Orient with gai lon and khan choy from the Far East, flavors from the tropics when you try carambola and manzano bananas, and much more—there's a veritable garden variety of unusual and delicious palate-pleasers at your grocery store year-round.

A glowing report

Looking good and feeling good are 2 positive results from including fruits and vegetables in your diet; produce is nature's energy source, fueling a healthy inner glow that's the unmistakable result of eating well and keeping fit.

The healthy choice

The vitamins and nutrients in produce promote healthy skin, teeth and gums, as well as many internal functions we can't see, such as proper connective tissue development, cell growth and nerve impulses.

Refueling

In addition to revving up your energy level, eating produce has other health benefits as well: A high-fiber, low-fat diet including lots of fruits and vegetables has been found to lower the risk of certain types of cancer, and to decrease the risk of high blood pressure, heart disease, stroke and the most common form of diabetes.

How low can you go

Almost all produce is naturally low in calories, fat and sodium, and the fiber many contain is helpful in keeping your digestive system healthy.

Respect authority

Leading health authorities agree that fruits and vegetables are an essential part of everyone's daily diet, and that eating 5 servings a day is important for maintaining good health.

When it comes to produce and nutrition, you already know a lot of the basics. If you want something with vitamin C, you head for an orange, right? But did you know that a kiwifruit ranks high in vitamin C, too? And then there's fiber. Just about everyone knows that prunes are a good source, but you can also find plenty of fiber in raspberries. Read on for a sampling of good sources of vitamins and other important nutritional values — some may surprise you.

High in Fiber

blackberries	grapefruit	kiwifruit	oranges	raspberries

Fruits and vegetables containing fiber do so much more than help to maintain a healthy digestive tract. Studies have shown that diets high in fiber (and low in fat) help to prevent high blood pressure, heart disease, stroke, certain types of cancer and the most common form of diabetes. A fiber-rich diet may also protect against colon cancer.

Top 12 High in Vitamin A

apricots	cantaloupes	carrots	collard greens	hot chile peppers	leaf lettuce
romaine lettuce	mangoes	nectarines	peaches	spinach	sweet potatoes

The old saying about carrots being good for your eyes is true. Carrots, like the other fruits and vegetables listed here, are high in vitamin A, which promotes good vision, especially in dim light. Vitamin A also helps to form and maintain healthy skin, teeth, mucous membranes, and skeletal and soft tissue. Some research indicates that vitamin A may increase resistance to infection in children.

Top 12 High in Vitamin C

broccoli	cabbage	cantaloupes	cauliflower	grapefruit	green peppers
brussel sprouts	kiwifruit	oranges	papayas	strawberries	mustard greens

This essential vitamin has multiple benefits: keeping teeth and gums healthy, aiding in iron absorption, maintaining normal connective tissue and healing wounds. Vitamin C may also help in preventing cataracts.

High in Iron

white beans	spinach

Good Source of Iron

chickpea	lentils	lima beans	pink bean	small white bean	winged beans

Iron is good for the blood; in particular, it's essential to the formation of hemoglobin, which carries oxygen in the blood, and myoglobin, which carries oxygen in muscles. To help your body absorb iron from fruits and vegetables, try to include a food item high in vitamin C in the same meal.

Top 12 Sodium-Free Favorites

apples	avocados	bananas	bell peppers	cucumbers	eggplant
grapefruit	kiwifruit	mushrooms	oranges	potatoes	summer squash

For those watching their sodium intake to reduce the risks of hypertension or high blood pressure, there is a wide variety of delicious, sodium-free fruits and vegetables that can be included in a sodium-free or low-sodium diet plan.

Cruciferous Vegetables

broccoli	Brussels sprouts	cabbage	cauliflower	kale	turnips

So named for the cross-like formation of the flowers produced by these types of plants, cruciferous vegetables are helpful in the prevention of certain types of cancer.

Top 12 Good Sources of Folate

asparagus	endive	lima beans	pigeon bean	pinto bean	strawberries
chickpea	lentils	mustard greens	pink bean	spinach	white bean

Essential to the growth and function of new cells, folate, also known as folacin or folic acid, is important in every diet, but especially for pregnant women. Folic acid may lower the rate of some birth defects such as spina bifida. It may also be helpful in the prevention of cancer of the cervix.

High & dry

As a general rule, it's a good idea to store produce unwashed until ready to use (the water from washing can encourage bacterial growth and speed decay). Wait until just before preparation to wash most produce.

An apple a day

To ripen stone fruit, as well as many other unripe fruits such as kiwis, place fruit in a loosely closed paper bag at room temperature. To further speed up the process, add an apple to the mix. The apple will release ethylene gas, which accelerates ripening. And here's another apple idea: To keep a cake fresher longer, add half an apple to the cake tin.

Cut to the chase

You can quickly slice small, firm mushrooms with an egg slicer.

When the time's ripe

Bananas ripen best when hanging, instead of simply resting on the kitchen counter. Instead of buying a special hanger, make your own by threading a piece of yarn or string through a banana bunch, and then looping it over a cabinet knob.

The core of the matter

To quickly and easily remove the core of a head of iceberg lettuce, hold the head core side down over the kitchen counter. Then firmly strike the core against the counter. It should then remove with a gentle pull. And remember, never cut lettuce — tear it. Cutting with a knife bruises and discolors the edges of lettuce.

Salad days

To allow greens to fully crisp before serving, wash thoroughly under cold running water, shake off the excess moisture, then blot with paper towels. Refrigerate an hour or so until ready to prepare.

There's the rub

A quick fix to onion or garlic odor on your hands: Rub them with a lemon wedge and rinse in cold water.

Potato panacea

Oops — if you've added too much salt to a soup or sauce, add half a peeled potato to the mix and cook for another 5 minutes or so. Remove the potato and discard.

Too cold for comfort

Never store tomatoes in the refrigerator; the chilly temperature destroys the flavor.

Citrus secrets

One medium lemon yields 2–3 tablespoons of juice; it takes 5–8 lemons to make a cup of juice. One lemon rind will give you about 1 tablespoon of grated peel; the rind of 1 medium orange will yield 2 tablespoons of grated peel. You can squeeze about 2–3 tablespoons of juice from a medium orange; 3–4 of them will deliver a cup of juice. (An extra hint: grate the peel before juicing the fruit and freeze for later use in recipes calling for zest.)

How sweet it is

Try poaching fresh fruit with corn syrup instead of sugar; corn syrup gives the fruit a bright appearance, and makes it fresher-tasting than sugar.

Oil's well

Instead of butter or margarine, try using a little olive oil on steamed vegetables. You'll get great flavor without all the extra fat.

Measure for measure

If a recipe calls for dried herbs, pick up some fresh herbs instead, then triple the quantity specified and enjoy the enhanced flavor.

Garlic power

The flavor of 1 clove of garlic is 10 times stronger when pushed through a garlic press than when it's minced with a sharp knife. More of the clove's essential oils are released when a garlic press is used. Keep this in mind when using garlic to flavor sauces and such. One clove of minced garlic yields about 1 teaspoon.

Soup's on

Waste not, want not: After cooking fruits or vegetables, use the nutrient-rich water as a base for soup.

**Wherever possible, FDA-approved nutritional information has been provided.
If this data is absent, please refer to the nutritional information
for a similar variety of the same item.**

**The nutritional values and information are approximate and have been provided because of consumer interest.
U.S. and Canadian nutritional data differs slightly because of differences in standard sizes of produce.
Try-Foods International, Inc. can make no warranty of their accuracy.**

COMMODITY	JAN	FEB	MAR	APR	MAY	JUN	JUL	AUG	SEP	OCT	NOV	DEC
Alfalfa Sprouts												
Apples												
Apricots												
Artichokes												
Asian Pears												
Avocados												
Bananas												
Beans												
Bean Sprouts												
Beets												
Belgian Endive												
Bitter Melons												
Blackberries												
Black-eyed Peas												
Blood Oranges												
Blueberries												
Bok Choy												
Boniato												
Breadfruit												
Broccoli												
Brussels Sprouts												
Burro Bananas												
Cabbage												
Calabaza												
Cantaloupe												
Carambola/Star Fruit												
Carrots												
Cauliflower												
Celery												
Chayote												
Cherimoyas												
Cherries												
Chinese Cabbage												
Chinese Long Beans												
Collard Greens												
Corn												
Cranberries												
Cucumbers												
Daikon												
Eggplant												
English Cucumber												
Escarole												
Feijoas												
Flowering Kale/Salad Savoy												
Garlic												
Ginger Root												
Grapefruit												
Grapes												
Guavas												
Honeydew												
Horned Melon/Kiwano												
Japanese Cucumbers												
Jicama												
Kale												
Kiwifruit												
Kohlrabi												
Kumquats												

Produce Marketing Association (PMA) availability guide

COMMODITY	JAN	FEB	MAR	APR	MAY	JUN	JUL	AUG	SEP	OCT	NOV	DEC
Leeks	●	●	●	●	●	●	●	●	●	●	●	●
Lemons	●	●	●	●	●	●	●	●	●	●	●	●
Lettuce, Iceberg	●	●	●	●	●	●	●	●	●	●	●	●
Lettuce, Leaf	●	●	●	●	●	●	●	●	●	●	●	●
Lettuce, Romaine	●	●	●	●	●	●	●	●	●	●	●	●
Limes	●	●	●	●	●	●	●	●	●	●	●	●
Malanga	●	●	●	●	●	●	●	●	●			
Mamey Sapotes				●	●	●	●	●	●			
Mango					●	●	●	●	●			
Melons	●	●	●	●	●	●	●	●	●	●	●	●
Mushrooms	●	●	●	●	●	●	●	●	●	●	●	●
Nectarines					●	●	●	●	●	●		
Okra	●	●	●	●	●	●	●	●	●	●	●	●
Onions, Dry	●	●	●	●	●	●	●	●	●	●	●	●
Onions, Green	●	●	●	●	●	●	●	●	●	●	●	●
Oranges	●	●	●	●	●	●	●	●	●	●	●	●
Papaya	●	●	●	●	●	●	●	●	●	●	●	●
Passion Fruit	●	●	●	●	●	●	●	●	●	●	●	●
Peaches					●	●	●	●	●	●		
Pearl Onions	●	●	●	●	●	●	●	●	●	●	●	●
Pears	●	●	●	●	●	●	●	●	●	●	●	●
Pepino Melons	●	●	●	●	●					●	●	●
Peppers, Bell	●	●	●	●	●	●	●	●	●	●	●	●
Peppers, Chili	●	●	●	●	●	●	●	●	●	●	●	●
Persimmons	●	●								●	●	●
Pineapple	●	●	●	●	●	●	●	●	●	●	●	●
Plantains	●	●	●	●	●	●	●	●	●	●	●	●
Plums					●	●	●	●	●	●		
Pomegranate								●	●	●	●	●
Potatoes	●	●	●	●	●	●	●	●	●	●	●	●
Prickly/Cactus Pears						●	●	●	●	●	●	●
Pummelos	●	●	●									
Radicchio	●	●	●	●	●	●	●	●	●	●	●	●
Radishes	●	●	●	●	●	●	●	●	●	●	●	●
Rapini/Broccoli Raab	●	●	●	●	●	●	●	●	●	●	●	●
Raspberries	●	●	●	●	●	●	●	●	●	●	●	●
Red Bananas	●	●	●	●	●	●	●	●	●	●	●	●
Rhubarb				●	●	●	●					
Salsify	●	●	●	●	●	●	●	●	●	●	●	●
Sapotes	●	●	●	●	●	●	●	●	●	●	●	●
Shallots	●	●	●	●	●	●	●	●	●	●	●	●
Snow Peas	●	●	●	●	●	●	●	●	●	●	●	●
Spinach	●	●	●	●	●	●	●	●	●	●	●	●
Squash	●	●	●	●	●	●	●	●	●	●	●	●
Strawberries	●	●	●	●	●	●	●	●	●	●	●	●
Sunchokes	●	●	●	●	●	●	●	●	●	●	●	●
Sun-Dried Tomatoes	●	●	●	●	●	●	●	●	●	●	●	●
Sweet Potatoes	●	●	●	●	●	●	●	●	●	●	●	●
Tamarillos				●	●	●	●	●	●			
Tamarindos	●	●	●	●	●	●	●	●	●	●	●	●
Taro Root	●	●	●	●	●	●	●	●	●	●	●	●
Tomatillos	●	●	●	●	●	●	●	●	●	●	●	●
Tomatoes	●	●	●	●	●	●	●	●	●	●	●	●
Turnips	●	●	●							●	●	●
Watercress	●	●	●	●	●	●	●	●	●	●	●	●
Watermelon					●	●	●	●	●	●		

Avocado Fruit Salad Recipe

Easy Recipe:
1 ripe avocado, peeled, pitted and cubed
4 tart apples (such as Granny Smith), peeled, cored and cubed
2 ripe nectarines (or peaches), pitted and cubed
½ grapefruit, peeled and cut into sections, then into bite-size pieces
1 tbsp. honey
1 tbsp. pecans, toasted and chopped
Lettuce leaves to cover four plates

Easy Steps:
❶ Gently toss together the avocado, apples, nectarines and grapefruit.
❷ Drizzle honey and lemon juice over fruit and toss again, lightly.
❸ Place lettuce on plates. Divide fruit between plates. Garnish with pecans.

Serves 4.
*If using peaches, blanch in boiling water for one minute, remove and plunge into ice water. Skin will peel easily with a knife.

Nutrient Analysis per Recipe Serving:
Calories-220, Total Carbohydrates-39g, Protein-2g, Cholesterol-0mg, Sodium-21mg, Fiber-7g, Total Fat-9g (36% of calories from fat)

Selection & Storage: Avocados ripen best off the tree. A ripe one will yield to gentle pressure. To speed ripening process, place avocados in a paper bag with an apple. Poke a few holes in bag and store at room temperature.

Preparation: Ripe avocados peel easily. Slice in half lengthwise and remove one side. Stick a fork in the large pit and twist to remove. Avocados discolor quickly, so rub lemon juice on surface or cut at the last moment.

Honeyed Calypso Fruit Recipe

Easy Recipe:
2 cups (1 pint) fresh blueberries
2 bananas, peeled and sliced
2 cups (1 pint) strawberries, hulled and halved
2 cups seedless grapes
2 nectarines, quartered
⅓ cup orange juice
2 tbsp. lemon juice
1½ tbsp. honey
½ cup slivered almonds, toasted

Easy Steps:
❶ Clean and combine fruit.
❷ Just before serving, mix together the orange juice, lemon juice and honey.
❸ Pour over the fruit. Garnish with almonds.

Serves 8.

Nutrient Analysis per Recipe Serving: Calories-164,
Total Carbohydrates-23g, Protein-3g, Cholesterol-0mg, Sodium-60mg, Total Fat-5g (27% of calories from fat)

Selection & Storage: Look for plump, firm, indigo-blue berries with a silvery frost. Avoid any carton with moldy berries. Do not wash until ready to use. To store, refrigerate, tightly covered, for one week. Or, freeze in a single layer for an hour and then keep in the freezer for six months.

Preparation: Rinse blueberries thoroughly. Discard any berries that are shriveled or moldy. Pick off any stems that are still attached.

Citrus Star Cups Recipe

Easy Recipe:
2 grapefruit
2 oranges, peeled and sliced into bite-size pieces
1 tangerine, peeled and sectioned
½ lb. red grapes
Shredded coconut

Easy Steps:
❶ Make sawtooth cuts all around grapefruit. Twist and pull grapefruit apart.
❷ Scoop out pulp and cut it into bite-size pieces. Set grapefruit shells aside.
❸ Toss all fruit in a bowl with coconut
❹ Evenly distribute fruit in the grapefruit shells. Serves 4.

Nutrient Analysis per Recipe Serving:
Calories-134,
Protein-2g, Total Carbohydrates-33g, Dietary Fiber-4g, Sodium-5mg, Cholesterol-0mg, Total Fat-1g (7% of calories from fat)

Selection & Storage: Choose heavy fruits with smooth, thin skins. Citrus can be kept at room temperature for several days. It will keep several weeks if refrigerated.

Preparation: Citrus fruit will be juicier if you roll it between your palm and the countertop a few seconds before using.

Kiwifruit & Cream Recipe

Easy Recipe:
1 10-oz. package of frozen raspberries or strawberries
1 tbsp. sweet wine, rum or orange liqueur
¾ cup confectioner's sugar
2 cups part-skim ricotta cheese
6 kiwifruit, peeled and sliced crosswise, then sliced in half

Easy Steps:
❶ Place frozen berries in bowl. Defrost on high in the microwave for 2 minutes.
❷ Purée berries in a blender. Pour berries through sieve. Discard seeds.
❸ Add liquor and ¼ cup of the sugar to the berries. Gently whip the ricotta with the remaining sugar.
❹ Place some kiwifruit slices in 4 dessert bowls. Add cheese, then berry sauce. Repeat, ending with a kiwifruit layer. Chill while eating dinner. Bring remaining sauce to the table. Serves 4.

Nutritional Analysis per Recipe Serving:
Calories-346, Carbohydrates-62g, Protein-11g, Cholesterol-25mg,

Selection & Storage: Choose fruit with unbroken and unbruised skin. A ripe kiwifruit will yield to gentle pressure. Most kiwifruit are sold hard. Ripen at room temperature.

Preparation: Peel skin with a sharp knife or a vegetable peeler. Kiwifruit will not discolor when exposed to air and are a perfect choice for salads or garnish. Their color will change if cooked.

NUTRITION FACTS

UNITED STATES	
Serving Size: 1 medium with skin	
Calories	80
Protein	0 g
Fat	0 g
Carbohydrates	22 g
Dietary Fiber	5 g
Sodium	0 mg

CANADA	
Serving Size: per 140 g (1 medium)	
Energy	83 cal.....350 kJ
Protein	0.3 g
Fat	0.5 g
Carbohydrates	21 g
Dietary Fibre	3 g
Sodium	0 mg
Potassium	161 mg

UNITED STATES	
Serving Size: 1 medium with skin	
Calories	80
Protein	0 g
Fat	0 g
Carbohydrates	22 g
Dietary Fiber	5 g
Sodium	0 mg

CANADA	
Serving Size: per 140 g (1 medium)	
Energy	83 cal.....350 kJ
Protein	0.3 g
Fat	0.5 g
Carbohydrates	21 g
Dietary Fibre	3 g
Sodium	0 mg
Potassium	161 mg

UNITED STATES	
Serving Size: 1 medium with skin	
Calories	80
Protein	0 g
Fat	0 g
Carbohydrates	22 g
Dietary Fiber	5 g
Sodium	0 mg

CANADA	
Serving Size: per 140 g (1 medium)	
Energy	83 cal.....350 kJ
Protein	0.3 g
Fat	0.5 g
Carbohydrates	21 g
Dietary Fibre	3 g
Sodium	0 mg
Potassium	161 mg

UNITED STATES	
Serving Size: 1 medium with skin	
Calories	80
Protein	0 g
Fat	0 g
Carbohydrates	22 g
Dietary Fiber	5 g
Sodium	0 mg

CANADA	
Serving Size: per 140 g (1 medium)	
Energy	83 cal.....350 kJ
Protein	0.3 g
Fat	0.5 g
Carbohydrates	21 g
Dietary Fibre	3 g
Sodium	0 mg
Potassium	161 mg

SOURCE: USDA

Braeburn

General Information: The Braeburn apple, developed in New Zealand, is red-flushed and striped over greenish-gold skin. The Braeburn is a good eating apple with firm, juicy flesh and sweet-tart flavor. They are also good for dicing and tossing into salads. U.S. Braeburn are available year-round.

Selection & Storage: Look for firm, smooth-skinned apples free of bruises and gouges. A dry brown patch on the skin (scald) does not affect the taste. Apples should have a fresh, not musty, smell. Store in a plastic bag in the refrigerator.

Preparation & Cooking Tips: Braeburns are excellent sliced raw with cheese and a good choice for cooking in pies and applesauce. If serving raw, be aware that cut apples will discolor. To keep apples from browning, toss with citrus or apple juice, or dip in acidulated water.

Cameo

General Information: Cameo apples are the do-it-all apples to eat out-of-hand or for baking and cooking. The cameo, a crisp, juicy, sweet-tart new variety is recognizable by its bi-coloring—red and yellow—and distinctive white speckles on the skin and a long stem. The flesh varies from white to cream. The cameo was tested for 20 years before its current popular debut. It is available in late autumn.

Selection & Storage: Look for firm, smooth-skinned apples, free of bruises and gouges. Scald, a dry brown patch on the skin, will not affect the taste. Apples should have a fresh, not musty smell. Store in a plastic bag in the refrigerator crisper or drawer away from vegetables. Apples can be kept in the refrigerator for up to six weeks.

Preparation & Cooking Tips: Cameo apples are slow to brown when cut, so they are perfect in fruit or green salads. Bake in pies or apple crisps. Cameos hold their shape and flavor well when baked. Test for doneness because cameos have an extra dense, crunchy flesh and may need a few extra minutes of baking time.

Cortland

General Information: Cortland apples are big in size with sweet flavor. With dark, reddish-purple skin and pure, white flesh, Cortlands are available September through spring.

Selection & Storage: Look for apples with firm texture and unbroken skin with no bruises. Brown freckling or streaks do not affect flavor or quality. Store in a plastic bag in the crisper section of the refrigerator.

Preparation & Cooking Tips: The flesh of Cortlands resists browning, making them perfect for slicing and serving raw. They are also delicious baked in pies. Wash apples thoroughly before using. An apple slicer, available at many grocery stores and specialty kitchen shops, is a fast and easy way to get perfect, evenly sized slices. If peeling is desired, use a vegetable peeler to remove as little flesh as possible.

Crispin/Mutsu

General Information: Developed in Japan as Mutsu, the Crispin was renamed for European and North American distribution. The Crispin is a large, greenish russet apple with a golden blush. The crisp, deep creamy flesh is honey flavored when ripe. When cooked, slices retain shape with a sweet, light taste. Crispin apples are available from December to March.

Selection & Storage: Look for firm, smooth-skinned apples free of bruises and gouges. A dry brown patch on the skin (scald) does not affect the taste. Apples should have a fresh, not musty, smell. Store in a plastic bag in the refrigerator.

Preparation & Cooking Tips: Excellent eating and cooking apples, Crispins are a good choice for pies and applesauce. If serving raw, remember that cut apples will discolor. To keep apples from browning, toss with citrus or apple juice, or dip in acidulated water.

Apples

Empire

General Information: Empire apples are named for New York State, where this apple was developed as a cross between the Red Delicious and the McIntosh. A good all-purpose apple, the Empire is like the McIntosh, but with firmer flesh. Available year-round.

Selection & Storage: Look for firm, smooth-skinned apples free of bruises and gouges. A dry brown patch on the skin (scald) does not affect the taste. Apples should have a fresh, not musty, smell. Store in a plastic bag in the refrigerator.

Preparation & Cooking Tips: Excellent eating and cooking apples, Empires are a good choice for pies and rosy applesauce. If serving raw, remember that cut apples will discolor. To keep apples from browning, toss with citrus or apple juice, or dip in acidulated water.

Fuji

General Information: Developed in Japan in the 1940s, this variety has American parents, Red Delicious and Ralls Janet. Fuji apples are small and round with a pretty, orange-red blush. Their flesh is crisp, firm, juicy and honey flavored. Available year-round.

Selection & Storage: Look for firm, smooth-skinned apples free of bruises and gouges. A dry brown patch on the skin (scald) does not affect the taste. Apples should have a fresh, not musty, smell. Store in a plastic bag in the refrigerator.

Preparation & Cooking Tips: Excellent eating and cooking apples, Fujis are a good choice for pies and applesauce. Cooked apples go well with pork and chicken. If serving raw, remember that cut apples will discolor. To keep apples from browning, toss with citrus or apple juice, or dip in acidulated water.

Gala

General Information: Like the Braeburn apple, Gala apples come from New Zealand. Galas are a hybrid apple created by crossing a British apple, Cox's Orange Pippen, with the Red Delicous apple. One strain of Gala is named Royal Gala, after Queen Elizabeth II declared her preference for it. The round Gala has creamy yellow skin striped with pink, and a honey perfume flavor. The Gala is available most of the year,

Selection & Storage: Look for firm, smooth-skinned apples free of bruises gouges. A dry brown patch on the skin (scald) does not affect the taste. Apples should have a fresh, not musty, smell. Store in a plastic bag in the refrigerator.

Preparation & Cooking Tips: Gala apples should be eaten raw because their texture disintegrates with heat. Remember, cut apples will discolor. To keep apples from browning, toss with citrus or apple juice or dip in acidulated water.

Golden Delicious

General Information: There are many varieties of Golden Delicious. With the older varieties, the color is a dull gold with a pink blush. Those developed later have a smooth, glossy, greener skin. The Golden Delicious apple tastes flowery sweet with moderate juiciness. Available year-round,

Selection & Storage: Look for firm, smooth-skinned apples free of bruises and gouges. A dry brown patch on the skin (scald) does not affect the taste. Apples should have a fresh, not musty, smell. Store in a plastic bag in the refrigerator.

Preparation & Cooking Tips: Golden Delicious apples will retain their shape when cooked, which makes them a good choice for pies and open tarts, but a poor choice for applesauce. To keep cut apples from browning, toss with citrus or apple juice, or dip in acidulated water.

NUTRITION FACTS

UNITED STATES
Serving Size: 1 medium with skin
Calories	80
Protein	0 g
Fat	0 g
Carbohydrates	22 g
Dietary Fiber	5 g
Sodium	0 mg

CANADA
Serving Size: per 140 g (1 medium)
Energy	83 cal....350 kJ
Protein	0.3 g
Fat	0.5 g
Carbohydrates	21 g
Dietary Fibre	3 g
Sodium	0 mg
Potassium	161 mg

UNITED STATES
Serving Size: 1 medium with skin
Calories	80
Protein	0 g
Fat	0 g
Carbohydrates	22 g
Dietary Fiber	5 g
Sodium	0 mg

CANADA
Serving Size: per 140 g (1 medium)
Energy	83 cal....350 kJ
Protein	0.3 g
Fat	0.5 g
Carbohydrates	21 g
Dietary Fibre	3 g
Sodium	0 mg
Potassium	161 mg

UNITED STATES
Serving Size: 1 medium with skin
Calories	80
Protein	0 g
Fat	0 g
Carbohydrates	22 g
Dietary Fiber	5 g
Sodium	0 mg

CANADA
Serving Size: per 140 g (1 medium)
Energy	83 cal....350 kJ
Protein	0.3 g
Fat	0.5 g
Carbohydrates	21 g
Dietary Fibre	3 g
Sodium	0 mg
Potassium	161 mg

UNITED STATES
Serving Size: 1 medium with skin
Calories	80
Protein	0 g
Fat	0 g
Carbohydrates	22 g
Dietary Fiber	5 g
Sodium	0 mg

CANADA
Serving Size: per 140 g (1 medium)
Energy	83 cal....350 kJ
Protein	0.3 g
Fat	0.5 g
Carbohydrates	21 g
Dietary Fibre	3 g
Sodium	0 mg
Potassium	161 mg

SOURCE: USDA

Apples

NUTRITION FACTS

UNITED STATES
Serving Size: 1 medium with skin
Calories 80
Protein..............................0 g
Fat ....0 g
Carbohydrates...............22 g
Dietary Fiber ....5 g
Sodium ....0 mg

CANADA
Serving Size: per 140 g (1 medium)
Energy...........83 cal.....350 kJ
Protein...........................0.3 g
Fat ....0.5 g
Carbohydrates ....21 g
Dietary Fibre ....3 g
Sodium ....0 mg
Potassium ....161 mg

UNITED STATES
Serving Size: 1 medium with skin
Calories 80
Protein..............................0 g
Fat ....0 g
Carbohydrates...............22 g
Dietary Fiber ....5 g
Sodium ....0 mg

CANADA
Serving Size: per 140 g (1 medium)
Energy...........83 cal.....350 kJ
Protein...........................0.3 g
Fat ....0.5 g
Carbohydrates ....21 g
Dietary Fibre ....3 g
Sodium ....0 mg
Potassium ....161 mg

UNITED STATES
Serving Size: 1 medium with skin
Calories 80
Protein..............................0 g
Fat ....0 g
Carbohydrates ....22 g
Dietary Fiber ....5 g
Sodium ....0 mg

CANADA
Serving Size: per 140 g (1 medium)
Energy...........83 cal.....350 kJ
Protein...........................0.3 g
Fat ....0.5 g
Carbohydrates ....21 g
Dietary Fibre ....3 g
Sodium ....0 mg
Potassium ....161 mg

UNITED STATES
Serving Size: 1 medium with skin
Calories 80
Protein..............................0 g
Fat ....0 g
Carbohydrates ....22 g
Dietary Fiber ....5 g
Sodium ....0 mg

CANADA
Serving Size: per 140 g (1 medium)
Energy...........83 cal.....350 kJ
Protein...........................0.3 g
Fat ....0.5 g
Carbohydrates ....21 g
Dietary Fibre ....3 g
Sodium ....0 mg
Potassium ....161 mg

SOURCE: USDA

Granny Smith

General Information: Granny Smith apples were discovered in Australia in 1868 by Mrs. Thomas Smith. Americans didn't get a taste of the Granny Smith until the 1950s, when they were imported from New Zealand and South Africa. Available most of the year, Granny Smiths are firm and tart with freckled, green skin.

Selection & Storage: Look for firm, smooth-skinned apples free of bruises and gouges. A dry brown patch on the skin (scald) does not affect the taste. Apples should have a fresh, not musty, smell. Store in a plastic bag in the refrigerator.

Preparation & Cooking Tips: Excellent eating and cooking apples, Granny Smiths are often specified in pie recipes because they hold their shape and flavor when cooked. They are a delicious accompaniment to pork or chicken. To keep cut apples from browning, toss with citrus or apple juice, or dip in acidulated water.

Idared

General Information: The mild-tasting Idared is a good all-purpose apple. Popular in the Northeast and Midwest, the Idared is a cross between Jonathan and Wagener apples. Idareds are greenish-yellow flushed with red, and available from September through spring.

Selection & Storage: Look for firm, smooth-skinned apples free of bruises and gouges. A dry brown patch on the skin (scald) does not affect the taste. Apples should have a fresh, not musty, smell. Store in a plastic bag in the refrigerator.

Preparation & Cooking Tips: Idared apples retain their shape when cooked, which makes them a good choice for pies and open tarts. If using Idared apples in a salad or snack, remember that cut apples will discolor. To keep cut apples from browning, toss with citrus or apple juice, or dip in acidulated water.

Jonagold

General Information: Jonagolds, a cross between Golden Delicious and Jonathan apples, are large, fine eating apples with rich, juicy, spicy flesh. Available from November through April, Jonagolds are golden-skinned, striped and blushed with red.

Selection & Storage: Look for firm, smooth-skinned apples free of bruises and gouges. A dry brown patch on the skin (scald) does not affect the taste. Apples should have a fresh, not musty, smell. Store in a plastic bag in the refrigerator.

Preparation & Cooking Tips: Excellent eating and cooking apples, Jonagolds are good in fresh salads or sliced with cheese. To keep cut apples from browning, toss with citrus or apple juice, or dip in acidulated water.

Jonathan

General Information: The Jonathan apple was discovered in 1800 in Woodstock, New York, by a man named Philip Rick. Originally called the "Rick" apple, the Jonathan was popularized by a man named Jonathan Hasbrouk, who took claim to the apple. Red-skinned, the Jonathan boasts highly aromatic, spicy flesh, with availability from mid-September through March.

Selection & Storage: Look for firm, smooth-skinned apples free of bruises and gouges. A dry brown patch on the skin (scald) does not affect the taste. The apples should have a fresh, not musty, smell. Store in a plastic bag in the refrigerator.

Preparation & Cooking Tips: Excellent eating and cooking apples, Jonathans are a good choice for pies and applesauce. To keep cut apples from browning, toss with citrus or apple juice, or dip in acidulated water.

Apples

Fruit

Lady

General Information: The petite Lady apple is the oldest apple, first recorded in 1628. Hailing from the French Renaissance, the oblong Lady apple is diminutive, flattened on both ends, and as small as an inch-and-a-half across. The skin of both varieties is a shiny, pale green with a red blush. Lady apples are delectably crisp and tart, with availability from November to March.

Selection & Storage: Look for firm, smooth-skinned apples free of bruises and holes. Apples should have a fresh, not musty, smell. Store in a plastic bag in the refrigerator.

Preparation & Cooking Tips: Excellent eating and cooking apples, Lady apples may be used in pies or applesauce. Their small size makes them a fun treat in children's lunch boxes or use as decoration. To keep cut apples from browning, toss with citrus or apple juice, or dip in acidulated water.

McIntosh

General Information: The McIntosh is the most popular apple in America. Discovered in the 1700s by a Canadian, John McIntosh, the McIntosh has bright-red skin tinged with green, crisp, strawberry sweet flesh, and year-round availability.

Selection & Storage: Look for firm, smooth-skinned apples free of bruises and gouges. A dry brown patch on the skin (scald) does not affect the taste. Apples should have a fresh, not musty, smell. Store in a plastic bag in the refrigerator.

Preparation & Cooking Tips: Although the McIntosh is considered an all-purpose apple, the texture disintegrates with heat. The McIntosh is best eaten out-of-hand. To keep apples from browning, toss with citrus or apple juice, or dip in acidulated water.

Pink Lady

General Information: This Aussie lady represents the finest Western Australian-based apples, also grown in the U.S. The pink lady is distinguished by her true pink coloring, crisp crunch and smooth texture. The pink lady has a sweet-tart flavor similar to the Granny Smith. She is the ultimate apple for dessert quality eating apples. Her best feature is that she is outstanding for eating fresh or for baking. Look for this variety in late September through February.

Selection & Storage: Look for firm, smooth-skinned apples, free of bruises and gouges. Scald, a dry brown patch on the skin, will not affect the taste. Apples should have a fresh, not musty smell. Store in a plastic bag in the refrigerator crisper or drawer away from vegetables. Apples can be kept in the refrigerator for up to six weeks.

Preparation & Cooking Tips: The flesh of the Pink lady is crisp and firm. It resists browning when cut, making it ideal for salads, fresh eating and baking. It is a cross between a Lady Williams and Golden Delicious and pairs nicely with bold cheeses.

Red Delicious

General Information: The character Johnny Appleseed is based on the life of John Chapman who wore a saucepan hat and propagated apple seedlings all over eastern America. The Western Red Delicious apple, large and bright red, is distinctive with its elongated shape and five knobs at the base. The Eastern variety has less pronounced characteristics. The Red Delicious is sweet and juicy. Red Delicious are available year-round.

Selection & Storage: Look for firm, smooth-skinned apples free of bruises and gouges. A dry brown patch on the skin (scald) does not affect the taste. The apples should have a fresh, not musty, smell. Store in a plastic bag in the refrigerator.

Preparation & Cooking Tips: Red Delicious apples should be eaten out-of-hand. The texture disintegrates with heat. To keep apples from browning, toss with citrus or apple juice, or dip in acidulated water.

NUTRITION FACTS

Lady

UNITED STATES
Serving Size: 1 medium with skin
Calories 80
Protein .... 0 g
Fat .... 0 g
Carbohydrates .... 22 g
Dietary Fiber .... 5 g
Sodium .... 0 mg

CANADA
Serving Size: per 140 g (1 medium)
Energy .... 83 cal ... 350 kJ
Protein .... 0.3 g
Fat .... 0.5 g
Carbohydrates .... 21 g
Dietary Fibre .... 3 g
Sodium .... 0 mg
Potassium .... 161 mg

McIntosh

UNITED STATES
Serving Size: 1 medium with skin
Calories 80
Protein .... 0 g
Fat .... 0 g
Carbohydrates .... 22 g
Dietary Fiber .... 5 g
Sodium .... 0 mg

CANADA
Serving Size: per 140 g (1 medium)
Energy .... 83 cal ... 350 kJ
Protein .... 0.3 g
Fat .... 0.5 g
Carbohydrates .... 21 g
Dietary Fibre .... 3 g
Sodium .... 0 mg
Potassium .... 161 mg

Pink Lady

UNITED STATES
Serving Size: 1 medium with skin
Calories 80
Protein .... 0 g
Fat .... 0 g
Carbohydrates .... 22 g
Dietary Fiber .... 5 g
Sodium .... 0 mg

CANADA
Serving Size: per 140 g (1 medium)
Energy .... 83 cal ... 350 kJ
Protein .... 0.3 g
Fat .... 0.5 g
Carbohydrates .... 21 g
Dietary Fibre .... 3 g
Sodium .... 0 mg
Potassium .... 161 mg

Red Delicious

UNITED STATES
Serving Size: 1 medium with skin
Calories 80
Protein .... 0 g
Fat .... 0 g
Carbohydrates .... 22 g
Dietary Fiber .... 5 g
Sodium .... 0 mg

CANADA
Serving Size: per 140 g (1 medium)
Energy .... 83 cal ... 350 kJ
Protein .... 0.3 g
Fat .... 0.5 g
Carbohydrates .... 21 g
Dietary Fibre .... 3 g
Sodium .... 0 mg
Potassium .... 161 mg

SOURCE: USDA

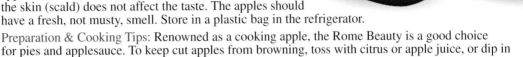

Apples

Rome Beauty

General Information: The name Rome comes from the Rome, Ohio, township where it was discovered. The Rome Beauty is a large, deep-red apple with yellow speckling. An excellent cooking and baking apple, the taste ranges from sweet to mildly tart. The Rome Beauty is available from late September to July.

Selection & Storage: Look for firm, smooth-skinned apples free of bruises and gouges. A dry brown patch on the skin (scald) does not affect the taste. The apples should have a fresh, not musty, smell. Store in a plastic bag in the refrigerator.

Preparation & Cooking Tips: Renowned as a cooking apple, the Rome Beauty is a good choice for pies and applesauce. To keep cut apples from browning, toss with citrus or apple juice, or dip in acidulated water.

NUTRITION FACTS

UNITED STATES	
Serving Size: 1 medium with skin	
Calories	80
Protein	0 g
Fat	0 g
Carbohydrates	22 g
Dietary Fiber	5 g
Sodium	0 mg

CANADA		
Serving Size: per 140 g (1 medium)		
Energy	83 cal	350 kJ
Protein		0.3 g
Fat		0.5 g
Carbohydrates		21 g
Dietary Fibre		3 g
Sodium		0 mg
Potassium		161 mg

Winesap

General Information: True to its name, the Winesap apple has a tangy flavor reminiscent of wine. Available October through July, Winesaps have a dark, reddish-purple skin and firm, juicy flesh.

Selection & Storage: Look for apples with firm texture and unbroken skin with no bruises. Brown freckling or streaks do not affect flavor or quality. Store in a plastic bag in the refrigerator.

Preparation & Cooking Tips: Winesaps are used in a variety of ways: out-of-hand, baked, and as applesauce. Wash apples thoroughly before using. An apple corer or slicer, available at many grocery stores and specialty kitchen shops, is a fast and easy way to get perfect, evenly sized slices. If peeling is desired, use a vegetable peeler to remove as little flesh as possible. To keep cut apples from browning toss with citrus or apple juice, or dip in acidulated water.

UNITED STATES	
Serving Size: 1 medium with skin	
Calories	80
Protein	0 g
Fat	0 g
Carbohydrates	22 g
Dietary Fiber	5 g
Sodium	0 mg

CANADA		
Serving Size: per 140 g (1 medium)		
Energy	83 cal	350 kJ
Protein		0.3 g
Fat		0.5 g
Carbohydrates		21 g
Dietary Fibre		3 g
Sodium		0 mg
Potassium		161 mg

Tasty Ideas for Berries

To enhance the flavor of fresh fruit, squeeze on a little lemon juice. For a special occasion, sprinkle fruit lightly with rum or brandy. If fruit doesn't look its best or is overripe, mash lightly with a fork and serve over vanilla ice cream or yogurt for a quick dessert.

To defrost frozen berries, thaw slowly in the refrigerator and serve while still slightly chilled. Defrost for only 30 minutes to use as decorations on desserts. If you need to defrost berries quickly, place the container holding berries into another dish of warm water until thawed. You can use frozen berries without thawing in smoothies or quick sorbet desserts. For sorbet, puree frozen berries in a food processor with confectioners sugar to taste. Spoon into chilled glasses and serve.

Berries

Blackberries

General Information: Sweet and juicy, blackberries grow on bramble bushes with needle-sharp prickers. Bumpy and purplish-black in color, blackberries are the largest of the wild berries. They are available May through September.

Selection & Storage: Choose firm, plump, dark-colored berries, avoiding berries with mold. Attached hulls are a sign the berries were picked while immature. To store, lay a paper towel on a baking sheet; place unwashed berries in a single layer. Cover with another towel and refrigerate for up to 2 days. Or, freeze for an hour on a baking sheet, then place in a container and freeze up to 9 months.

Preparation & Cooking Tips: Do not wash blackberries until ready for use or they will become waterlogged. If used in a cake, be sure the batter is thick or the berries will sink to the bottom. Blackberries improve with cooking, which intensifies the flavor and softens the seedy texture.

NUTRITION FACTS

UNITED STATES	
Serving Size: 1 cup	
Calories	70
Protein	1 g
Fat	0.5 g
Carbohydrates	18 g
Dietary Fiber	7 g
Sodium	0 mg

CANADA		
Serving Size: per 145 g (250 mL/1 cup)		
Energy	75 cal	320 kJ
Protein		1 g
Fat		0.6 g
Carbohydrates		14 g
Dietary Fibre		7.3 g
Sodium		0 mg
Potassium		284 mg

SOURCE: USDA

Berries

Blueberries

General Information: Wild blueberries are smaller than the cultivated variety. Cultivated berries, available from May to October, are grown in Michigan, New Jersey, Maine, Washington and North Carolina. Whether wild or cultivated, blueberries are high in vitamin C.

Selection & Storage: Look for plump, firm, indigo-blue berries with a silvery frost, avoiding moldy berries. Do not wash until ready to use. To store, refrigerate, tightly covered, for 1 week. Or, place berries in a single layer on a paper towel on a baking sheet; freeze berries for an hour, then place in a container and freeze for up to 9 months.

Preparation & Cooking Tips: Rinse blueberries thoroughly, discarding shriveled or moldy berries. Pick off any stems that are still attached. If used in muffins, toss the berries into the batter at the last moment. Fresh berries will not bleed unless their skins are broken.

Boysenberries

General Information: A hybrid of raspberry and blackberry, boysenberries have a tart, sweet flavor that combines the best qualities of both berries. Summertime is the peak season for boysenberries.

Selection & Storage: Choose plump, firm boysenberries that are uniform in color. If sold in packages, check for leaking or stains, an indication that the berries have been damaged or are overripe. Remove berries from packaging; discard any that are moldy or crushed. Blot with paper towels and store in a single layer on a tray covered with paper towels. Refrigerate for no more than 2 days.

Preparation & Cooking Tips: Boysenberries are delicious in fresh fruit salads, stirred into yogurt or on top of ice cream. They also make tasty pies.

Photo Courtesy of Hurst's Berry Farm

Cranberries

General Information: Everyone remembers cranberries for holiday meals. Distinctively tart, firm, red fresh cranberries perk up summer compotes, salads, meat dishes, muffins and even cocktails. The peak market period is from October through December.

Selection & Storage: Cranberries come in plastic packages. Look for bags of brightly colored, dark-red cranberries. Refrigerated cranberries can be stored for 1 month. Frozen cranberries may be kept for 1 year.

Preparation & Cooking Tips: Rinse thoroughly. Discard any berries that are soft, shriveled or discolored. Cook cranberries only until they pop. Longer cooking will result in mushy, bitter berries. You can make an uncooked cranberry sauce by grinding berries in a food processor with apples, oranges or dried apricots.

Fuyu Persimmon

General Information: Persimmons taste like a sweet combination of pumpkin, plum and honey. The Fuyu is shaped like a tomato with a distinctive, four-leafed, capped stem. Unlike most persimmons, which would curl your tongue if eaten unripe, the Fuyu has no tannin and can be eaten when crisp to hard. The smooth skin of Fuyus ranges from yellow to orange-red. They are available from October to February.

Selection & Storage: Ripe Fuyus should yield to gentle pressure. Ripen in a pierced paper bag with an apple. When ripe, place persimmons in a plastic bag in the refrigerator, but use quickly.

Preparation & Cooking Tips: Of all the varieties of persimmons, the Fuyu is the best choice for salads because of its firm texture. Rinse fruit. To peel, cut out the leaf base, then cut persimmon in half lengthwise. Insert a sharp paring knife between the flesh and the skin and peel skin away from the fruit.

NUTRITION FACTS

UNITED STATES
Serving Size: 1 cup
Calories	80
Protein	1 g
Fat	0.5 g
Carbohydrates	20 g
Dietary Fiber	4 g
Sodium	10 mg

CANADA
Serving Size: per 150 g (250 mL/1 cup)
Energy	84 cal	350 kJ
Protein	1.0 g	
Fat	0.6 g	
Carbohydrates	21 g	
Dietary Fibre	3.9 g	
Sodium	9 mg	
Potassium	134 mg	

UNITED STATES
Serving Size: 1 cup
Calories	66
Protein	1.5 g
Fat	0.3 g
Carbohydrates	16 g
Dietary Fiber	5 g
Sodium	1.3 mg

CANADA
Serving Size: per 145 g (250 mL/1 cup)
Energy	66 cal	276 kJ
Protein	0.4 g	
Fat	0.2 g	
Carbohydrates	12.6 g	
Dietary Fibre	4.1 g	
Sodium	1 mg	
Potassium	183 mg	

UNITED STATES
Serving Size: ½ cup
Calories	25
Protein	2 g
Fat	0 g
Carbohydrates	6 g
Dietary Fiber	2 g
Sodium	0 mg

CANADA
Serving Size: per 50 g (125 mL/½ cup)
Energy	25 cal	100 kJ
Protein	0.2 g	
Fat	0.1 g	
Carbohydrates	6.3 g	
Dietary Fibre	2.1 g	
Sodium	1 mg	
Potassium	36 mg	

UNITED STATES
Serving Size: 1 medium
Calories	60
Protein	0 g
Fat	0 g
Carbohydrates	17 g
Dietary Fiber	2 g
Sodium	0 mg

CANADA
Serving Size: per 150 g (1 medium)
Energy	105 cal	440 kJ
Protein	0.9 g	
Fat	0.3 g	
Carbohydrates	28 g	
Dietary Fibre	2.6 g	
Sodium	2 mg	
Potassium	242 mg	

SOURCE: USDA

Berries

Fruit

Gooseberries

General Information: Some gooseberries are the size of a blueberry; others are the size of a cherry tomato. The skin can be fuzzy, prickly or satin-smooth. The color varies from white to green to purple. Once a staple in the American Colonial larder, tart gooseberries are rarely eaten by Americans today. From November to January, choose the large New Zealand gooseberries. In the summer months, American gooseberries come to market.

Selection & Storage: Select hard, dry berries. Pinkish-purple berries are less tart. Gooseberries stay firm for 2 weeks in the refrigerator; then they soften and turn pinkish. When they turn purplish, use in purées.

Preparation & Cooking Tips: Clip off the little stems and tops unless you intend to sieve the berries after cooking. Gooseberries are highly acidic and tend to be tart. If cooking gooseberries, use the smaller variety. Larger gooseberries will lose flavor when cooked.

Hachiya Persimmon

General Information: Most Americans have never tasted a persimmon — unique taste combination of pumpkin, plum and honey. The Hachiya is shaped like a long acorn with smooth, deep-orange skin. If eaten before it is ripe, the Hachiya is bitter beyond words. They are in season from October to February.

Selection & Storage: Look for Hachiya persimmons that are softer than a baby's cheek, nearly liquid. Choose fruits that are deep orange with no trace of yellow. If buying unripe persimmons, place them in a paper bag with an apple and eat when ripe. Hachiya persimmons may take several weeks to ripen

Preparation & Cooking Tips: Rinse fruit. Peeling is optional, but recommended for salads. Some Hachiyas have black seeds that should be removed. Do not cook Hachiyas or they will be tough and tasteless. They are best eaten by cutting off the top and scooping out the fruit with a spoon.

Raspberries

General Information: Raspberries come in three colors: red, black and gold. They are formed of many connecting drupelets, which are individual sections of fruit. The seeds in each drupelet provide high fiber content. Raspberries are available year-round, with peaks in June and early September.

Selection & Storage: Select fragrant, plump, intensely colored berries. Choose raspberries without hulls. Discard any with mold or bruises. To store, lay a paper towel on a baking sheet; place unwashed berries in a single layer. Cover with another towel and refrigerate for up to 3 days. Or, freeze for an hour on baking sheet, then place in a container and freeze for up to 9 months.

Preparation & Cooking Tips: Raspberries should be washed right before use. To make raspberry sauce, purée fresh or frozen berries. Push through a sieve to remove seeds. Add 1 tablespoon each of confectioner's sugar and Grand Marnier or orange juice.

Red Currants

General Information: Red currants are tiny, glossy scarlet berries that grow on vines. Fresh currants are different from dried currants, which are actually dried Zante grapes. Fresh red currants deliver an immediate jolt of color and flavor to meat dishes. Red currants are available from June to August and from December to February.

Selection & Storage: For fresh usage, choose deeply red, shiny berries. For jams and jellies, choose paler berries. Refrigerate currants on a paper towel in clusters for no more than 3 days.

Preparation & Cooking Tips: Rinse currants in a bowl of water. Using a fork, pull the currants from their stems. Currants can add zest to a dish just as lemons and limes do. Add to meat dishes, salads or vegetables.

NUTRITION FACTS

UNITED STATES
Serving Size: ½ cup
Calories	35
Protein	1 g
Fat	0 g
Carbohydrates	8 g
Dietary Fiber	3 g
Sodium	0 mg

CANADA
Serving Size: per 75 g (125 mL/½ cup)
Energy	33 cal.....140 kJ
Protein	0.7 g
Fat	0.4 g
Carbohydrates	7.6 g
Dietary Fibre	3.2 g
Sodium	1 mg
Potassium	149 mg

UNITED STATES
Serving Size: 1 medium
Calories	120
Protein	1 g
Fat	0 g
Carbohydrates	31 g
Dietary Fiber	5 g
Sodium	0 mg

CANADA
Serving Size: per 75 g (1/2 fruit)
Energy	53 cal.....238 kJ
Protein	0.5 g
Fat	0.0 g
Carbohydrates	13.9 g
Dietary Fibre	n/a
Sodium	.75 mg
Potassium	120 mg

UNITED STATES
Serving Size: 1 cup
Calories	60
Protein	1 g
Fat	0.5 g
Carbohydrates	14 g
Dietary Fiber	8 g
Sodium	0 mg

CANADA
Serving Size: per 50 g (250 mL/1 cup)
Energy	61 cal.....250 kJ
Protein	1.1 g
Fat	0.7 g
Carbohydrates	15 g
Dietary Fibre	6.1 g
Sodium	0 mg
Potassium	190 mg

UNITED STATES
Serving Size: ½ cup
Calories	30
Protein	1 g
Fat	0 g
Carbohydrates	8 g
Dietary Fiber	2 g
Sodium	0 mg

CANADA
Serving Size: per 50 g (125 mL/½ cup)
Energy	34 cal.....140 kJ
Protein	0.8 g
Fat	0.1 g
Carbohydrates	8.3 g
Dietary Fibre	2.6 g
Sodium	1 mg
Potassium	165 mg

SOURCE: USDA

Berries

Strawberries

General Information: The strawberry is sometimes called the "inside-out" fruit because its seeds are on the surface rather than inside. As Samuel Butler said of the strawberry, "Doubtless God could have made a better berry, but doubtless God never did." Strawberries are available year-round. Their peak season is April to June.

Selection & Storage: Look for brightly colored, plump berries with a strong scent. Small berries are the tastiest. Strawberries do not ripen after they have been picked. Do not wash berries before storing. Place in a single layer on a paper towel in a moisture-proof container. In the refrigerator, they will last 2 to 3 days.

Preparation & Cooking Tips: Rinse berries thoroughly. With a small, sharp knife, remove the hull. To get maximum juice, slice strawberries, sprinkle with sugar and let sit at room temperature for 2 hours. Use strawberries in salads, soufflés, breads, preserves, tarts and frozen confections.

NUTRITION FACTS

UNITED STATES	
Serving Size: 8 medium	
Calories	45
Protein	1 g
Fat	0 g
Carbohydrates	12 g
Dietary Fiber	4 g
Sodium	0 mg

CANADA		
Serving Size: per 120 g (8 medium)		
Energy	36 cal	150 kJ
Protein		0.7 g
Fat		0.4 g
Carbohydrates		8.4 g
Dietary Fibre		2.6 g
Sodium		1 mg
Potassium		199 mg

Delicious Citrus Tips

A pat of flavored butter melting over hot, freshly cooked vegetables is a delicious finishing touch. And flavored butters are easy to make. Just put 4 ounces of unsalted butter in a mixing bowl and beat with a wooden spoon or electric mixer until soft. Add 2 teaspoons of fresh orange or lime juice or 1 teaspoon lemon juice and the grated zest of 1 orange, lime or lemon. Try different combinations for exciting taste sensations.

Another citrus tip. Cut a lemon, lime or orange in half with a zigzag edge and trim the base to sit flat. Then dip the points into fresh chopped parsley. Serve this with your favorite fish entree.

Citrus

Blood Orange

General Information: The flesh of the blood orange is a sumptuous red, purple or burgundy. Blood oranges have a subtle taste of raspberry — sweet and less acidic than regular oranges. Originally brought to the United States by Spanish and Italian immigrants, 2 varieties, the Ruby Red and the Moro, are grown in California and Florida. They are available December through May.

Selection & Storage: Select blood oranges that are heavy for their size, as they will be the juiciest. The skin of a blood orange may be tinged with red, and either smooth or pitted. Store blood oranges in a loosely wrapped plastic bag in the refrigerator for up to 1 week.

Preparation & Cooking Tips: Some blood oranges are seedless. If the variety you have picked has seeds, remove them before serving. The unexpected color of blood oranges makes them especially attractive as a garnish or in salads.

NUTRITION FACTS

UNITED STATES	
Serving Size: 1 medium	
Calories	62
Protein	1 g
Fat	0 g
Carbohydrates	15 g
Dietary Fiber	1 g
Sodium	0 mg

CANADA		
Serving Size: per 130 g (1 medium)		
Energy	61 cal	260 kJ
Protein		1.2 g
Fat		0.2 g
Carbohydrates		15 g
Dietary Fibre		2.3 g
Sodium		0 mg
Potassium		235 mg

Grapefruit

General Information: Grapefruit grows in clusters like grapes. The first grapefruit tree in Florida was planted by a French nobleman in 1823. It wasn't until after World War I that grapefruit was eaten as a breakfast food. Two varieties of the sweet-tart fruit are grown in the United States: white, and pink or red. Fresh grapefruit is available year-round.

Selection & Storage: Choose heavy fruit with smooth, thin skins. Grapefruit will not ripen after picking. Grapefruit can be kept at room temperature for 6 days, but keeps several weeks if refrigerated.

Preparation & Cooking Tips: Grapefruit is juicier if rolled between your palm and the countertop a few seconds before eating. To remove pith easily, drop the whole grapefruit in boiling water. Remove from heat and let sit for 4 minutes. When you peel the grapefruit, the pith should come off with the skin. For dessert, dot grapefruit halves with brown sugar and broil. For salads, add grapefruit sections for color and piquant flavor.

UNITED STATES	
Serving Size: ½ medium	
Calories	60
Protein	1 g
Fat	0 g
Carbohydrates	16 g
Dietary Fiber	6 g
Sodium	0 mg

CANADA		
Serving Size: per 120 g (1/2 medium)		
Energy	38 cal	160 kJ
Protein		0.8 g
Fat		0.1 g
Carbohydrates		9.7 g
Dietary Fibre		2.1 g
Sodium		0 mg
Potassium		167 mg

SOURCE: USDA

Juice Orange

General Information: A glass of freshly squeezed orange juice is the perfect start to the day. Not only does it taste delicious, but the orange pulp provides fiber to lower your cholesterol. Florida produces most of the juice oranges in the United States. In 1835, a freeze destroyed most of the orange trees in Florida. Only the Indian River variety survived. The entire Florida orange industry had to start again, using this variety of orange.

Selection & Storage: Bright color is not necessarily an indication of ripeness. Pick oranges that are firm and heavy for their size. Often, ripe oranges will have a slight greening. Oranges will last up to 2 weeks when refrigerated in a loosely wrapped plastic bag.

Preparation & Cooking Tips: Juice oranges are best when squeezed and consumed as a refreshing beverage.

Kumquat

General Information: Kumquats are a strange breed of fruit. Unlike their cousin — oranges — kumquats have a sweet, pungent rind and a bitter, dry flesh. The skin and flesh are eaten together. Fresh kumquats are available from November to March.

Selection & Storage: Choose firm, dry, fully orange fruit with stems. The rounded variety is generally sweeter and milder than the oval variety. Wash and dry thoroughly. Store in a loosely wrapped plastic bag in the refrigerator.

Preparation & Cooking Tips: Remove stem; rinse and dry fruit. For a more uniform, tender texture and mellow flavor, drop kumquats in boiling water for 20 seconds, drain and chill in ice water. Dry fruit and refrigerate. To use, slice in half and remove seeds with knife tip. They are wonderful preserved in syrup or brandy. Kumquats make tangy sauces for meat or poultry.

Lemon

General Information: The tart zing of a lemon rousts the laziest palate. Lemons are the spark of many a dish: stews, cakes, tarts, soups, fish, vinaigrettes and drinks. Packed with vitamin C, the lemon is practically calorie-free. Lemons are available year-round.

Selection & Storage: Choose bright-yellow, thin-skinned lemons. If you intend to make candied lemon peel, choose the thicker-skinned lemons. Depending on their freshness when purchased, lemons can be refrigerated for 2 to 3 weeks. If you have leftover lemon juice, freeze it. Refrigerated juice loses its flavor faster than frozen juice.

Preparation & Cooking Tips: To increase the amount of juice, lemons should be at room temperature; place your palm on top of the lemon and roll it slowly, but firmly, across the countertop. Six medium lemons produce 1 cup of juice. One medium lemon yields 2 to 3 teaspoons of zest and 3 tablespoons of juice.

Lime

General Information: The lime was responsible for nicknaming a navy! When the British Navy ruled the seas, the sailors ate vitamin C-rich limes to prevent scurvy. Soon the sailors came to be known as "limeys." Limes enhance the flavors of fish, fruit, vegetables and chicken. Lime adds flavor without fat or sodium and can be used as a substitute for salt in many dishes. Available year-round, their peak season is May through August.

Selection & Storage: Select brightly colored, smooth-skinned, heavy limes. Some limes have small brown patches on their skin (russeting). This does not affect flavor. Do not buy limes that are hard or shriveled. Store limes in the refrigerator for up to 10 days.

Preparation & Cooking Tips: Six medium limes will yield about a half-cup of juice. Place your palm on the lime and roll it slowly across the countertop. Slice in half. Stick a fork into the fruit of the lime and twist back and forth to release juice.

NUTRITION FACTS

Juice Orange

UNITED STATES
Serving Size: 1 medium
Calories	70
Protein	1 g
Fat	0 g
Carbohydrates	17 g
Dietary Fiber	4 g
Sodium	0 mg

CANADA
Serving Size: per 150 g (1 medium)
Energy	64 cal.....290 kJ
Protein	1.1 g
Fat	0.3 g
Carbohydrates	17 g
Dietary Fibre	4.4 g
Sodium	0 mg
Potassium	254 mg

Kumquat

UNITED STATES
Serving Size: 3 medium
Calories	35
Protein	1 g
Fat	0 g
Carbohydrates	9 g
Dietary Fiber	4 g
Sodium	0 mg

CANADA
Serving Size: per 60 g (3 medium)
Energy	36 cal.....150 kJ
Protein	0.5 g
Fat	0.1 g
Carbohydrates	9.4 g
Dietary Fibre	2.1 g
Sodium	3 mg
Potassium	111 mg

Lemon

UNITED STATES
Serving Size: 1 medium
Calories	15
Protein	0 g
Fat	0 g
Carbohydrates	5 g
Dietary Fiber	1 g
Sodium	5 mg

CANADA
Serving Size: per 60 g (1 medium)
Energy	17 cal.....70 kJ
Protein	0.7 g
Fat	0.2 g
Carbohydrates	5.6 g
Dietary Fibre	1.3 g
Sodium	1 mg
Potassium	83 mg

Lime

UNITED STATES
Serving Size: 1 medium
Calories	20
Protein	0 g
Fat	0 g
Carbohydrates	7 g
Dietary Fiber	2 g
Sodium	0 mg

CANADA
Serving Size: per 70 g (1 medium)
Energy	21 cal.....90 kJ
Protein	0.5 g
Fat	0.1 g
Carbohydrates	7.4 g
Dietary Fibre	1.5 g
Sodium	1 mg
Potassium	71 mg

SOURCE: USDA

Mandarin/Tangerine

General Information: The most common mandarin orange found in the United States is the tangerine. The first such mandarin orange came to Europe via Tangiers; hence the name. Other varieties of mandarins are the Clementine, Dancy and Satsuma oranges. Their fruit is as sweet as juice or eating oranges, but less acidic. Many varieties of mandarins are seedless. Depending on the variety, mandarins may be found at the market from November through June.

Selection & Storage: Choose mandarins that are plump and heavy for their size, as these will be juiciest. They should be soft, but firm to the touch. The color may vary from light to deep orange, but the skin should be glossy. Mandarins may be kept for up to 1 week in the refrigerator.

Preparation & Cooking Tips: Mandarins are best eaten raw. If you must cook mandarins, heat gently and do not boil or they will lose their flavor. Mandarins are good in salads, on custards, or as side dishes with candied lemon zest.

Navel Orange

General Information: Navel oranges are excellent eating oranges — sweet, juicy and seedless. Eating an orange boosts body absorption of iron from plant foods by as much as 400 percent. The navel orange came to California from Bahia, Brazil, in 1873. It was dubbed the "belly-button orange" because of the bump at the blossom end of the fruit. The navel orange is available from November through late spring.

Selection & Storage: Pick oranges that are firm and heavy for their size. Russeting, a rough brown spot on the skin, does not affect the flavor. Often, ripe oranges will have a slight greening. Oranges will keep for up to 2 weeks when refrigerated.

Preparation & Cooking Tips: Navel oranges are best eaten raw. With a sharp knife, cut through the skin and remove the "navel." Score the skin in 3 places from the navel to the bottom. Gently pull away the skin.

Tangelo

General Information: Tangelo sounds like a dance step, but is actually a hybrid fruit — a cross between a tangerine and a grapefruit. Tangelos are juicy with a sweetly tart citrus flavor. They are a loose-skinned fruit, which makes them easy to peel. Tangelos have distinctive bumps on one end. The skin ranges from smooth to coarse and the color from yellowy-orange to deep orange. The most common variety of tangelo available in North America is the Minneola, grown in Florida. Tangelos are available from November to March.

Selection & Storage: Choose heavy fruit. Much like grapefruit, a tangelo should give with slight pressure. Keep tangelos at room temperature for consumption within 5 days. Otherwise, refrigerate for up to 2 weeks.

Preparation & Cooking Tips: Tangelos will lose much of their flavor if cooked. Eat them raw in segments or add to salads or desserts.

Temple Orange

General Information: Also known as a Royal mandarin, temple oranges are tangors — a cross between a tangerine and an orange. Sweet and juicy, they look like a large tangerine with a flavor similar to oranges. They are available January through March.

Selection & Storage: Choose temple oranges that are firm and heavy for their size. Superficial green or brown patches do not affect flavor. Temple oranges can be refrigerated or stored at room temperature for up to 2 weeks.

Preparation & Cooking Tips: Peel or cut into sections and enjoy out-of-hand. Or, remove membranes and add segments to fruit and green salads and gelatin molds. Segments dipped in yogurt make a healthy snack.

NUTRITION FACTS

UNITED STATES
Serving Size: 1 medium
Calories 37
Protein.....................1 g
Fat ....0 g
Carbohydrates ....9 g
Dietary Fiber ....2 g
Sodium ....1 mg

CANADA
Serving Size: per 130 g (2 medium)
Energy..........57 cal....239 kJ
Protein....................1.1 g
Fat ....0.3 g
Carbohydrates ....14.6 g
Dietary Fibre ....1.7 g
Sodium ....2 mg
Potassium ....204 mg

UNITED STATES
Serving Size: 1 medium
Calories 70
Protein.....................1 g
Fat ....0 g
Carbohydrates.................21 g
Dietary Fiber ....7 g
Sodium ....0 mg

CANADA
Serving Size: per 140 g (1 medium)
Energy..........64 cal....270 kJ
Protein....................1.4 g
Fat ....0.1 g
Carbohydrates ....16 g
Dietary Fibre ....3.4 g
Sodium ....1 mg
Potassium ....249 mg

UNITED STATES
Serving Size: 1 medium
Calories 45
Protein.....................1 g
Fat ....0 g
Carbohydrates................11 g
Dietary Fiber ....2 g
Sodium ....0 mg

CANADA
Serving Size: per 85 g (1 medium)
Energy..........37 cal....160 kJ
Protein....................0.5 g
Fat ....0.1 g
Carbohydrates ....9.4 g
Dietary Fibre ....0.8 g
Sodium ....1 mg
Potassium ....132 mg

UNITED STATES
Serving Size: 1 medium
Calories 62
Protein.....................1 g
Fat ....0.1 g
Carbohydrates ....15 g
Dietary Fiber ....3 g
Sodium ....0 mg

CANADA
Serving Size: per 130 g (1 medium)
Energy..........61 cal....260 kJ
Protein....................1.2 g
Fat ....0.2 g
Carbohydrates ....15 g
Dietary Fibre ....2.3 g
Sodium ....0 mg
Potassium ....235 mg

SOURCE: USDA

Ugli®Fruit

General Information: The Ugli® Fruit is homely with its odd pear shape, thick skin and greenish-yellow color. But inside, what a beauty! It tastes like honeyed tangerine and tart grapefruit. A member of the "loose-skinned" citrus family, thus easily peeled, the Ugli® Fruit is native to Jamaica and available from winter through spring.

Selection & Storage: Choose heavy Uglis® with no sign of drying at the stem end. Much like grapefruit, the Ugli® should give with slight pressure. Uglis® have a coarse skin with many surface blemishes. The color ranges from lime green to light orange. Keep at room temperature for consumption within 5 days. Or, store for up to 3 weeks in the refrigerator.

Preparation & Cooking Tips: Uglis® lose much of their flavor if cooked, but boiling down the juice in a non-aluminum pan creates an intense syrup. Eat them raw in segments or with a grapefruit spoon.

Valencia Orange

General Information: The most widely grown oranges, Valencias comprise about half the total number of oranges grown each year. Valencias are medium to large in size, and have smooth, thin skins. They are available February through June.

Selection & Storage: Choose Valencia oranges that are firm and heavy for their size. Superficial green or brown patches do not affect flavor. Valencia oranges can be refrigerated or stored at room temperature for up to 2 weeks.

Preparation & Cooking Tips: Peel or cut into sections and enjoy out-of-hand. Or, add segments to fruit and green salads and gelatin molds. Valencias, especially the Florida variety, are considered the best oranges for juicing. Squeeze juice from Valencia halves and enjoy, or use to marinate meat, fish or poultry before cooking.

Ideas for Storing and Serving Grapes

To store grapes, wrap bunches of grapes loosely in newsprint and keep them in the dark. For a tasty treat, freeze whole grapes and snack on them straight from the freezer. Grapes are lovely additions to party trays to add a light, delicious, colorful touch as a garnish and healthy finger food. For another simple hors d'oeuvre, mix equal parts of blue cheese and butter. Sandwich mixture between large, cut, red seedless grapes. To cut grapes, slice lengthwise in half.

Grapes

Black

General Information: Grapes are divided into two color categories: black and white. Black grapes are sometimes called red because their color varies from deep rose-pink to purple to black. Most of the flavor resides in the skin. Black Hamburg grapes, grown in hothouses, are fat, juicy and very fragrant. Concord grapes, blue-black with a dusting of silver, are eaten out-of-hand and used in jellies and juices.

Selection & Storage: Choose grapes that are plump, full-colored and firmly attached, with no brown area at stem connections. Store grapes, unwashed, in the refrigerator for up to 1 week. Grapes also may be frozen for up to 1 week. Wash, dry, and place in a single layer on a baking sheet. Freeze for 1 hour and then put grapes in an airtight container.

Preparation & Cooking Tips: Wash grapes thoroughly before use. Ideally, grapes should be served at 60°F.

NUTRITION FACTS

UNITED STATES
Serving Size: 1 medium
Calories 37
Protein............................1 g
Fat ....0 g
Carbohydrates..................10 g
Dietary Fiber ....0 g
Sodium ....1 mg

CANADA

NUTRITION FACTS
NOT AVAILABLE

UNITED STATES
Serving Size: 1 medium
Calories 59
Protein.........................1.25 g
Fat ....0.3 g
Carbohydrates...................14 g
Dietary Fiber ....3 g
Sodium ....0 mg

CANADA
Serving Size: per 120 g (1 medium)
Energy...........59 cal.....250 kJ
Protein...........................1.3 g
Fat ....0.4 g
Carbohydrates ....14 g
Dietary Fibre ....3.0 g
Sodium ....0 mg
Potassium ....215 mg

NUTRITION FACTS

UNITED STATES
Serving Size: 1½ cups
Calories 90
Protein............................1 g
Fat ....1 g
Carbohydrates ....24 g
Dietary Fiber ....1 g
Sodium ....0 mg

CANADA
Serving Size: per 140 g (375 mL/1½ cups)
Energy...........88 cal.....370 kJ
Protein...........................0.9 g
Fat ....0.5 g
Carbohydrates ....24 g
Dietary Fibre ....1.3 g
Sodium ....3 mg
Potassium ....267 mg

SOURCE: USDA

Grapes

Champagne

General Information: Also known as Black Corinth grapes, Champagne grapes are named for their sweet, wine-like flavor. These small, seedless purple grapes are available July to October.

Selection & Storage: Grapes are picked and sold when ripe; they will not ripen further after picking. Look for firm, plump grapes firmly attached to flexible, not dry, stems. The silvery-white "bloom" found on grapes is a clear indication of freshness. After discarding any overripe grapes, refrigerate, unwashed, in a perforated plastic bag for up to 1 week.

Preparation & Cooking Tips: Champagne grapes are best chilled and eaten out-of-hand. Or, add them to fruit and green salads, or stir into yogurt for a flavorful treat.

Concord

General Information: Sweet-tart Concord grapes are often used to make preserves and grape juice. These plump, round, blue-black grapes are available in September and October.

Selection & Storage: Grapes are picked and sold when ripe; they will not ripen further after picking. Look for firm, plump grapes firmly attached to flexible, not dry, stems. The silvery-white "bloom" found on grapes is a clear indication of freshness. After discarding any overripe grapes, refrigerate, unwashed, for no more than 1 week.

Preparation & Cooking Tips: Concord grapes are best chilled and eaten out-of-hand, or try them frozen. Remove from stems, wash and place in a single layer on a tray. Freeze until hard for a refreshing snack. Or, add them to salads and gelatin molds, or stir halved grapes into yogurt for a flavorful treat.

Green

General Information: Green grapes are actually white grapes. The color of white grapes varies from pale green to amber-yellow. Most of the flavor resides in the skin. The amber-green Muscat grape is renowned for its sweet flavor and musky aroma. Almeria is another popular grape. Availability depends on the variety of grape.

Selection & Storage: Choose grapes that are plump, full-colored and firmly attached, with no brown area at stem connections. Store grapes, unwashed, in the refrigerator for up to 1 week. Grapes also may be frozen for up to 1 week. Wash, dry, and place in a single layer on a baking sheet. Freeze for 1 hour and then put grapes in an airtight container. Frozen grapes are a great treat.

Preparation & Cooking Tips: Wash grapes thoroughly before eating. Ideally, grapes should be served at 60°F.

Red

General Information: There are two categories of grapes: black and white. Red grapes are actually black grapes. Their color varies from deep rose-pink to purplish red. Most of the flavor resides in the skin. The Cardinal grape has a sweet, musky flavor. The Ruby, available from August through January, is dark red, thin-skinned and has an oval shape. Large and tart, Flame Seedless grapes are second only to green Thompson Seedless grapes in popularity.

Selection & Storage: Choose grapes that are plump, full-colored and firmly attached, with no brown area at stem connections. Store grapes, unwashed, in the refrigerator for up to 1 week.

Preparation & Cooking Tips: Wash grapes thoroughly before use. Red grapes are wonderful as a snack or in salads. Ideally, grapes should be served at 60°F.

NUTRITION FACTS

Champagne

UNITED STATES
Serving Size: 1½ cups
Calories	90
Protein	1 g
Fat	1 g
Carbohydrates	24 g
Dietary Fiber	1 g
Sodium	0 mg

CANADA
Serving Size: per 140 g (375 mL/1½ cups)
Energy	114 cal.....475 kJ
Protein	1.05 g
Fat	0.9 g
Carbohydrates	28 g
Dietary Fibre	1.6 g
Sodium	3.2 mg
Potassium	0 mg

Concord

UNITED STATES
Serving Size: 1½ cups
Calories	87
Protein	1 g
Fat	0.5 g
Carbohydrates	24 g
Dietary Fiber	1 g
Sodium	3 mg

CANADA
Serving Size: per 140 g (375 mL/1½ cups)
Energy	62 cal.....258 kJ
Protein	0.6 g
Fat	0.3 g
Carbohydrates	16 g
Dietary Fibre	0.9 g
Sodium	1.8 mg
Potassium	257 mg

Green

UNITED STATES
Serving Size: 1 ½ cups
Calories	90
Protein	1 g
Fat	1 g
Carbohydrates	24 g
Dietary Fiber	1 g
Sodium	0 mg

CANADA
Serving Size: per 140 g (375 mL/1 ½ cups)
Energy	88 cal.....370 kJ
Protein	0.9 g
Fat	0.5 g
Carbohydrates	24 g
Dietary Fibre	1.3 g
Sodium	3 mg
Potassium	267 mg

Red

UNITED STATES
Serving Size: 1½ cups
Calories	90
Protein	1 g
Fat	1 g
Carbohydrates	24g
Dietary Fiber	1 g
Sodium	0 mg

CANADA
Serving Size: per 140 g (375 mL/1½ cups)
Energy	88 cal.....370 kJ
Protein	0.9 g
Fat	0.5 g
Carbohydrates	24 g
Dietary Fibre	1.3 g
Sodium	3 mg
Potassium	267 mg

SOURCE: USDA

Grapes

Seedless

NUTRITION FACTS

UNITED STATES	
Serving Size: 1½ cups	
Calories	90
Protein	1 g
Fat	1 g
Carbohydrates	24 g
Dietary Fiber	1 g
Sodium	0 mg

CANADA		
Serving Size: per 140 g (375 mL/1½ cups)		
Energy	88 cal	370 kJ
Protein		0.9 g
Fat		0.5 g
Carbohydrates		24 g
Dietary Fibre		1.3 g
Sodium		3 mg
Potassium		267 mg

General Information: The most popular variety of seedless grape in the United States is the Thompson Seedless. Most of the raisins in the United States are made from Thompson Seedless grapes. Other varieties of seedless grapes are the Perlette, Flame and Ruby. The round, frosty-green Perlette has a short, early season. Their flesh is mildly sweet with a firm texture. Flame and Ruby are red seedless grapes.

Selection & Storage: Choose grapes that are plump, full-colored and firmly attached, with no brown area at stem connections. Store grapes, unwashed, in the refrigerator for up to 1 week.

Preparation & Cooking Tips: Wash grapes thoroughly before use. Ideally, grapes should be served at 60°F. Serve with ripe, creamy cheeses such as Brie.

Ripeness Test for Melons

When is a melon ripe? Should you sniff it? What about knocking on it for explicit resonance? Is it wise to bounce a melon on a floor for a ripeness test? It is simple to test for ripeness. Hold the melon firmly in both hands and lightly press the area immediately around the tip of the melon at the opposite end from the stem. The surface should give slightly. Another hint for ripeness is a pleasantly sweet aroma.

Melons

Cantaloupe

NUTRITION FACTS

UNITED STATES	
Serving Size: ¼ medium	
Calories	56
Protein	1 g
Fat	0 g
Carbohydrates	16 g
Dietary Fiber	1 g
Sodium	25 mg

CANADA		
Serving Size: per 135 g (¼ medium)		
Energy	47 cal	200 kJ
Protein		1.2 g
Fat		0.4 g
Carbohydrates		11 g
Dietary Fibre		0.9 g
Sodium		12 mg
Potassium		417 mg

General Information: Cantaloupes are of European origin and named for a papal villa, Cantaloupo, near Rome. The European melon has a warty rind and scented, yellow flesh. It is not exported. North America cantaloupe is actually a muskmelon and features raised, netted skin and sweet, orange flesh. They are available June to November.

Selection & Storage: Cantaloupes picked before they mature never reach full flavor. Check the stem end for a clean, smooth indentation, known as a "full slip." If the edge is jagged, the cantaloupe was picked before maturity. A good melon is symmetrical and the blossom end gives with slight pressure. Avoid overripe melons with lumps or soft spots. Cantaloupes become more yellow as they ripen. Store ripe in the refrigerator for up to 5 days.

Preparation & Cooking Tips: Slice cantaloupe in half. Scrape seeds out. Cantaloupe halves may be eaten with a spoon. Cantaloupe is so sweet it goes well with salty meats such as prosciutto.

Casaba

NUTRITION FACTS

UNITED STATES	
Serving Size: 1 cup	
Calories	45
Protein	2 g
Fat	0 g
Carbohydrates	11 g
Dietary Fiber	1 g
Sodium	20 mg

CANADA		
Serving Size: per 180 g (250 mL/1 cup)		
Energy	47 cal	200 kJ
Protein		1.6 g
Fat		0.2 g
Carbohydrates		11 g
Dietary Fibre		1.4 g
Sodium		22 mg
Potassium		378 mg

General Information: Casabas are large, deep-ridged, golden-yellow skinned melons. The cream-colored flesh is juicy with a distinctive mild taste likened to cucumber. Weighing between 4 and 7 pounds, the casaba's round shape is pointed at the stem end. Casabas are available from September to November.

Selection & Storage: Casaba melons picked before maturity never reach full flavor. Choose uniformly yellow casabas. The blossom end should give with slight pressure. Avoid rock-hard melons and overripe melons with lumps or soft spots. Wrap ripe melons in a plastic bag and refrigerate up to 5 days.

Preparation & Cooking Tips: Slice the casaba in half. Scrape out seeds and strings. Slice halves into pieces. With a sharp knife, slice the flesh and the rind. Casabas are good plain or with a sprinkle of lime juice.

SOURCE: USDA

Melons

Crenshaw

General Information: Melon connoisseurs say that the Crenshaw is the most sweetly succulent melon in the world. A hybrid cross of the casaba and cantaloupe, the Crenshaw melon is rounded at the blossom end and pointed at the stem end. The skin of a Crenshaw is dark green and, as it ripens, the skin becomes yellow. Crenshaws are large, from 5 to 9 pounds. They are available from July to October.

Selection & Storage: Melons picked before maturity never reach full flavor. A good melon gives with slight pressure. Avoid rock-hard melons and overripe melons with lumps or soft spots. Ripe Crenshaws give off a spicy fragrance and have springy, not mushy, skin. Store melons at room temperature until ripe. Wrap ripe melons in a plastic bag and refrigerate up to 5 days.

Preparation & Cooking Tips: Slice melon in half. Scrape out seeds and strings. Slice halves into pieces. With a sharp knife, slice between the flesh and the rind.

Honeydew

General Information: Sweet and succulent, the honeydew has pale, greenish-white skin and pale-green flesh. Of the muskmelon family, honeydews weigh from 4 to 8 pounds and are available year-round.

Selection & Storage: Honeydew melons picked before maturity never reach full flavor. A good melon is symmetrical and the blossom end gives with slight pressure. Avoid rock-hard melons and overripe melons with lumps or soft spots. Perfectly ripe honeydews have an almost imperceptible wrinkling on the skin's surface that can be felt. Wrap ripe melons in a plastic bag and refrigerate up to 5 days.

Preparation & Cooking Tips: Slice honeydew in half. With a spoon, scrape out the seeds. Slice halves into 4 or more pieces. With a sharp knife, slice between the whitish-green flesh and the deeper-green rind. Honeydew is excellent plain or with a sprinkle of fresh lime juice. Honeydews should not be cooked.

Juan Canary

General Information: The Juan Canary melon, a variation of the casaba melon, has a brilliant yellow, roughly furrowed skin. Unlike the casaba, the Juan Canary is oblong-shaped with slightly pointed ends and slightly larger than a cantaloupe. The flesh is creamy white, tinged with pink around the seed cavity. It is in season from July to November.

Selection & Storage: Juan Canary melons picked before maturity never reach full flavor. Choose those of a uniform, deep-yellow color. The blossom end should give with slight pressure. Avoid rock-hard melons and overripe melons with lumps or soft spots.

Preparation & Cooking Tips: Slice in half. With a spoon, scrape out seeds and any strings. Slice halves into 4 pieces. Slice between the creamy white flesh and the pale-green rind. Juan Canary melons are good plain or with a sprinkle of fresh lime juice. Juan Canary melons should not be cooked.

Pepino

General Information: With its waxy, ivory skin streaked with deep purple, the Pepino looks more like an eggplant than a melon. Ranging in size from a plum to a large papaya, the entire pepino is edible — skin, seeds and yellow flesh. Sweet and firm, the flesh tastes like a combination of pear and banana. The Pepino is also known as mellowfruit and treemelon. They are available from late fall to mid-spring.

Selection & Storage: Look for fragrant, firm, unblemished Pepino melons. Ripen at room temperature. The fragrance intensifies and the background color becomes deep golden upon ripening. Store ripe pepino melons in a plastic bag in the refrigerator for up to 3 days.

Preparation & Cooking Tips: Eat Pepinos when just ripened. Peel before eating out-of-hand. Add zest with lemon or lime juice, basil, salt and pepper.

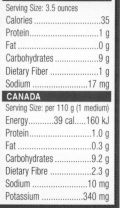

NUTRITION FACTS

UNITED STATES
Serving Size: 3.5 ounces
Calories 35
Protein..................1 g
Fat ....0 g
Carbohydrates ....9 g
Dietary Fiber ....1 g
Sodium ....17 mg

CANADA
Serving Size: per 110 g (1 medium)
Energy..........39 cal.....160 kJ
Protein..................1.0 g
Fat ....0.3 g
Carbohydrates ....9.2 g
Dietary Fibre ....2.3 g
Sodium ....10 mg
Potassium ....340 mg

UNITED STATES
Serving Size: 1/10 medium
Calories 50
Protein..................1 g
Fat ....0 g
Carbohydrates ....13 g
Dietary Fiber ....1 g
Sodium ....35 mg

CANADA
Serving Size: per 130 g (1/10 medium)
Energy..........46 cal.....190 kJ
Protein..................0.6 g
Fat ....0.1 g
Carbohydrates ....12 g
Dietary Fibre ....1 g
Sodium ....13 mg
Potassium ....352 mg

UNITED STATES
Serving Size: 1 medium with skin
Calories 80
Protein..................0 g
Fat ....0 g
Carbohydrates ....22 g
Dietary Fiber ....5 g
Sodium ....0 mg

CANADA
Serving Size: 1/4 cup, dry
Energy..........80 cal.....258 kJ
Protein..................0 g
Fat ....0 g
Carbohydrates ....22 g
Dietary Fibre ....5 g
Sodium ....0 mg
Potassium ....176 mg

UNITED STATES
Serving Size: 1 medium with skin
Calories 80
Protein..................0 g
Fat ....0 g
Carbohydrates ....22 g
Dietary Fiber ....5 g
Sodium ....0 mg

CANADA
Serving Size: 1/4 cup, dry
Energy..........80 cal.....258 kJ
Protein..................0 g
Fat ....0 g
Carbohydrates ....22 g
Dietary Fibre ....5 g
Sodium ....0 mg
Potassium ....176 mg

SOURCE: USDA

Persian

General Information: The Persian melon is a large, grayish-green muskmelon with delicate netting on the rind. They weigh about 5 pounds. The rich, salmon-colored flesh is sweet and delectable. Available from July through October, they peak in late summer.

Selection and Storage: Persian melons picked before they are mature never reach full flavor. A good melon is symmetrical and the blossom end gives with slight pressure. When a Persian melon is ripe, the skin turns slightly golden, the netting lightens in color and its perfumed fragrance becomes more pronounced. Ripen at room temperature. Store ripe Persian melons in a plastic bag in the refrigerator for up to 5 days.

Preparation & Cooking Tips: Eat Persians when just ripened. Slice melon in half. Scrape out the seeds and any strings. Slice halves into 4 or more pieces. With a sharp knife, slice between the flesh and the rind.

Watermelon

General Information: Watermelons are oblong and large, up to 30 pounds. The rind is hard, and dark or light green, depending on the variety. Smaller, round watermelons are sometimes called "icebox" melons. Yellow or golden watermelon tastes the same as red, but has bright-yellow flesh. Watermelons are available from May through September.

Selection & Storage: Avoid melons with a flat side. The skin should be dull, not shiny. Slap the melon and listen for a hollow thump. Refrigerate for no more than a week.

Preparation & Cooking Tips: Most seeds are in concentric circles. Cut melon into circular slices. Use cookie cutter to remove seedless center. With a sharp knife, remove the ring of seeds. Cut remaining ring at inner rind. Cube reserved fruit into 1-inch cubes. Serve watermelon chunks tossed with orange juice, mint leaves, a little sugar and toasted almonds.

Poach Pears – with Port or Purée

Poached pears are another perfect way to serve this seasonal fruit. Peel the fruit, but do not cut or core. Slice up to, but not through, the stem end to create a pear-shaped fan. Cook gently in a little water and lemon juice until just tender. Cook over low heat to retain flavor and shape. For a special occasion, pour port over a single layer of poached pears and chill. To puree poached pears, core and puree fruit in a food processor until smooth.

Pears

Anjou

General Information: The Anjou pear is the second most popular pear in America after the Bartlett. Egg-shaped and relatively hardy, red Anjous are russet-colored. Anjous are available from October through May.

Selection & Storage: Pears are tricky: If allowed to ripen on the tree, most pears turn mushy and grainy. On the other hand, a pear picked too early never ripens. After harvest, a pear requires 5 to 10 days at room temperature to fully ripen. Select firm, unblemished pears. The ripening process is hastened by placing pears in a pierced paper bag with an apple or banana. When ripe, pears are fragrant and the flesh at the stem yields to gentle pressure. Store ripe pears in a plastic bag in the refrigerator for up to 5 days.

Preparation & Cooking Tips: Anjous are considered firmer than Bartletts, but less flavorful. The flesh of an Anjou stands up well to cooking, but pear skin darkens and toughens when heated. Remove skin before cooking.

NUTRITION FACTS (Persian)

UNITED STATES — Serving Size: 1 cup
Calories 56; Protein 1 g; Fat 0 g; Carbohydrates 16 g; Dietary Fiber 1 g; Sodium 14 mg

CANADA — Serving Size: per 160 g (250 mL/1 cup)
Energy 56 cal / 230 kJ; Protein 1.4 g; Fat 0.5 g; Carbohydrates 13 g; Dietary Fibre 0.5 g; Sodium 14 mg; Potassium 494 mg

NUTRITION FACTS (Watermelon)

UNITED STATES — Serving Size: 1/18 medium
Calories 80; Protein 1 g; Fat 0 g; Carbohydrates 27 g; Dietary Fiber 2 g; Sodium 10 mg

CANADA — Serving Size: per 170 g (250 mL/1 cup)
Energy 54 cal / 230 kJ; Protein 1.1 g; Fat 0.7 g; Carbohydrates 12 g; Dietary Fibre 0.7 g; Sodium 3 mg; Potassium 197 mg

NUTRITION FACTS (Anjou)

UNITED STATES — Serving Size: 1 medium
Calories 100; Protein 1 g; Fat 1 g; Carbohydrates 25 g; Dietary Fiber 4 g; Sodium 0 mg

CANADA — Serving Size: per 160 g (1 medium)
Energy 94 cal / 400 kJ; Protein 0.6 g; Fat 0.6 g; Carbohydrates 24 g; Dietary Fibre 4.8 g; Sodium 0 mg; Potassium 200 mg

SOURCE: USDA

Pears

Asian

General Information: Most Asian pears are grown in Japan. Although technically a member of the pear family, the Asian pear resembles an apple in shape and texture. Crisp, grainy, slightly sweet and juicy, Asian pears are delicious. Varying in size and color from gold to green, there are over a 100 varieties of Asian pears. Some are smooth skinned, while others are dappled with russet spots. Asian pears are available from late summer through early fall.

Selection & Storage: Ripe Asian pears are hard. Choose the most fragrant pears available. Store ripe pears in the refrigerator. They will last up to 2 weeks.

Preparation & Cooking Tips: Asian pears may be eaten peeled or unpeeled. All but the slim center core is edible. If they are to be eaten raw, serve them chilled. When sliced paper-thin, the nectar surfaces on each slice. When cooked, the flavor of Asian pears intensifies and the flesh remains firm.

Bartlett

General Information: Seventy-five percent of all pears grown in the United States are Bartlett pears. Bartlett is the standard against which all other pears are measured. Much of the Bartlett harvest goes to canning. Red Bartletts taste similar to the yellow Bartletts, but cost more. They are harvested in July and August.

Selection & Storage: Bartletts bruise easily. Look for firm, unmarked and unbruised fruit. When ripe, a red Bartlett goes from dark green with reddish blush to brilliant red. They are fragrant and the flesh at the stem yields to gentle pressure. Ripen pears at room temperature. The process is hastened by placing pears in a pierced paper bag with an apple or banana. Store ripe pears in a plastic bag in the refrigerator for up to 5 days.

Preparation & Cooking Tips: Bartletts are better eaten out-of-hand, but can be used in cooked dishes. When heated, pear skin will darken and toughen, so remove before cooking.

Bosc

General Information: Most Americans have never tasted a perfectly ripe pear. The French claim that Americans lack the patience a pear requires. Pears can go from not quite ripe to mushy in a day. The skin of a Bosc is a russeted yellow. Boscs are slow to ripen, but reward patience with a creamy, sweet and spicy flesh. They are available September through May.

Selection & Storage: Select firm, unblemished Boscs. Ripen pears at room temperature. The process is hastened by placing pears in a pierced paper bag with an apple or banana. Ripened Boscs are fragrant and the flesh at the stem yields to gentle pressure. Store ripe pears in a plastic bag in the refrigerator for up to 5 days.

Preparation & Cooking Tips: Boscs are an excellent choice for poaching, with their elegant shape and firm flesh. Pear skin will darken and toughen when heated, so remove skin before cooking.

Comice

General Information: Known as the "Queen of Pears," the Comice is generally considered to be the best eating pear on the face of the earth. Large and exquisite, this pear has a buttery smooth, sweet flesh and fruity fragrance. It is available from October through February.

Selection & Storage: Comice pears are very delicate, must be handled carefully, and are generally wrapped in paper for protection. Choose firm greenish-yellow pears with occasional russet specks. Ripen at room temperature. When ripe, the skin turns yellow, the fragrance intensifies, and the neck yields to slight pressure. Ripe Comice pears will keep a day or 2 in the refrigerator.

Preparation & Cooking Tips: Wash ripe pears and gently dry. Serve Comice pears at room temperature with a rich cheese, such as Brie or Gorgonzola. Do not cook Comice pears.

NUTRITION FACTS

UNITED STATES
Serving Size: 1 medium

Calories	50
Protein	1 g
Fat	0 g
Carbohydrates	13 g
Dietary Fiber	4 g
Sodium	0 mg

CANADA
Serving Size: per 120 g (1 medium)

Energy	51 cal	200 kJ
Protein		0.6 g
Fat		0.3 g
Carbohydrates		13 g
Dietary Fibre		4.4 g
Sodium		0 mg
Potassium		198 mg

UNITED STATES
Serving Size: 1 medium

Calories	98
Protein	1 g
Fat	1 g
Carbohydrates	25 g
Dietary Fiber	5 g
Sodium	0 mg

CANADA
Serving Size: per 160 g (1 medium)

Energy	94 cal	400 kJ
Protein		0.6 g
Fat		0.6 g
Carbohydrates		24 g
Dietary Fibre		4.8 g
Sodium		0 mg
Potassium		200 mg

UNITED STATES
Serving Size: 1 medium

Calories	86
Protein	1 g
Fat	1 g
Carbohydrates	22 g
Dietary Fiber	5 g
Sodium	0 mg

CANADA
Serving Size: per 145 g (1 medium)

Energy	85 cal	360 kJ
Protein		0.6 g
Fat		0.6 g
Carbohydrates		22 g
Dietary Fibre		4.4 g
Sodium		0 mg
Potassium		181 mg

UNITED STATES
Serving Size: 1 medium

Calories	122
Protein	1 g
Fat	1 g
Carbohydrates	31 g
Dietary Fiber	5 g
Sodium	0 mg

CANADA
Serving Size: per 160 g (1 medium)

Energy	94 cal	400 kJ
Protein		0.6 g
Fat		0.6 g
Carbohydrates		24 g
Dietary Fibre		4.8 g
Sodium		0 mg
Potassium		200 mg

SOURCE: USDA

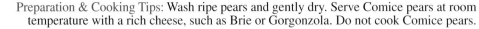

NUTRITION FACTS

UNITED STATES
Serving Size: 1 medium
Calories..........................98
Protein...............................1 g
Fat ....1 g
Carbohydrates ....25 g
Dietary Fiber ....5 g
Sodium ....0 mg

CANADA
Serving Size: per 160 g (1 medium)
Energy...........94 cal.....400 kJ
Protein............................0.6 g
Fat ....0.6 g
Carbohydrates ....24 g
Dietary Fibre ....4.8 g
Sodium ....0 mg
Potassium ....200 mg

UNITED STATES
Serving Size: 1 medium
Calories 98
Protein...............................1 g
Fat ....1 g
Carbohydrates ....25 g
Dietary Fiber ....5 g
Sodium ....0 mg

CANADA
Serving Size: per 160 g (1 medium)
Energy...........94 cal.....400 kJ
Protein............................0.6 g
Fat ....0.6 g
Carbohydrates ....24 g
Dietary Fibre ....4.8 g
Sodium ....0 mg
Potassium ....200 mg

UNITED STATES
Serving Size: 1 medium
Calories 98
Protein...............................1 g
Fat ....1 g
Carbohydrates ....25 g
Dietary Fiber ....5 g
Sodium ....0 mg

CANADA
Serving Size: per 160 g (1 medium)
Energy...........94 cal.....400 kJ
Protein............................0.6 g
Fat ....0.6 g
Carbohydrates ....24 g
Dietary Fibre ....4.8 g
Sodium ....0 mg
Potassium ....200 mg

SOURCE: USDA

Forelle

General Information: The green and red speckled Forelle pear is also known as the "trout pear." (Forelle is the German word for trout.) The Forelle originated in Saxony in the early eighteenth century. Distinguished by its spectacular color, the Forelle is the size and shape of a small Bartlett. Forelles are sometimes tricky to ripen, but can be very sweet and juicy. They are available at Christmas time.

Selection & Storage: Choose pears with good color that are unbruised and firm, but not hard. Ripen pears at room temperature. The process will be hastened if pears are placed in a pierced paper bag with an apple or banana. Forelles deepen in color when ripe and the flesh at the stem yields to gentle pressure. Store ripe pears in a plastic bag in the refrigerator for up to 5 days.

Preparation & Cooking Tips: Pear skin darkens and toughens when heated, so remove skin before cooking. Pears discolor when exposed to air. To retard this process, dip sliced pears into acidulated water.

Packham

General Information: The Packham pear, originally bred in Australia in 1897, is the pear of choice Down Under. A late-season pear, Packhams have the overall shape and size of an Anjou, but with bumpy green skin. When fully ripe, they are juicy and sweet. They are available March to July.

Selection & Storage: Choose firm, unblemished pears. When ripe, the green skin develops a yellow undercast, the fragrance intensifies, and the flesh at the stem yields to gentle pressure. Ripen pears at room temperature. Hasten ripening by placing pears in a pierced paper bag with an apple or banana. Store ripe pears in a plastic bag in the refrigerator for up to 5 days.

Preparation & Cooking Tips: Packham pears are excellent eaten out-of-hand, but are suitable for cooking. When cooking Packhams, select slightly underripe, firm pears. Pear skin darkens and toughens when heated, so remove skin before cooking.

Seckel

General Information: The smallest of all commercially grown pears, the Seckel has olive-green skin with a prominent red blush. Spicy sweet, the Seckel has firm flesh, which makes it an excellent pear for cooking or canning. The texture of the Seckel is grainier than other European pears, giving it the nickname "sand pear." Some find the Seckel too crisp for out-of-hand eating. The Seckel is available from late August through December.

Selection & Storage: Seckels are rock-hard at the store. Ripen pears at room temperature. Hasten ripening by placing pears in a pierced paper bag with an apple or banana. Seckel pears are ripe when a golden blush appears in the green and the flesh at the stem yields to gentle pressure. Store in a plastic bag in the refrigerator for up to 5 days.

Preparation & Cooking Tips: Seckels are an excellent canning or pickling pear. Pear skin darkens and toughens when heated, so remove before cooking.

Stone Fruit Salsa and Sauce

For a quick, fun twist to a plain meal, add a savory fruit salsa. Cut up 6 nectarines or peaches, mince ½ small red onion, add a handful of chopped fresh cilantro and toss together with the juice of 2 limes. This salsa adds a boost of color and unexpected flavor to your meal. Serve with grilled meat or fish.

French toast and waffles can be healthy. Top with sliced peaches and a sauce made from 1 cup of non-fat vanilla yogurt mixed with a tablespoon of brown sugar or maple syrup. Dust fruited waffles with cinnamon.

Stone Fruit

Apricot

General Information: A relative of the almond and the peach, the apricot is a buttery sweet, intensely flavored fruit. Four thousand years ago, apricots grew wild in the mountains of China. To be at their best, apricots must be picked when ripe and plump. Unfortunately, that is when they are at their most fragile for shipping. Sixty percent of the domestic crop is canned and another twenty-five percent is dried. They are available May through August.

Selection & Storage: Buy plump, firm, but not hard, apricots. Depending on the variety, ripe apricots are pale yellow to burnt orange. Avoid apricots with a greenish tinge or bruises. Store apricots at room temperature until ripe. Once ripe, wrap apricots in a plastic bag and store in the refrigerator for up to 3 days. Apricots are very perishable and lose flavor quickly.

Preparation & Cooking Tips: To prepare, just wash and slice in half. Serve with Roquefort or Camembert cheese.

Bing Cherries

General Information: Bing cherries are large, plump and juicy. Their glossy skin ranges from garnet to almost black. Native to Eurasia, cherries arrived in North America with the first English settlers. Cherries do not keep well without their stem, so they must be harvested by hand. They are available May through August.

Selection & Storage: Look for firm, plump cherries with green stems. If the stem or skin around the stem is brown, the fruit is not fresh. Highly perishable, wash cherries when ready to eat them. Keep cherries in a plastic bag in the refrigerator for 2 to 3 days. Cherries may be frozen, with or without pits, for up to 1 year. Rinse and dry cherries and place in zip-seal plastic bag. Close all but 1 inch, insert straw and suck out air; then fully seal.

Preparation & Cooking Tips: Pit cherries with a cherry pitter or with the tip of a vegetable peeler. Add a few drops of pure almond extract to baked cherries to intensify cherry taste.

Nectarine

General Information: The luscious nectarine is a relative of the peach, and may be used interchangeably in recipes. The chief difference between a peach and a nectarine is the skin. Nectarines are available year-round. Domestic nectarines are available from May to October.

Selection & Storage: Avoid nectarines that have a greenish hue or are rock-hard. When ripe, a nectarine is fragrant and yields slightly to the touch. Let stand at room temperature until ripe. Hasten the process by putting nectarines in a paper bag. Refrigerate up to 5 days.

Preparation & Cooking Tips: Nectarines do not need to be peeled before eating. They are an excellent substitution for strawberries in a shortcake recipe. Nectarines are good fresh or as a cooking fruit.

Peach

General Information: Peaches fall into two categories: clingstone and freestone. In a clingstone peach, the pit "clings" to the flesh. Freestone peaches, the most common, have pits that falls away easily. Peaches range in color from pink-blushed white to gold with red blush. They are available from May to October.

Selection & Storage: A red blush on a peach does not indicate ripeness. The background color should be overall creamy or yellow. A green background means the peach was picked too soon and will not ripen further. Buy peaches with unbruised and unwrinkled skin. Ripen at room temperature in a paper bag. When soft to the touch and fragrant, store peaches, unwashed, in the refrigerator for up to 2 weeks. Check frequently for brown spots.

Preparation & Cooking Tips: Remove from the refrigerator 1 hour before eating. Wash peaches and gently rub them with a towel to remove the fuzziness. The flavor intensifies when warm.

NUTRITION FACTS

UNITED STATES
Serving Size: 4 medium
Calories	70
Protein	2 g
Fat	0.5 g
Carbohydrates	16 g
Dietary Fiber	3 g
Sodium	0 mg

CANADA
Serving Size: per 110 g (3 medium)
Energy	53 cal.....220 kJ
Protein	1.5 g
Fat	0.4 g
Carbohydrates	12 g
Dietary Fibre	2.1 g
Sodium	1 mg
Potassium	326 mg

UNITED STATES
Serving Size: 1 cup
Calories	90
Protein	2 g
Fat	0 g
Carbohydrates	22 g
Dietary Fiber	3 g
Sodium	0 mg

CANADA
Serving Size: per 150 g (250 mL/1 cup)
Energy	108 cal.....450 kJ
Protein	1.8 g
Fat	1.4 g
Carbohydrates	25 g
Dietary Fibre	1.7 g
Sodium	0 mg
Potassium	336 mg

UNITED STATES
Serving Size: 1 medium
Calories	70
Protein	1 g
Fat	0 g
Carbohydrates	16 g
Dietary Fiber	2 g
Sodium	0 mg

CANADA
Serving Size: per 140 g (1 medium)
Energy	69 cal.....290 kJ
Protein	1.3 g
Fat	0.6 g
Carbohydrates	17 g
Dietary Fibre	2.2 g
Sodium	0 mg
Potassium	297 mg

UNITED STATES
Serving Size: 1 medium
Calories	40
Protein	1 g
Fat	0 g
Carbohydrates	10 g
Dietary Fiber	2 g
Sodium	0 mg

CANADA
Serving Size: per 160 g (2 medium)
Energy	69 cal.....290 kJ
Protein	1.1 g
Fat	0.1 g
Carbohydrates	18 g
Dietary Fibre	3.0 g
Sodium	0 mg
Potassium	315 mg

SOURCE: USDA

NUTRITION FACTS

UNITED STATES	
Serving Size: 2 medium	
Calories	80
Protein	1 g
Fat	1 g
Carbohydrates	19 g
Dietary Fiber	2 g
Sodium	0 mg

CANADA		
Serving Size: per 130 g (2 medium)		
Energy	72 cal	300 kJ
Protein		1.0 g
Fat		0.8 g
Carbohydrates		17 g
Dietary Fibre		2.1 g
Sodium		0 mg
Potassium		224 mg

UNITED STATES	
Serving Size: 5 medium	
Calories	100
Protein	1 g
Fat	0 g
Carbohydrates	26 g
Dietary Fiber	3 g
Sodium	0 mg

CANADA		
Serving Size: per 40 g (5 medium)		
Energy	95 cal	400 kJ
Protein		1.0 g
Fat		0.2 g
Carbohydrates		25 g
Dietary Fibre		2.9 g
Sodium		2 mg
Potassium		298 mg

UNITED STATES	
Serving Size: 1 cup	
Calories	96
Protein	2 g
Fat	0 g
Carbohydrates	22 g
Dietary Fiber	3 g
Sodium	0 mg

CANADA		
Serving Size: per 150 g (250 mL/1 cup)		
Energy	108 cal	450 kJ
Protein		1.8 g
Fat		1.4 g
Carbohydrates		25 g
Dietary Fibre		1.7 g
Sodium		0 mg
Potassium		336 mg

SOURCE: USDA

Plum

General Information: Plums are remarkably diverse. Color ranges include yellow, green, red, purple and indigo blue. Sizes vary from 1 to 3 inches in diameter. Depending on the variety, the flesh tastes sweet to tart. All prunes are plums, but not all plums are prunes. Prunes come from a sugary European variety of plum that can be dried without fermenting. Plums are available from May through October, with peak supplies between July and September.

Selection & Storage: Choose firm plums that give slightly to palm pressure. Avoid plums with cracks, soft spots or brown spots (an indication of sunburn). Ripen at room temperature, or put in a paper bag. Ripe plums should be placed in a plastic bag in the refrigerator for up to 5 days.

Preparation & Cooking Tips: Wash plums, cut in half and remove pit. For an easy dessert, sauté quartered plums and brown sugar in a little butter until soft.

Prunes

General Information: While it is true that all prunes are plums, very few plums can be prunes. In order to be a prune, a plum must be capable of drying with its pit in place. Most plums will ferment at the pit. The plum destined to become a prune stays on the tree until fully ripe in order to develop enough sugar. The plum must also have a freestone pit. Prunes are delicious, high-energy, high-fiber morsels that have been around since the days of early Rome. Dried prunes are available year-round, fresh fruits are available in the fall.

Selection & Storage: Prunes are pre-packaged according to size (small to jumbo) and condition (pitted or unpitted). They can be refrigerated for up to 6 months.

Preparation & Cooking Tips: Fresh prunes are a good out-of-hand fruit. Dried prunes can be steeped in warm sherry or fruit juice to be plumped. When puréed, prunes are an excellent fat substitute in baking.

Rainier Cherries

General Information: Available for 5 short weeks in May and June, the Rainier cherry is considered the most delectable of all sweet cherries. Large, sweet and juicy, the Rainier has yellow skin with a pink blush and pinkish-white flesh. The Rainier cherry is grown in California and Washington.

Selection & Storage: Rainier cherries, picked ripe, are highly perishable and must be handled carefully. Buy firm, plump cherries with green stems attached. Enjoy Rainier cherries as soon as possible after purchasing. Keep unwashed cherries in a bowl in the refrigerator. Place a paper towel on top of the cherries to absorb excess moisture. They may be frozen for nearly a year. Stem, rinse and dry cherries and place in a zip-seal plastic bag. Remove excess air from bag before sealing.

Preparation & Cooking Tips: Cherries can be pitted with a cherry pitter or with the tip of a vegetable peeler. Rainier cherries may be cooked, but they are excellent eaten out-of-hand.

Decorative Ideas for Tropical Fruit

Pineapple lends itself to many decorative preparations such as to rings, spears, cubes and even boats. For a boat, cut a pineapple in half and scoop out the flesh. Cut the pineapple flesh into neat, even pieces and put them back in the pineapple halves. Flavor with 1 to 2 tablespoons of brandy or rum and a little sugar to taste. Toss the fruit to mix; cover tightly and chill. This makes a wonderful appetizer served with cheeses or a delicious light dessert addition to ice creams and custards.

Tropical Fruit

Banana

General Information: Although the banana has been around for thousands of years, it arrived in North America in 1804. At the Philadelphia Centennial Exposition in 1876, bananas were sold as exotic fruit. Today, the banana is the world's most popular fruit. Bananas come in a variety of colors, including yellow, purple, green, red and black. Each has its own particular taste, shape, size and texture. Bananas are available year-round.

Selection & Storage: Select plump, evenly colored bananas. Bananas are cut from the tree when green. Tiny brown speckles indicate the banana is ripe. Store at room temperature. If refrigerated, the skin darkens, but the fruit remains edible.

Preparation & Cooking Tips: To prepare a banana, just peel it. If cooking with bananas, choose slightly underripe fruit (green at their tips); they hold their shape better. Overripe bananas can be frozen, if wrapped airtight, for up to 6 months.

Burro Banana

General Information: Burro bananas, chunkier than regular bananas, come from Mexico. Despite their inelegant shape, they hold a luscious secret. The soft, creamy flesh of a burro banana tastes slightly lemony.

Selection & Storage: Select plump, evenly colored bananas. Avoid cracked or bruised fruit. Bananas are cut from the tree when green. They ripen in transit to the market. Never eat an unripened burro banana. When ripe, heavy black spots will form along the ribs. Note: burro bananas go from green to ripe much quicker than regular bananas. Hasten the ripening process by placing the bananas in a paper bag. Store at room temperature.

Preparation & Cooking Tips: Preparing a burro banana is easy: just peel it. Overripe bananas can be frozen, if wrapped airtight, for up to 6 months. Or, mash the bananas, add 1 teaspoon of lemon juice for each banana and freeze in an airtight container.

Carambola/Star Fruit

General Information: The carambola is a stunning fruit, both in appearance and taste. Glossy yellow with prominent ribs, the carambola forms star shapes when sliced horizontally. (The carambola is marketed as star fruit.) The taste of a carambola is a flowery combination of plums, McIntosh apples and Concord grapes, with a touch of citrus. The edible skin is thin and slightly waxy. Carambolas are available from summer's end to mid-winter.

Selection & Storage: When choosing carambolas, look for wide ribs on evenly colored fruit. Narrow-ribbed carambolas tend to be tart. Avoid fruit with browned or squished ribs. If green, store at room temperature until yellow and fruit has a full, floral-fruity fragrance. Ripe carambolas keep in the refrigerator for up to 2 weeks.

Preparation & Cooking Tips: Rinse and slice thinly. Carambolas need not be skinned, but if the ribs are dark, peel with a vegetable peeler. Carambolas do not discolor when exposed to air, so they are perfect for salads.

Coconut

General Information: Coconuts are hard work, but the sweet flesh is well worth the effort. A coconut is multi-layered. A smooth, thick, hard, tan shell is removed before exporting. The next layer is the hairy, brown husk, then a tough brown membrane and finally the sweet, white coconut. Fresh coconuts are available year-round.

Selection & Storage: Choose a coconut that is heavy for its size. Shake the coconut to hear liquid movement. The 3 "eyes" should not be wet. Store whole coconuts in the refrigerator for several weeks. Store coconut liquid for only 1 day. Store cut chunks or grated coconut in an airtight container for up to 2 weeks in the refrigerator.

Preparation & Cooking Tips: To crack a coconut, first puncture the "eyes" and drain out the juice (this is not coconut milk). Heat the coconut in a 350°F oven for 15 minutes. Let stand until warm, wrap in a towel and crack with a hammer. One medium coconut yields 3 to 4 cups of grated coconut for sprinkling over salads or in desserts.

NUTRITION FACTS

UNITED STATES
Serving Size: 1 medium
Calories 110
Protein........................1 g
Fat ....0 g
Carbohydrates ....29 g
Dietary Fiber ....4 g
Sodium ....0 mg

CANADA
Serving Size: per 115 g (1 medium)
Energy.........106 cal.....440 kJ
Protein...........................1.2 g
Fat ....0.6 g
Carbohydrates ....27 g
Dietary Fibre ....2 g
Sodium ....1 mg
Potassium ....455 mg

UNITED STATES
Serving Size: 1 medium with skin
Calories 80
Protein........................0 g
Fat ....0 g
Carbohydrates ....22 g
Dietary Fiber ....5 g
Sodium ....0 mg

CANADA
Serving Size: 1/4 cup, dry
Energy...........80 cal.....258 kJ
Protein...........................0 g
Fat ....0 g
Carbohydrates ....22 g
Dietary Fibre ....5 g
Sodium ....0 mg
Potassium ....176 mg

UNITED STATES
Serving Size: 1 medium
Calories 40
Protein........................1 g
Fat ....0 g
Carbohydrates ....10 g
Dietary Fiber ....3 g
Sodium ....0 mg

CANADA
Serving Size: per 130 g (1 medium)
Energy...........43 cal.....180 kJ
Protein...........................0.7 g
Fat ....0.5 g
Carbohydrates ....10 g
Dietary Fibre ....2.2 g
Sodium ....3 mg
Potassium ....212 mg

UNITED STATES
Serving Size: 1 ounce
Calories 110
Protein........................1 g
Fat ....10 g
Carbohydrates ....5 g
Dietary Fiber ....3 g
Sodium ....5 mg

CANADA
Serving Size: per 30 g (1 ounce)
Energy.........106 cal.....440 kJ
Protein...........................1.0 g
Fat ....10 g
Carbohydrates ....4.6 g
Dietary Fibre ....2.7 g
Sodium ....6 mg
Potassium ....107 mg

SOURCE: USDA

NUTRITION FACTS

UNITED STATES	
Serving Size: 1 medium	
Calories	45
Protein	1 g
Fat	0.5 g
Carbohydrates	11 g
Dietary Fiber	5 g
Sodium	0 mg

CANADA	
Serving Size: per 90 g (1 medium)	
Energy	46 cal.....191 kJ
Protein	0.7 g
Fat	0.5 g
Carbohydrates	11 g
Dietary Fibre	4.9 g
Sodium	3 mg
Potassium	256 mg

UNITED STATES	
Serving Size: 2 medium	
Calories	100
Protein	2 g
Fat	1 g
Carbohydrates	24 g
Dietary Fiber	4 g
Sodium	0 mg

CANADA	
Serving Size: per 160 g (2 medium)	
Energy	98 cal.....410 kJ
Protein	1.6 g
Fat	0.7 g
Carbohydrates	24 g
Dietary Fibre	5.4 g
Sodium	8 mg
Potassium	531 mg

UNITED STATES	
Serving Size: 1/2 medium	
Calories	70
Protein	1 g
Fat	0 g
Carbohydrates	18 g
Dietary Fiber	2 g
Sodium	0 mg

CANADA	
Serving Size: per 110 g (1/2 medium)	
Energy	72 cal....300 kJ
Protein	0.6 g
Fat	0.3 g
Carbohydrates	19 g
Dietary Fibre	2.2 g
Sodium	2 mg
Potassium	172 mg

UNITED STATES	
NUTRITION FACTS NOT AVAILABLE	

CANADA	
NUTRITION FACTS NOT AVAILABLE	

SOURCE: USDA

Guava

General Information: Ripe guavas have a tantalizing scent, shifting from musk when unripe to flowery sweet when ripe. This pungent fruit is often confused with its cousin, the feijoa, but it is a completely different fruit. The guava is an egg-shaped fruit that tastes of honey, melon and strawberries. The season lasts from late spring to early fall.

Selection & Storage: Guavas ripen quickly at room temperature, so look for firm fruit. Avoid fruit with bruises or soft spots. Look for good color and a strong smell. Use as soon as fruit ripens. Refrigerate for 1 day when fully ripened.

Preparation & Cooking Tips: Guavas are traditionally used for jellies, preserves and chutney. Guavas deliver a burst of flavor when used with other fruits in salads, sauces or desserts. To prepare, slice off the top, halve lengthwise and cut into chunks. Remove seeds, if any.

Kiwifruit

General Information: Covered with a fuzzy brown skin, the egg-shaped kiwifruit has a dramatic interior. A pale center is surrounded by emerald flesh, flecked with tiny black edible seeds. The taste has been likened to a combination of cantaloupe, strawberry and citrus. Kiwifruit, originally an export of New Zealand, was named for their famous kiwi bird. It is available year-round.

Selection & Storage: Choose fruit with unbroken and unbruised skin. A ripe kiwifruit yields to gentle pressure. Most kiwis are sold hard and must be ripened at home. Ripen at room temperature, out of the sun. Refrigerate ripe kiwifruit for up to 1 week.

Preparation & Cooking Tips: Peel skin with a sharp knife or a vegetable peeler. Slice crosswise. Kiwifruit will not discolor when exposed to air and are a perfect choice for salads or garnish. Heating is not recommended, as the kiwifruit turns an unappetizing shade of olive green.

Mango

General Information: The fragrant, juicy sweetness of a ripe mango is one of life's true pleasures. Many aficionados claim the only way to eat a mango is over a sink — they're that juicy! Mangos are in season from January through October.

Selection & Storage: When ripe, a mango yields to gentle pressure like a ripe avocado, and the stem end has a gentle aroma. Choose plump mangos, avoiding those with shriveled or bruised skin. Ripen at room temperature, uncovered, out of direct sunlight. Refrigerate ripe mangoes in a plastic bag for up to 3 days.

Preparation & Cooking Tips: To peel and pit a mango, place it stem-side up. With a long knife, make a vertical slice starting at ¼ inch to the right of the stem. Repeat on the other side. Lightly score the flesh of the mango into diamonds. When scoring, go down to, but not through, the skin. Buckle the skin, pushing the flesh outward so that it resembles a porcupine. Slice off the cubes. When cooking, heat gently.

Manzano Banana

General Information: One of hundreds of specialty bananas, the Manzano banana is also known as an apple or finger banana. It is a stocky, pale yellow banana, measuring about 4 inches long or finger length. Its flavor has apple and strawberry overtones. Manzano bananas are available year-round.

Selection & Storage: Look for firm, pale-yellow bananas without bruises or cracks. Manzanos are ripe when their yellow skin turns completely black. Store at room temperature until ripe. Overripe bananas can be frozen, if wrapped airtight, for up to 6 months. Or, mash the bananas, add 1 teaspoon of lemon juice for each banana and freeze in an airtight container.

Preparation & Cooking Tips: Manzanos can be eaten fresh, but they cook well. Halve them lengthwise and sauté in butter with brown sugar; flambé with rum. Manzanos are the perfect size for fritters.

Tropical Fruit

Niño Banana

General Information: So called because bunches of these dimunitive bananas look like a child's chubby hand ("niño" is Spanish for "child), Niño bananas are plump and sweet. They are also known as baby, ladyfinger or finger bananas, but should not be confused with Manzanos. They are available year-round.

Selection & Storage: Bananas ripen best off the tree, so they are picked unripe. Choose niño bananas that are firm and plump with no bruises or splits in the skin. Avoid those with a dull or grayish skins, as they will not ripen properly.

Preparation & Cooking Tips: Niño bananas are delicious eaten out of hand, or slice and top cereals, yogurt, waffles and pancakes. They are also good baking bananas; simply place in a baking dish and brush with fruit juice or honey and bake at 350°F until tender – about 15 minutes. Niño bananas are popular in Asian and Hispanic cuisines.

Papaya

General Information: Papayas range from 1 to 20 pounds. The variety most often found in the United States is the Solo. Six inches long and about a pound-and-a-half in weight, the Solo is pear-shaped with a vivid golden skin. The flesh, also golden, is juicy and smooth, with an exotic sweet-tart flavor. The center cavity is packed with gelatin-covered seeds. Papayas are available year-round.

Selection & Storage: A blotchy, deeply colored papaya often packs more flavor. Test for ripeness by touch; it should yield to gentle pressure. A green papaya ripens quickly at room temperature. Refrigerate ripe fruit and use as soon as possible.

Preparation & Cooking Tips: Ripe papayas are best eaten raw. Green papaya can be cooked as a vegetable. Halve the papaya and remove seeds. Seeds are edible, but very peppery. The skin is easily removed with a vegetable peeler. Serve papaya halved with lime or cubed with other fruits.

Pineapple

General Information: The exquisite flavor and aroma of pineapple make it a welcome addition to any cook's table. The British thought the fruit's bumpy, diamond-shaped pattern resembled a pine cone and so called it pineapple. Fresh pineapple is available year-round.

Selection & Storage: Pineapples must be picked ripe because, once off the tree, the starch will not turn to sugar. Choose a pineapple that is plump and slightly   soft to the touch. The stem end should have a sweet aroma. Fresh, deep-green leaves are a good sign. Store whole ripe pineapples, tightly sealed, in the refrigerator for 3 days. Once cut, tightly sealed pineapple can remain in the refrigerator for 3 more days.

Preparation & Cooking Tips: To prepare pineapple, cut a thick slice from the top and the bottom. Pare skin from the top downward. Next, remove the eyes by cutting diagonal grooves. Finally, cut into eighths and remove the core section from each.

Plantain

General Information: This delicious tropical fruit holds up well during cooking and offers culinary pleasures at every stage of ripeness. When green to near-yellow, the flavor is bland and the texture is starchy; perfect for boiling and frying. When the plantain is yellow to brown, it has a slight fruitiness and firm texture that suits any part of the meal. Black, ripe plantains are sweeter and ideal for dessert.

Selection & Storage: Occasionally, plantains harden instead of ripening; discard them. Refrigerate green plantains. Keep yellow to black plantains at cool room temperature, out of the sun and well ventilated. Eat black fruit soon. Plantains produce a ripening gas, so store away from other fruits.

Preparation & Cooking Tips: Peel black, ripe plantains like a banana. Other stages require another technique. Rinse the fruit and slice off the tips. Cut into sections, then slit the very thick, stiff peel lengthwise along its four ridges and remove each strip.

NUTRITION FACTS

UNITED STATES
Serving Size: 1 small
Calories 75
Protein...........................0.8 g
Fat ....0.4 g
Carbohydrates ....19 g
Dietary Fiber ....2 g
Sodium ....0.8 mg
CANADA
Serving Size: 1 small
Energy...........75 cal.....312 kJ
Protein...........................0.8 g
Fat ....0.4 g
Carbohydrates ....19 g
Dietary Fibre ....2 g
Sodium ....0.8 mg
Potassium ....467 mg

UNITED STATES
Serving Size: ½ medium
Calories 60
Protein...............................1 g
Fat ....0 g
Carbohydrates ....15 g
Dietary Fiber ....3 g
Sodium ....0 mg
CANADA
Serving Size: per 155 g (½ medium)
Energy...........60 cal.....250 kJ
Protein...........................1.0 g
Fat ....0.2 g
Carbohydrates ....15 g
Dietary Fibre ....2.3 g
Sodium ....5 mg
Potassium ....398 mg

UNITED STATES
Serving Size: 2 slices,3"diameter,¾"thick
Calories 60
Protein...............................1 g
Fat ....0 g
Carbohydrates ....16 g
Dietary Fiber ....1 g
Sodium ....10 mg
CANADA
Serving Size: per 160 g (250mL/1 cup)
Energy...........78 cal.....330 kJ
Protein...........................0.6 g
Fat ....0.7 g
Carbohydrates ....20 g
Dietary Fibre ....1.9 g
Sodium ....1.6 mg
Potassium ....181 mg

UNITED STATES
Serving Size: 1 medium
Calories 220
Protein...............................2 g
Fat ....0.5 g
Carbohydrates ....57 g
Dietary Fiber ....4 g
Sodium ....5 mg
CANADA
Serving Size: per 160 g (1 medium)
Energy.........195 cal....820 kJ
Protein...........................2.1 g
Fat ....0.6 g
Carbohydrates ....51 g
Dietary Fibre ....3.7 g
Sodium ....6 mg
Potassium ....798 mg

SOURCE: USDA

Tropical Fruit

Fruit

Red Banana

General Information: The red banana, sweeter than its yellow cousin, has a slight taste of raspberries. The skin of a red banana is a dark, winey-red streaked with black. Inside, the pink flesh is creamy and fragrant. Red bananas are usually about 5 inches long and stockier than yellow bananas.

Selection & Storage: When ripe, red bananas have a purplish hue with black patches and very sweet, slightly sticky flesh. Do not buy red bananas that have cracks. Store at room temperature until ripe. Ripe bananas can be stored in the refrigerator. The skin will turn black, but the flesh will be fine. Overripe bananas can be frozen, if wrapped airtight, for up to six months. Or, mash the bananas, add 1 teaspoon of lemon juice for each banana and freeze in an airtight container.

Preparation & Cooking Tips: Peel red bananas and eat. If slicing, sprinkle with lemon juice to prevent browning.

Banana or Mango Sorbet

Combine ½ cup sugar and ¾ cup water in saucepan and bring to a boil, stirring to dissolve the sugar. Cool syrup. Puree a large mango, peeled and cubed, with 4 tablespoons of orange juice or 2 tablespoons of lemon juice. Puree in a blender or food processor. Add to the cooled syrup and mix well. Freeze until firm. Alternately, puree 4 large bananas and add to syrup instead of mango.

Other Fruit

Dates

General Information: The date has a long, narrow seed, papery-thin skin and extremely sweet flesh. Dates grow in thick clusters on giant date palm trees. Their length varies from 1 to 2 inches, depending on the variety. Their color also varies when ripe, from golden brown to deep brown. Fresh dates are available from late summer through mid-fall.

Selection & Storage: Choose fresh dates that are plump and soft, with a smooth, shiny skin. Avoid shriveled, moldy or crystallized dates. Store fresh dates in a plastic bag in the refrigerator for up to 2 weeks.

Preparation & Cooking Tips: If dates are bunched together in a solid mass, put them in a microwave oven and heat at medium (50% power) for 45 seconds. Allow to stand for 1 minute before separating. Or, place dates on a baking pan and heat at 300°F for 5 minutes. Dates are a good natural sweetener.

Figs

General Information: A member of the mulberry family, the fig is shaped like a small pear. Inside is a seedy, sweet pulp. Figs vary in color from green to yellow, brown, purple or black. Fresh figs are available from June to October.

Selection & Storage: Figs are extremely perishable and should be eaten soon after purchase. Choose figs that are plump and heavy for their size. The fig should be firm, not too hard or too soft. Handle with care, for they bruise easily. Old figs will smell sour. Store fresh figs for no more than 2 days in the refrigerator, on a plate lined with a paper towel. Dried figs may be stored in an airtight container for up to 6 months.

Preparation & Cooking Tips: Trim off the stems of fresh or dried figs. Fresh figs may be sliced for toppings, or eaten out-of-hand at room temperature for full flavor. Dried figs may need to be simmered for a couple of minutes in fruit juice to make them plump.

NUTRITION FACTS

UNITED STATES
Serving Size: 3.5 ounces

Calories	90
Protein	1 g
Fat	0 g
Carbohydrates	23 g
Dietary Fiber	2 g
Sodium	0 mg

CANADA
Serving Size: per 115 g (1 large)

Energy	106 cal.....440 kJ
Protein	1.2 g
Fat	0.6 g
Carbohydrates	25 g
Dietary Fibre	1.0 g
Sodium	1 mg
Potassium	455 mg

NUTRITION FACTS

UNITED STATES
Serving Size: 5 medium

Calories	110
Protein	1 g
Fat	0 g
Carbohydrates	31 g
Dietary Fiber	3 g
Sodium	1 mg

CANADA
Serving Size: per 40 g (5 medium)

Energy	110 cal.....460 kJ
Protein	0.8 g
Fat	0.2 g
Carbohydrates	29 g
Dietary Fibre	3.4 g
Sodium	1 mg
Potassium	261 mg

UNITED STATES
Serving Size: 1 medium

Calories	35
Protein	0 g
Fat	0 g
Carbohydrates	10 g
Dietary Fiber	2 g
Sodium	0 mg

CANADA
Serving Size: per 110 g (2 medium)

Energy	81 cal.....340 kJ
Protein	0.8 g
Fat	0.3 g
Carbohydrates	21 g
Dietary Fibre	3.6 g
Sodium	1 mg
Potassium	255 mg

SOURCE: USDA

23

Other Fruit

Florida Avocado

General Information: The avocados grown in Florida are very different from those grown in California. The Florida avocado, with its smooth green skin, is nicknamed "alligator pear." Cookbook author, Steve Raichlen, claims, "Florida avocados are sweeter, lighter and moister than most from California. And best of all, according to *Eating Well* magazine, they contain only ½ the fat and ⅔ the calories (112 in a 3.5- ounce serving)." Florida avocados come to market from August to January.

Selection & Storage: Avocados ripen best off the tree. To speed the ripening process, place avocados in a paper bag with an apple. Poke a few holes in bag and store at room temperature. A ripe Florida avocado yields to gentle pressure. Once ripe, keep avocados in the refrigerator for up to a week.

Preparation & Cooking Tips: Ripe avocados peel easily. Slice in half and remove one side. Stick a fork in the large pit and twist to remove. Avocados discolor quickly, so rub lemon juice on the surface or cut just before serving.

Haas Avocado

General Information: Rich and buttery, the avocado boasts a sweet, nutty flavor. The Haas avocado has dark, pebbly skin and is smaller and creamier than the Florida avocado. Many people think of the avocado as a vegetable, but it is a fruit. In Hawaii and South Africa, the avocado is served with sugar and lime juice for breakfast. The peak season is from February to October.

Selection & Storage: Avocados ripen best off the tree. To speed the ripening process, place avocados in a paper bag with an apple. Poke a few holes in the bag and store at room temperature. Ripe avocados yield to gentle pressure. They also change color from green to purple-black. Once ripe, keep avocados in the refrigerator for up to a week.

Preparation & Cooking Tips: Ripe avocados peel easily. Slice in half and remove 1 side. Stick a fork in the large pit and twist to remove. Avocados discolor quickly, so rub lemon juice on the surface or cut at the last moment. Purists claim that the Haas variety is the only avocado to use when making guacamole.

Passion Fruit

General Information: The inside of a passion fruit is filled with tear-shaped, yellow-green or yellow-orange gelatinous seed sacks. The scent is definitely tropical and intense — full of jasmine, honey, lemon and floral aromas. The taste is potent as well: Think of it as a flavoring like vanilla beans — a little goes a long way in creating a spectacular dish. Look for passion fruit year-round.

Selection & Storage: Choose firm, smooth passion fruits that are heavy for their size. Ripen at room temperature. Dark purple passion fruit is ripe when wrinkled but not cracked. Yellow, pink to red or lavender passion fruit is barely dimpled when ripe. Passion fruit can be frozen whole, wrapped tightly in plastic. Defrost until soft enough to cut; scoop out pulp.

Preparation & Cooking Tips: Cut the tip off the passion fruit as if it were a soft boiled egg. Scoop out pulp. To remove seeds, purée with a teaspoon of sugar and water. Strain and use.

NUTRITION FACTS

UNITED STATES
Serving Size: ⅒ medium

Calories	35
Protein	0 g
Fat	2.5 g
Carbohydrates	3 g
Dietary Fiber	3 g
Sodium	0 mg

CANADA
Serving Size: per 30 g (⅒ medium)

Energy	34 cal.....140 kJ
Protein	0.5 g
Fat	2.7 g
Carbohydrates	2.7 g
Dietary Fibre	0.8 g
Sodium	2 mg
Potassium	148 mg

UNITED STATES
Serving Size: ⅕ medium

Calories	50
Protein	0 g
Fat	5 g
Carbohydrates	3 g
Dietary Fiber	3 g
Sodium	0 mg

CANADA
Serving Size: per 40 g (⅕ medium)

Energy	65 cal.....270 kJ
Protein	0.8 g
Fat	6.2 g
Carbohydrates	3 g
Dietary Fibre	1 g
Sodium	4 mg
Potassium	240 mg

UNITED STATES
Serving Size: 1 medium

Calories	140
Protein	3 g
Fat	1 g
Carbohydrates	34 g
Dietary Fiber	15 g
Sodium	40 mg

CANADA
Serving Size: per 100 g (125mL/1/2 cup)

Energy	106 cal.....450 kJ
Protein	2.4 g
Fat	0.8 g
Carbohydrates	26 g
Dietary Fibre	1.7 g
Sodium	31 mg
Potassium	383 mg

SOURCE: USDA

Keeping Beautiful Fresh Fruit Color

If exposed to the air for very long, cut flesh of fresh fruit starts to turn brown such as apples, bananas, peaches and avocados. So if prepared fruit has to wait before being served or cooked, sprinkle the cut surfaces with lemon juice. Or you can immerse hard fruit in water and lemon juice. Be careful not to soak fruit so that it becomes soggy.

Vegetables (side tab)

NUTRITION FACTS

UNITED STATES
Serving Size: ¼ cup, dry

Calories	170
Protein	10 g
Fat	0.5 g
Carbohydrates	30 g
Dietary Fiber	7 g
Sodium	0 mg

CANADA
Serving Size: per 1 cup, dry

Energy	661 cal.....2768 kJ
Protein	41.9 g
Fat	2.7 g
Carbohydrates	120.9 g
Dietary Fibre	29.4 g
Sodium	9.7 mg
Potassium	2877 mg

UNITED STATES
Serving Size: per 1 cup, boiled

Calories	198
Protein	13 g
Fat	1 g
Carbohydrates	36 g
Dietary Fiber	16 g
Sodium	7 mg

CANADA
Serving Size: per 1 cup, raw

Energy	130 cal.....546 kJ
Protein	4.2 g
Fat	0.5 g
Carbohydrates	27.4 g
Dietary Fibre	7.2 g
Sodium	5.8 mg
Potassium	624 mg

UNITED STATES
Serving Size: ¼ cup

Calories	140
Protein	10 g
Fat	0.5 g
Carbohydrates	26 g
Dietary Fiber	0 g
Sodium	5 mg

CANADA
Serving Size: per 35 g (60 mL/¼ cup)

Energy	125 cal.....521 kJ
Protein	0.1 g
Fat	0.0 g
Carbohydrates	31 g
Dietary Fibre	0.2 g
Sodium	4 mg
Potassium	4 mg

UNITED STATES
Serving Size: ¼ cup, dry

Calories	160
Protein	11 g
Fat	0.5 g
Carbohydrates	29 g
Dietary Fiber	0 g
Sodium	0 mg

CANADA
Serving Size: per 50 g (60 mL/¼ cup, dry)

Energy	168 cal.....350 kJ
Protein	11 g
Fat	0.6 g
Carbohydrates	30 g
Dietary Fibre	1.4 g
Sodium	3 mg
Potassium	666 mg

SOURCE: USDA

Black Beans

General Information: Few foods are more versatile, economical and flavorful than dried beans. They are rich in protein and fiber, yet low in fat. Black beans are also known as turtle beans, or in Hispanic markets as *frijoles negros.*

Selection & Storage: Trays of rehydrated black beans are sold dated for freshness. Rehydrated black beans are highly perishable and must be refrigerated. Dried black beans can be kept for 1 year in an airtight container.

Preparation & Cooking Tips: Rehydrated beans do not need to be soaked. Dried beans do. Place beans in a large bowl. Cover with 3 inches of water. Refrigerate 4 hours or overnight, then drain and rinse well. Place beans in stockpot and cover with 3 inches of water. Add an onion and a bay leaf. (Do not add salt or acidic ingredients, such as tomatoes, until the end or the beans will toughen.) Bring to a boil. Reduce heat and simmer until tender, about 1 to 2 hours. If you want soft beans, cook with the lid on; for firmer beans, keep the lid off while cooking.

Black-Eyed Peas

General Information: A good source of protein, black-eyed peas are small beige beans with a black "eye" in the middle. They are also called cowpeas. Black-eyed peas are sold fresh or dried.

Selection & Storage: Packages of fresh peas are dated for freshness and must be refrigerated. Store dried black-eyed peas in an airtight container for up to 1 year.

Preparation & Cooking Tips: Fresh black-eyed peas do not need to be soaked, but need to cook slowly for hours. Dried beans must be soaked. Place beans in a large bowl. Cover with water to three inches above the beans. Refrigerate for 4 to 12 hours. Drain and rinse well. Place beans in stockpot and add water to 3 inches above the beans. Add an onion and a bay leaf. (Do not add salt or acidic ingredients, such as tomatoes, until the end or the beans will toughen.) Bring to a boil. Reduce heat and simmer until tender, about 1 to 2 hours. If you want soft beans, cook with the lid on; for firmer beans, keep the lid off.

Chinese Long Beans

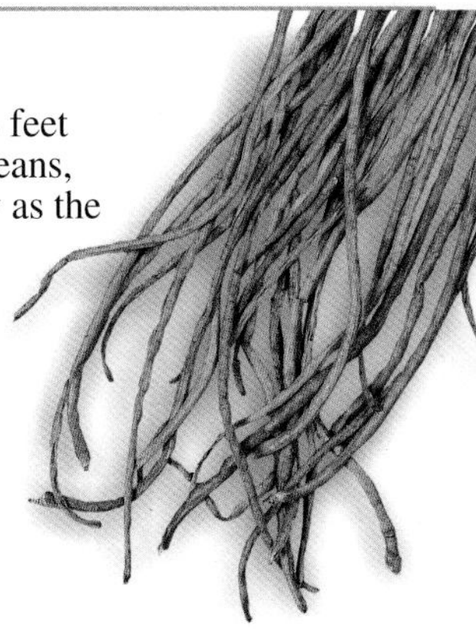

General Information: Chinese long beans are pencil thin and can grow to 3 feet in length, although they are usually harvested at 18 inches. Chinese long beans, also known as yard-long beans, and are a member of the same plant family as the black-eyed pea. Chinese long beans are crunchy, but not juicy. They are available year-round with their peak season in the fall.

Selection & Storage: Look for smaller, thin beans, for they will be younger and more tender. There are two varieties: deep green or pale green tinged with yellow. The paler variety is best for quick-cooking dishes, such as stir-fries. It is also sweeter. The dark-green variety becomes fibrous when cooked. They are good in slow-cooked, braised dishes. Keep Chinese long beans in the warmest part of the refrigerator for no more than 3 days.

Preparation & Cooking Tips: Rinse the beans. Line up the beans on a cutting board and trim the ends; cut to desired length, usually 2 inches.

Cranberry Beans

General Information: There's no mistaking a cranberry bean pod. Unlike other shelled beans, the pod of a cranberry bean is not green. It is large, knobby and beige with cranberry-red splotches. Inside, the beans, shaped like lima beans, are creamy white with cranberry-red streaks. Cranberry beans have a rich, nutty flavor that makes them worth seeking. When cooked, the shelled cranberry beans lose their red color. They are available fresh in the summer and dried year-round.

Selection & Storage: Cranberry beans are usually sold in their pods. Look for plump, firm pods; avoid limp or shriveled pods. Keep unshelled pods in a plastic bag in the refrigerator for no more than 3 days.

Preparation & Cooking Tips: Cranberry beans must be shelled before they are cooked. Press on the inside curve of the pod and split it open. Remove beans. Drop beans into a large pot of boiling water. Return to a boil, then reduce temperature and simmer until tender.

Fava Beans

General Information: North Americans are just discovering the fava bean's many charms. Fava beans are widely consumed in China, Europe, Africa and South America. Fava beans have a pea-like flavor and a tender, not starchy, texture. They grow in pods 8 to 12 inches long. The fava bean has a tough skin that must be removed. The fresh fava bean is available in spring and summer. Note: Certain people of Mediterranean origin have a toxic reaction to fava beans.

Selection & Storage: Choose the smallest, greenest fava bean pods with even coloring available. Refrigerate, unwashed, in a single layer for a few days.

Preparation & Cooking Tips: To shell fava beans, cut the tips from the pod and pull open along the seams. Remove the beans, leaving stems behind. Drop into boiling, salted water for 30 seconds. Drain and drop in ice water. When cool to the touch, slice skin with a fingernail and pop the bean out of the skin. Fava beans are good cooked with butter and savory.

French Green Beans

General Information: Known in France as *haricots verts* (airy-CO-vare), they are baby green beans. Their flavor is more intense than regular green beans, and they have no strings. French green beans are ¼ inch wide and 5 to 7 inches long. French green beans are sporadically available from May through March.

Selection & Storage: Choose beans that are deep green, smooth and crisp. If you must store the beans, wrap them in a slightly damp paper towel and then place inside a plastic bag. Refrigerate for no more than 2 days.

Preparation & Cooking Tips: Wash and drain. Snap off each end. Drop French green beans into a large pot of boiling, salted water. Cover to bring back the boil, then remove cover. Boil for 2 to 3 minutes. Test for doneness; they should be just tender. Immediately drain into a colander and run cold water over the beans to stop the cooking process. They are wonderful hot with lemon butter, or cold with a vinaigrette.

Garbanzo Beans

General Information: Garbanzo beans are shaped somewhat like a hazelnut: buff-colored, slightly lumpy and larger than a pea. Garbanzos are also known as chickpeas and ceci. Their flavor is rich and nuttier than most beans. Garbanzo beans keep their shape when cooked.

Selection & Storage: Choose plump beans. Discard beans that are discolored and shriveled. Dried garbanzo beans can be kept for 1 year in an airtight container.

Preparation & Cooking Tips: Place beans in a large bowl. Cover with water 3 inches above the beans. Refrigerate overnight. Drain beans and rinse well. Place beans in stockpot and cover with water, again, to 3 inches above the beans. (Do not add salt or acidic ingredients, such as tomatoes, until the end or the beans will toughen.) For soft beans, cook with the lid on; for firmer beans, keep the lid off while cooking. Bring to a boil. Reduce heat and simmer until tender, about 3 hours. Test by tasting. The texture should be smooth, but not mushy.

Green Beans

General Information: Fresh green beans taste nothing like their canned or frozen counterparts. When fresh, green beans have snap and texture. Green beans used to be called string beans, but the fibrous string has been mostly bred out of them. Green beans are available year-round.

Selection & Storage: Choose brightly colored beans with a smooth surface. Avoid those that are leathery or withered. If the bean can be bent at a 90° angle without snapping it, the bean is past its prime. Select green beans of equal size to facilitate even cooking. Refrigerate, unwashed, in an airtight bag for up to 4 days.

Preparation & Cooking Tips: To prepare, wash in cool water, drain and remove stems. Remove strings if necessary. The tip does not have to be trimmed. Drop green beans in boiling, salted water for 3 minutes or until just tender. Plunge them into a bowl of ice water to stop the cooking process. Drain and pat dry. When ready to serve, reheat in lemon-dill butter.

NUTRITION FACTS

UNITED STATES
Serving Size: ¼ cup, dry
Calories	43
Protein	10 g
Fat	0.5 g
Carbohydrates	22 g
Dietary Fiber	9 g
Sodium	0 mg

CANADA
Serving Size: per 32 g (.125mL, dry)
Energy	109 cal	454 kJ
Protein	8.3 g	
Fat	0.5 g	
Carbohydrates	18.7 g	
Dietary Fibre	n/a	
Sodium	5 mg	
Potassium	340 mg	

UNITED STATES
Serving Size: ½ cup, boiled
Calories	111
Protein	6 g
Fat	1 g
Carbohydrates	21 g
Dietary Fiber	na
Sodium	5 mg

CANADA
Serving Size: per 1 cup, boiled
Energy	243 cal	1017 kJ
Protein	13.2 g	
Fat	1.5 g	
Carbohydrates	45.1 g	
Dietary Fibre	n/a	
Sodium	11.3 mg	
Potassium	696 mg	

UNITED STATES
Serving Size: ¼ cup, dry
Calories	180
Protein	10 g
Fat	3 g
Carbohydrates	30 g
Dietary Fiber	9 g
Sodium	10 mg

CANADA
Serving Size: per 1 cup, raw
Energy	728 cal	3046 kJ
Protein	38.6 g	
Fat	12 g	
Carbohydrates	121.3 g	
Dietary Fibre	34.8 g	
Sodium	48 mg	
Potassium	1750 mg	

UNITED STATES
Serving Size: ¾ cup, cut
Calories	25
Protein	1 g
Fat	0 g
Carbohydrates	5 g
Dietary Fiber	3 g
Sodium	0 mg

CANADA
Serving Size: per 85 g (175 mL/¾ cup)
Energy	26 cal	110 kJ
Protein	1.6 g	
Fat	0.1 g	
Carbohydrates	6.1 g	
Dietary Fibre	1.5 g	
Sodium	5 mg	
Potassium	178 mg	

SOURCE: USDA

Vegetables

UNITED STATES
Serving Size: ½ cup
Calories 60
Protein.............................9 g
Fat ....0 g
Carbohydrates............10 g
Dietary Fiber ....4 g
Sodium ....0 mg
CANADA
Serving Size: per 75 g (125 mL/½ cup)
Energy...........61 cal.....250 kJ
Protein..........................4.1 g
Fat ....0.3 g
Carbohydrates ....11 g
Dietary Fibre ....3.8 g
Sodium ....4 mg
Potassium ....183 mg

UNITED STATES
Serving Size: ¼ cup, dry
Calories 150
Protein..............................10 g
Fat ....0 g
Carbohydrates............28 g
Dietary Fiber ....8 g
Sodium ....10 mg
CANADA
Serving Size: per 1 cup, raw
Energy.......601 cal.....2516 kJ
Protein........................38.1 g
Fat ....1.2 g
Carbohydrates ....112.8 g
Dietary Fibre...............33.8 g
Sodium ....32 mg
Potassium.................3068 mg

UNITED STATES
Serving Size: ¼ cup, dry
Calories 160
Protein..............................10 g
Fat ....0.5 g
Carbohydrates............31 g
Dietary Fiber ....12 g
Sodium ....0 mg
CANADA
Serving Size: per 50 g (125 mL/¼ cup. dry)
Energy.........170 cal.....350 kJ
Protein............................10 g
Fat ....0.5 g
Carbohydrates ....32 g
Dietary Fibre ....12 g
Sodium ....5 mg
Potassium ....664 mg

UNITED STATES
Serving Size: 1 cup
Calories 34
Protein...............................2 g
Fat ....0.1 g
Carbohydrates ....8 g
Dietary Fiber ....4 g
Sodium ....7 mg
CANADA
Serving Size: per 1 cup, dry, raw
Energy...........34 cal....143 kJ
Protein...............................2 g
Fat ....0.1 g
Carbohydrates ....7.8 g
Dietary Fibre ....3.7 g
Sodium ....6.6 mg
Potassium............229.9 mg

SOURCE: USDA

Green Peas

General Information: A favorite throughout North America, fresh peas are sweet and tender, and taste nothing at all like their starchy, bland canned cousins. The green garden pea is also known as the English pea. Fresh green peas are available from March through May, and August through November.

Selection & Storage: Look for round, full, bright-green pods with a satiny, fresh look. Avoid any pods that are hard, dull, pale or shriveled. It is important to buy them fresh because green peas start the sugar-to-starch conversion the instant they are picked. They are best if used right away. Refrigerate in a plastic bag for no more than 2 days.

Preparation & Cooking Tips: Do not shell peas until ready to cook. Snap off the stem end and unzip the pod by pulling on the string. Run a finger under the peas to free them from the pod. The ideal texture after cooking is tender, yet crisp.

Lima Beans

General Information: Lima beans are known for their rich, buttery flavor. This explains why they are also called butter beans. There are two distinct varieties of lima bean: the Fordhook, which is larger, and the baby lima. Fordhooks are not mature baby limas. Both varieties are pale-green, plump and sport a kidney-like curve. They are available from June to September.

Selection & Storage: Lima beans are usually sold in their pods. Look for plump, firm and dark-green beans. If pods are pale or shriveled, do not buy. Refrigerate, unshelled, in a plastic bag for no more than 1 week.

Preparation & Cooking Tips: Do not shell beans until ready to cook. Snap off the stem end and unzip the pod by pulling on the string. Use scissors to cut off part of the inner edge. Remove beans. In a heavy saucepan, soak fresh beans ½ hour in cold water. Drain. Simmer 1 lb. fresh lima beans in boiling salted water until tender. Add salt, pepper and butter to taste. Properly cooked beans will be tender, with a bit of firmness.

Pinto Beans

General Information: Pinto beans, grown in the American Southwest, are pale pink with streaks of reddish brown. Like most dried beans, pinto beans are also available in cans. Dried beans are better than canned for two reasons: they are lower in sodium, and have firmer texture.

Selection & Storage: Pick through dried beans and discard any that are discolored or shriveled. Dried pinto beans will keep in an airtight container for 1 year.

Preparation & Cooking Tips: Place beans in a large bowl. Cover with water 3 inches over the beans. Refrigerate overnight. Drain beans and rinse well. Place beans in stockpot and cover with water, again, to 3 inches above the beans. (Do not add salt or acidic ingredients, such as tomatoes, until the end or the beans will toughen.) For soft beans, cook with the lid on; for firmer beans, keep the lid off. Bring to a boil. Reduce heat and simmer until tender—about 2 hours. If more water is needed, make sure it is boiling hot. Test by tasting. The texture should be smooth, but not mushy.

Pole Beans

General Information: Pole beans are the pods of a vinelike plant and are often called snap beans because the crisp pods make a snapping sound when the ends are removed. They are available year-round, but the best supplies can be found in the summer and early fall.

Selection & Storage: Choose pole beans of uniform size for even cooking. Look for straight, slender, brightly colored pods with a velvety feel. Avoid beans that are very stiff or if the seeds are visible. Refrigerate, unwashed, in the crisper section for 3 to 5 days.

Preparation & Cooking Tips: After washing, snap off the ends of the beans and leave whole or cut into 1- or 2-inch lengths. Blanch, microwave, steam or stir-fry until crisp-tender; don't overcook.

Beans & Peas

Red Beans

General Information: Also called kidney beans, they are best known as an ingredient in red beans and rice and in chili con carne. The skin is dark red, and flesh is cream-colored. Dried beans are better than canned beans for two reasons: they are lower in sodium, and their texture is firmer. Dried beans are packed with protein, calcium, phosphorous and iron.

Selection & Storage: Pick through dried kidney beans and discard any that are shriveled. They will keep in an airtight container for 1 year.

Preparation & Cooking Tips: Place beans in a large bowl. Cover with water to 3 inches above the beans. Refrigerate for at least 4 hours or overnight. Drain beans and rinse well. Place beans in a stockpot and cover with water, again, to 3 inches above the beans. (Do not add salt or acidic ingredients until the end or the beans will toughen.) Bring to a boil. For soft beans, cook with the lid on; for firmer beans, keep the lid off. Reduce heat and simmer until tender—about 1 to 2 hours.

Snow Peas

General Information: The snow pea pod is thin and crisp. The seeds inside are tender and sweet. The French call snow peas *mange-tout* (which means "eat all"), because both the pod and the peas can be eaten. The Chinese have long used snow peas in stir-fries. Snow peas must be harvested when immature or the pea and pod will be tough. Snow peas are available year-round.

Selection & Storage: Look for bright-green, flexible pods. Avoid those that are yellowing or withered. Purchase ¼ pound of snow peas per person. Store unwashed snow peas in a plastic bag in the refrigerator for up to 3 days.

Preparation & Cooking Tips: To prepare pods for use, trim both ends and remove strings. Blanch snow pea pods in boiling salted water for 30 seconds. Remove and plunge into ice water. The pea pods will turn a brilliant emerald green and be ready to use in salads. In stir-fries, add the snow peas in the last 3 minutes of cooking time. Snow peas are delicious with shrimp, garlic and ginger.

Sugar Snap Peas

General Information: Sugar snap peas are sweet and crunchy. A hybrid cross of the English pea and the snow pea, sugar snap peas are entirely edible. The pods are rounded, thick and mature. Unlike snow peas that toughen with maturity, sugar snap peas remain tender and flavorful. Sugar snap peas can be served raw. Brief cooking underscores their sweetness, but it must be very brief, or the crunch will be lost. They are available in spring and fall.

Selection & Storage: Select small sugar snap pea pods, as they will be the most tender. If the stem is not in good condition, do not buy. Sugar snap peas are best if eaten on the day of purchase. They will keep a few days in a plastic bag in the refrigerator.

Preparation & Cooking Tips: Remove strings on both seams before cooking. To cook, drop in boiling, salted water and cook for 2 minutes only; or, steam for no more than 4 minutes. They can be served warm or chilled.

Yellow Wax Beans

General Information: Yellow wax beans are green beans that are cultivated for their pale yellow color. Wax beans look just like green beans that have lost their color. Waxy in texture and slightly more bitter in flavor, yellow wax beans can be substituted for green beans in most recipes. They are available in summer.

Selection & Storage: Choose brightly colored beans with a smooth surface. Avoid those with bulging seeds, brown spots, large scars or withered ends. Select beans of equal size to facilitate even cooking. Store unwashed beans in an airtight bag in the refrigerator for up to 4 days.

Preparation & Cooking Tips: To prepare, wash in cool water, drain and remove stems and strings. The tips do not have to be trimmed. Drop yellow wax beans in boiling, salted water for 3 minutes or until just tender. Drain and pat dry. When ready to serve, reheat in lemon-dill butter; or toss with melted butter and chopped scallions.

NUTRITION FACTS

UNITED STATES
Serving Size: ¼ cup, dry
Calories 160
Protein...........................10 g
Fat ....0 g
Carbohydrates.............28 g
Dietary Fiber ....7 g
Sodium ....5 mg

CANADA
Serving Size: per 50 g (125 mL/¼ cup, dry)
Energy.........169 cal.....710 kJ
Protein.......................11.3 g
Fat ....0.5 g
Carbohydrates ....31 g
Dietary Fibre ....3.7 g
Sodium ....6 mg
Potassium ....680 mg

UNITED STATES
Serving Size: 1 cup, steamed
Calories 67
Protein.........................5 g
Fat ....0 g
Carbohydrates.............11 g
Dietary Fiber ....4 g
Sodium ....6 mg

CANADA
Serving Size: per 75 g (125 mL/½ cup)
Energy...........32 cal.....130 kJ
Protein.......................2.1 g
Fat ....0.2 g
Carbohydrates ....5.7 g
Dietary Fibre ....2.0 g
Sodium ....3 mg
Potassium ....150 mg

UNITED STATES
Serving Size: 1 cup, steamed
Calories 67
Protein.........................5 g
Fat ....0 g
Carbohydrates.............11 g
Dietary Fiber ....4 g
Sodium ....6 mg

CANADA
Serving Size: per 150 g (250 mL/¼ cup)
Energy...........63 cal.....360 kJ
Protein.......................4.2 g
Fat ....0.3 g
Carbohydrates ....11 g
Dietary Fibre ....3.9 g
Sodium ....6 mg
Potassium ....300 mg

UNITED STATES
Serving Size: 1 cup, boiled
Calories 25
Protein.........................2 g
Fat ....0 g
Carbohydrates.............6 g
Dietary Fiber ....5 g
Sodium ....0 mg

CANADA
Serving Size: per 100 g (250 mL/1 cup)
Energy...........31 cal.....130 kJ
Protein.......................1.8 g
Fat ....0.1 g
Carbohydrates ....7.1 g
Dietary Fibre ....1.8 g
Sodium ....6 mg
Potassium ....209 mg

SOURCE: USDA

Common

General Information: The cucumber is a long, cylindrical, green-skinned member of the gourd family. Inside, crisp white flesh surrounds the seeded core. Cucumbers are usually eaten raw. Cucumbers are available year-round.

Selection & Storage: Choose firm, unblemished cucumbers. Check for soft spots, especially at ends. Avoid cucumbers with yellow streaks, as they are past their prime. Refrigerate, unwashed, in a plastic bag for up to 1 week.

Preparation & Cooking Tips: Wash the cucumber well or, if necessary, peel to remove the waxy coating. If the cucumber is very young, the seeds are tender and do not need to be removed. As the cucumber matures, the seeds become bigger and more bitter. To remove seeds, slice in half lengthwise. Drag a spoon through the seeds to remove them. Slice an inch from each end of the cucumber, as bitterness tends to gather there.

English/Burpless

General Information: English cucumbers can grow as long as 2 feet. They are nearly seedless. Seeds can cause indigestion, so English cucumbers are also known as Burpless. Their skin is deep green and their flesh creamy to crisp white. They are available year-round.

Selection & Storage: Choose firm, unblemished cucumbers. Check for soft spots, especially at ends. Avoid cucumbers with yellow streaks, as these indicate the cucumbers are past their prime. Refrigerate, unwashed, in a plastic bag for up to 1 week.

Preparation & Cooking Tips: Cucumbers are often commercially waxed to preserve their moisture content. Peel with a vegetable peeler if the skin is waxed. Wash well in cold water. English cucumbers can be used in gazpacho or other cold soups, salads, sandwiches or dips. Cook English cucumbers over low heat until just tender.

Japanese

General Information: The Japanese cucumber is a mild slicing cucumber. The cucumber has been used for thousands of years as a natural coolant for the palate. Thought to have originated in India or Thailand, the Japanese cucumber is a staple of Eastern and Western cooking. The Japanese cucumber is slender and deep green with a bumpy, ridged skin. Its taste is mild. Japanese cucumbers can be used in salads or for pickling. They are available year-round.

Selection & Storage: Choose firm, unblemished cucumbers. Check for soft spots. Avoid cucumbers with yellow streaks. Store cucumbers, unwashed, in a plastic bag in the refrigerator for up to 1 week.

Preparation & Cooking Tips: Wash cucumbers well or, if necessary, peel to remove waxy preservative. Slice an inch from each end, as bitterness tends to gather there. Japanese cucumbers can be gently cooked. Never cook over high heat or the cucumber will turn to mush.

Kirby

General Information: Kirby cucumbers, also known as pickling cucumbers, are small – ranging from 3 to 6 inches long. They are often irregularly shaped and have bumpy skin with tiny white or black dotted spines. Kirby cucumbers are never waxed. Their skin can be creamy yellow to pale or dark green. They are great for pickling, and are available year-round.

Selection & Storage: Choose firm, unwrinkled, unblemished cucumbers. Check for soft spots, especially at ends. Refrigerate, unwashed, in a plastic bag for up to 1 week.

Preparation & Cooking Tips: Scrub Kirby cucumbers gently with a soft brush or a washcloth. Bitterness accumulates in the ends of cucumbers, so trim ½ inch at each end. Kirby cucumbers have a natural affinity for cider vinegar, dill and celery seeds. Putting up jars of pickles is a well-rewarded effort. Kirby cucumbers may also be cooked with Japanese seasonings and then chilled or served at room temperature.

NUTRITION FACTS

UNITED STATES
Serving Size: ⅙ medium
Calories	15
Protein	1 g
Fat	0 g
Carbohydrates	3 g
Dietary Fiber	1 g
Sodium	0 mg

CANADA
Serving Size: per 110 g (⅙ med.)
Energy	13 cal	50 kJ
Protein		0.5 g
Fat		0.1 g
Carbohydrates		2.9 g
Dietary Fibre		0.7 g
Sodium		2 mg
Potassium		149 mg

UNITED STATES
Serving Size: ½ cup
Calories	7
Protein	0 g
Fat	0 g
Carbohydrates	0 g
Dietary Fiber	0 g
Sodium	1 mg

CANADA
Serving Size: per 70 g (125mL/½ cup)
Energy	9 cal	40 kJ
Protein		0.4 g
Fat		0.1 g
Carbohydrates		2.0 g
Dietary Fibre		0.5 g
Sodium		1 mg
Potassium		10 mg

UNITED STATES

NUTRITION FACTS
NOT AVAILABLE

CANADA

NUTRITION FACTS
NOT AVAILABLE

UNITED STATES

NUTRITION FACTS
NOT AVAILABLE

CANADA

NUTRITION FACTS
NOT AVAILABLE

SOURCE: USDA

Italian

General Information: Once reserved for eggplant Parmesan, eggplant is a key ingredient in Italian, Indian, Middle Eastern and Asian dishes. Italian eggplant resembles the common purple eggplant, except it is much smaller. Its skin is thinner and its flesh more delicate. Italian eggplant is available year-round.

Selection & Storage: Look for firm eggplants that are heavy for their size with taut, unwrinkled skin. When squeezed, they should be springy, not spongy. Pits, dents or wrinkles are signs that the eggplant is bitter. Eggplants are very perishable; do not refrigerate. Store them in a cool— not cold— place in a plastic bag for up to 2 days.

Preparation & Cooking Tips: Most Italian eggplants just require a rinse and a trim of the stem and green cap. Always cook eggplant before eating. Italian eggplants are a good choice for grilling, stuffing or for forming eggplant rolls wrapped around prosciutto and mozzarella.

Japanese

General Information: Japanese eggplants are a wonderful variation of the common eggplant. Small and narrow, they have a lovely, sweet taste. Their shape is similar to a chubby cucumber. Baby Japanese eggplants are a more tender variety. Their color ranges from solid purple to striated shades of purple. The skin is thin and does not have to be peeled. Japanese eggplants are available year-round.

Selection & Storage: Look for firm eggplants that are heavy for their size with taut, unwrinkled skin. Lightly press the eggplant to test for springy, not spongy, texture. Pits, dents or wrinkles are signs that the eggplant is bitter. Do not refrigerate. Use them right away, or store in a cool— not cold—place in a plastic bag for up to 2 days.

Preparation & Cooking Tips: Rinse Japanese eggplants and cut off stem and cap. Always cook eggplant before eating. Japanese eggplants are good halved lengthwise, brushed lightly with oil and grilled until fork-tender.

Purple

General Information: The most commonly available eggplant is large, cylindrical or pear-shaped, with a glossy, deep-purple skin. Eggplant is a vegetarian's delight, as its meaty, firm texture is an excellent substitute for meat in many dishes. Eggplant is available year-round.

Selection & Storage: Look for firm eggplants that are heavy for their size. Small or medium eggplants are less likely to be bitter. Eggplants are very perishable. Do not refrigerate. Use them right away, or store in a cool— not cold—place in a plastic bag for up to 2 days.

Preparation & Cooking Tips: The skin of small eggplants is edible. Large eggplants should be peeled. Eggplant discolors when exposed to air, so either peel right before using or dip pieces in acidulated water. Always cook eggplant before eating. Salting is recommended to draw out bitter juices, to reduce the moisture content and to prevent the eggplant from absorbing too much oil when cooked. Recipes will vary on the amount of salting required.

White

General Information: White eggplants are smaller and more firmLy textured than the common purple eggplant. They are denser, creamier and less bitter, even though they can have more seeds. White eggplants are available seasonally.

Selection & Storage: Look for firm eggplants that are heavy for their size with taut, unwrinkled skin. Lightly press the eggplant to test for springy, not spongy, texture. Pits, dents or wrinkles are signs that the eggplant is bitter. Do not buy waxed eggplants. Do not refrigerate. Use them right away, or store in a cool— not cold — place in a plastic bag for up to 2 days.

Preparation & Cooking Tips: Always cook eggplant before eating. The skin of a white eggplant is tough and must be peeled. Peel with a sharp knife or vegetable peeler. White eggplant is a good choice for dishes that require a firm texture. White eggplant holds its shape when fried, baked or steamed.

NUTRITION FACTS

UNITED STATES
Serving Size: ½ cup
Calories 13
Protein..............................0 g
Fat ....0 g
Carbohydrates..............3 g
Dietary Fiber ....1 g
Sodium ....2 mg

CANADA
Serving Size: per 85 g (250 mL/1 cup)
Energy............22 cal.....90 kJ
Protein...........................0.9 g
Fat ....0.1 g
Carbohydrates ....5.3 g
Dietary Fibre ....2.1 g
Sodium ....3 mg
Potassium ....186 mg

UNITED STATES
Serving Size: 3.5 ounces
Calories 25
Protein..............................1 g
Fat ....0 g
Carbohydrates...................6 g
Dietary Fiber ....10 g
Sodium ....2 mg

CANADA
Serving Size: per 100 g (3.5 oz.)
Energy............26 cal....110 kJ
Protein...........................1.1 g
Fat ....0.1 g
Carbohydrates ....6.3 g
Dietary Fibre ....2.5 g
Sodium ....4 mg
Potassium ....219 mg

UNITED STATES
Serving Size: 1 cup, diced
Calories 20
Protein..............................1 g
Fat ....0 g
Carbohydrates...................5 g
Dietary Fiber ....2 g
Sodium ....0 mg

CANADA
Serving Size: per 85 g (250 mL/1 cup)
Energy............22 cal....92 kJ
Protein...........................0.9 g
Fat ....0.1 g
Carbohydrates ....5.3 g
Dietary Fibre ....2.1 g
Sodium ....3 mg
Potassium ....186 mg

UNITED STATES

NUTRITION FACTS
NOT AVAILABLE

CANADA

NUTRITION FACTS
NOT AVAILABLE

SOURCE: USDA

NUTRITION FACTS

UNITED STATES
Serving Size: 2 heads

Calories	18
Protein	1 g
Fat	0 g
Carbohydrates	4 g
Dietary Fiber	3 g
Sodium	5 mg

CANADA
Serving Size: per 55 g (1 head)

Energy	8.3 cal....30 kJ
Protein	0.1 g
Fat	0.1 g
Carbohydrates	1.8 g
Dietary Fibre	1.7 g
Sodium	4 mg
Potassium	100 mg

UNITED STATES
Serving Size: 1/2 head

Calories	10
Protein	1 g
Fat	0 g
Carbohydrates	2 g
Dietary Fiber	1 g
Sodium	0 mg

CANADA
Serving Size: per 60 g (250 mL/1 cup)

Energy	7.8 cal....30 kJ
Protein	0.8 g
Fat	0.1 g
Carbohydrates	1.4 g
Dietary Fibre	0.6 g
Sodium	3 mg
Potassium	154 mg

UNITED STATES
Serving Size: 1 cup

Calories	9
Protein	1 g
Fat	0 g
Carbohydrates	2 g
Dietary Fiber	1 g
Sodium	46 mg

CANADA
Serving Size: per 75 g (250 mL/1 cup)

Energy	9.8 cal....40 kJ
Protein	1.1 g
Fat	0.2 g
Carbohydrates	1.6 g
Dietary Fibre	0.8 g
Sodium	49 mg
Potassium	189 mg

UNITED STATES
Serving Size: ½ head

Calories	10
Protein	1 g
Fat	0 g
Carbohydrates	2 g
Dietary Fiber	1 g
Sodium	0 mg

CANADA
Serving Size: per 60g (250 mL/1 cup)

Energy	7.8 cal....30 kJ
Protein	0.8 g
Fat	0.1 g
Carbohydrates	1.4 g
Dietary Fibre	0.6 g
Sodium	3 mg
Potassium	154 mg

SOURCE: USDA

Belgian Endive

General Information: Belgian endive grows in elegant tapered bundles, 4 to 6 inches long. The leaves are creamy white in the middle and yellow-green on the edges. It is grown in total darkness to prevent it from turning green. Belgian endive has a slightly bitter taste, a crunchy bite, and is available when many other interesting greens are in short supply. Its peak season is November through April.

Selection & Storage: Avoid Belgian endive with browning edges, rusted spots or slimy feel. Store Belgian endive, unwashed, wrapped in a paper towel inside a plastic bag in the refrigerator for up to 1 day.

Preparation & Cooking Tips: Wash Belgian endive with a damp cloth. Do not submerge in water. Trim the stem and, depending on use, cut the endive in half lengthwise or in strips crosswise. Belgian endive has a very distinctive taste — a little goes a long way. Use in salads, baked or braised; the inner leaves make edible scoops for dips.

Bibb Lettuce

General Information: Bibb lettuce is a butterhead lettuce. Butterheads have small, round and loosely formed heads and buttery, soft leaves. The outer leaves are pale green and the inner leaves are pale yellow. Bibb is prized for its sweet, subtle taste, and is available year-round.

Selection & Storage: Check the heads to be sure the leaves are supple and firmLy attached. Bibb lettuce requires gentle handling. Remove leaves and soak in a sink full of cold water. Swish the leaves around and then let sit for a bit so any sand can sink. Dry the leaves in a salad spinner, a few at a time. Wrap the dry leaves in paper towels and seal in a plastic bag. Try to remove most of the air from the bag. Bibb lettuce will keep up to 1 week in the refrigerator.

Preparation & Cooking Tips: Bibb lettuce is good in combination with other salad greens such as Boston, romaine, Belgian endive, sorrel and radicchio.

Bok Choy

General Information: Bok choy is a cruciferous vegetable. It is often incorrectly called Chinese cabbage. Unlike American cabbages, bok choy is not a round-head cabbage. Bok choy has wide-stemmed, white stalks with full, green leaves. The stalks are crunchy, mild, and juicy, while the leaves are tender and have a more cabbage-like taste. Bok choy is available year-round.

Selection & Storage: Selection depends on intended use. For soup, select the large-leafed variety. For stir-fries, choose those with longer and narrower stalks. Refrigerate, unwashed, in a perforated plastic bag for up to 3 days.

Preparation & Cooking Tips: Bok choy can be used in slaws, but Chinese cabbage is a better choice. Bok choy's flavor is enhanced with heat. It cooks quickly to the crisp-tender stage. The stalks are good stir-fried with seared seafood, chicken, beef or pork. Slivered bok choy leaves are good in soups.

Butterhead/Boston

General Information: Boston lettuce is a butterhead lettuce. Butterheads have small, round and loosely formed heads and buttery, soft leaves. The outer leaves are pale green and the inner leaves are pale yellow. Boston lettuce is available year-round.

Selection & Storage: Check the heads to be sure the leaves are supple and firmLy attached. Boston lettuce requires gentle handling, but it can be very sandy, so wash well. Remove leaves and soak in a sink full of cold water. Swish the leaves around and then let sit for a bit so any sand can sink. Dry the leaves in a salad spinner, a few at a time. Wrap the dry leaves in paper towels and seal in a plastic bag. Try to remove most of the air from the bag and refrigerate up to 1 week.

Preparation & Cooking Tips: Boston lettuce is good in combination with other salad greens such as watercress. Dress it with a buttermilk dressing, a raspberry vinaigrette, or with orange juice, olive oil and tarragon vinegar.

Greens

Cabbage

General Information: Cabbage comes in many forms: round, conical or flat. The heads can be loose or compact, the leaves curly or plain. The most common cabbage in markets is the head cabbage, a tight ball of waxy leaves. The green head is slightly less sweet than red cabbage. When shredded, cabbage can be eaten raw (coleslaw), simmered in soups and stews, pickled (sauerkraut) or sautéed. Larger chunks can be braised, boiled or steamed. Cabbage is available year-round.

Selection & Storage: Choose cabbages that are heavy for their size with crisp, tightly packed leaves. Tightly wrap in plastic and store in the refrigerator for up to 1 week.

Preparation & Cooking Tips: Cabbage steam can have a strong odor. Place a piece of bread, a walnut or a sprig of parsley in the cooking water to reduce the aroma. Cabbage should be cooked until it is just tender. Overcooked cabbage will be soggy and can have a strong, acrid taste.

Cabbage, Red

General Information: With more vitamin C than green cabbage, just 3 1/2 ounces of red cabbage provide nearly 100% of the RDA. It is also one of the super-healthy cruciferous vegetables. It is available year-round.

Selection & Storage: Buy red cabbage heads that are heavy and solid, with only a few loose outer leaves. Outer leaves should be flexible but firm, with a closely trimmed stem free from cracks or dryness. Place in a perforated plastic bag and store, unwashed, in the crisper section of the refrigerator for 2 weeks.

Preparation & Cooking Tips: Prepare cabbage right before eating or cooking, and rinse after leaves have been cut. Red cabbage is good shredded in salads and slaws, and may also be boiled, braised, microwaved, steamed or stuffed.

Chicory/Curly Endive

General Information: Chicory is the name of a wide variety of greens, including Belgian endive, escarole, frisée and radicchio. When listed as an ingredient, it generally refers to curly endive. Chicory/curly endive is crisp, with curly green leaves and a pale heart. Chicory is best eaten when young, as it increases in bitterness with age. It is usually considered too strong to be eaten alone and is mixed with other, milder, greens. Chicory/curly endive is available year-round.

Selection & Storage: Choose chicory that has crisp, fresh leaves with no signs of deterioration. Refrigerate, unwashed, in an airtight container for up to 3 days.

Preparation & Cooking Tips: Combine washed chicory with Bibb, Boston and loose-leaf lettuce. Serve with a warm bacon-and-red-wine vinaigrette, topped with garlic croutons.

Chinese Cabbage

General Information: Trying to describe Chinese cabbage is like trying to describe lettuce — there are so many varieties it's hard to know where to start. However, the two most commonly available Chinese cabbages in North America have two distinct forms: one is dark green, long and narrow with leaf tips fanning outward; the other is apple-green, shorter, thicker and has leaves that curve inward. While both are more tender than the common round cabbages, the narrow cabbage has crunchier leaves. One form or another is available year-round.

Selection & Storage: Look for firm heads with crisp leaves and no sign of browning. Tightly wrapped Chinese cabbage can be kept in the refrigerator. For salads, use within 4 days. For cooking, it will last up to 2 weeks.

Preparation & Cooking Tips: Chinese cabbage can be eaten raw in salads or slaws. It is excellent cooked in soups or stir-fries. Chinese cabbage leaves are also good blanched and then wrapped around spicy foods.

NUTRITION FACTS

UNITED STATES
Serving Size: 1/2 head
Calories	25
Protein	1 g
Fat	0 g
Carbohydrates	5 g
Dietary Fiber	2 g
Sodium	20 mg

CANADA
Serving Size: per 75 g (1/10 head)
Energy	18 cal.....80 kJ
Protein	0.9 g
Fat	0.1 g
Carbohydrates	4 g
Dietary Fibre	1.4 g
Sodium	14 mg
Potassium	185 mg

UNITED STATES
Serving Size: 1 cup, chopped
Calories	24
Protein	1 g
Fat	0.2 g
Carbohydrates	5 g
Dietary Fiber	2 g
Sodium	9 mg

CANADA
Serving Size: per 75 g (1/10 head)
Energy	18 cal.....80 kJ
Protein	0.9 g
Fat	0.1 g
Carbohydrates	4 g
Dietary Fibre	1.4 g
Sodium	14 mg
Potassium	185 mg

UNITED STATES
Serving Size: 1/2 cup, chopped
Calories	20
Protein	2 g
Fat	0 g
Carbohydrates	4 g
Dietary Fiber	4 g
Sodium	40 mg

CANADA
Serving Size: per 60 g (75 mL/1/3 cup)
Energy	14 cal.....60 kJ
Protein	1.0 g
Fat	0.2 g
Carbohydrates	2.8 g
Dietary Fibre	2.4 g
Sodium	27 mg
Potassium	252 mg

UNITED STATES
Serving Size: 1 cup, shredded
Calories	10
Protein	1 g
Fat	0 g
Carbohydrates	2 g
Dietary Fiber	1 g
Sodium	29 mg

CANADA
Serving Size: 1 cup shredded, raw
Energy	9 cal.....37 kJ
Protein	1 g
Fat	0.1 g
Carbohydrates	1.5 g
Dietary Fibre	0.7 g
Sodium	45.5 mg
Potassium	176 mg

SOURCE: USDA

NUTRITION FACTS

UNITED STATES
Serving Size: 2 cups, chopped
Calories 20
Protein..............................1 g
Fat ....0 g
Carbohydrates...............5 g
Dietary Fiber ....3 g
Sodium ....15 mg

CANADA
Serving Size: per 75 g (500 mL/2 cups)
Energy...........23 cal.....100 kJ
Protein............................1.2 g
Fat ....0.2 g
Carbohydrates ....5.3 g
Dietary Fibre ....2.7 g
Sodium ....15 mg
Potassium ....127 mg

Collard Greens

General Information: Collard greens are a non-head, Old World cabbage that tastes like a combination of cabbage and kale. Its intense green leaves are far more nutritious than paler-leafed cabbages. Traditionally in the Southern United States, collard greens are boiled with a piece of salt pork or ham hock. They are available from December through April.

Selection & Storage: Choose collard greens that are relatively small and firm. Avoid those with any sign of yellowing or holes. Store collard greens in damp paper towels inside a plastic bag. Collard greens can go limp quickly, so use within a few days.

Preparation & Cooking Tips: Collard greens tend to be gritty. Wash well in a sink full of water. The ribs are too tough to eat, so strip the ribs from leaves. Stack leaves in a pile and chop to desired size. Collards can be cooked long and slowly, or quickly like spinach. The latter method preserves the high vitamin C content.

UNITED STATES
Serving Size: 1 cup
Calories 5
Protein.........................0.4 g
Fat ....0 g
Carbohydrates ....1 g
Dietary Fiber ....1 g
Sodium ....7 mg

CANADA
Serving Size: per 55 g (250 mL/1 cup)
Energy...........9.4 cal.....39 kJ
Protein.........................0.7 g
Fat ....0.1 g
Carbohydrates ....1.8 g
Dietary Fibre ....0.8 g
Sodium ....12 mg
Potassium ....173 mg

Escarole

General Information: Escarole is a member of the endive family. It is sometimes called Batavian endive. A lettuce-like salad green, escarole is prized in France and Italy for its slightly nutty, bitter flavor. Its leaves are bright green and flare outwards. Its inner leaves are a softer green. Escarole is high in calcium and is available year-round.

Selection & Storage: Escarole leaves are fleshier than lettuce leaves. Look for heads that are loose and shaggy but have a well-defined heart. Avoid escarole that appears limp or has yellowing leaves. Refrigerate, wrapped in plastic, for only a few days.

Preparation & Cooking Tips: Escarole tends to be very dirty. Wash well in a sink full of cold water. Drain and wash again. Use escarole with other salad greens such as bibb, red leaf and spinach. Dress with a lemon vinaigrette and top with toasted hazelnuts or pine nuts, or a warm bacon-and-red-wine vinaigrette. Escarole is wonderful in soups, with beans or sautéed with lots of garlic and olive oil.

UNITED STATES
Serving Size: 1 cup
Calories 100
Protein............................34 g
Fat ....0.5 g
Carbohydrates ....59 g
Dietary Fiber ....0 g
Sodium ....1 mg

CANADA
Serving Size: per 90 g (250 mL/1 cup)
Energy...........18 cal.....80 kJ
Protein............................2.3 g
Fat ....0.3 g
Carbohydrates ....3 g
Dietary Fibre ....1.7 g
Sodium ....1 mg
Potassium ....199 mg

Fiddlehead Fern

General Information: There is no such plant as the fiddlehead fern. The term "fiddlehead" refers to a stage in the life of all ferns when they poke up through the soil but have not yet uncurled. Fiddlehead ferns are prized for their their delicate flavor: a combination of asparagus, artichokes and mushrooms. They are available from April until June.

Selection & Storage: Look for jade-green, tightly coiled fiddleheads that are no more than an $1^1/_2$ inches across, with tails no more than 2 inches in length. (Longer tails indicate the fiddlehead will be tough and stringy.) Fiddleheads do not store well. Use immediately.

Preparation & Cooking Tips: Trim tails to $^1/_4$ inch. If the fiddleheads still have papery scales, rub them between your palms to remove. Rinse well. Drop fiddleheads into rapidly boiling, salted water. Boil until tender throughout, about 5 minutes. Do not undercook or the unique flavor of the fiddlehead will not fully emerge. Drain well and drizzle with lemon butter or raspberry vinaigrette.

UNITED STATES
Serving Size: 1½ cups, shredded
Calories 15
Protein..............................1 g
Fat ....0 g
Carbohydrates...............4 g
Dietary Fiber ....2 g
Sodium ....30 mg

CANADA
Serving Size: per 90 g (250 mL/1 cup)
Energy...........11 cal.....50 kJ
Protein.........................0.8 g
Fat ....0.2 g
Carbohydrates ....2.1 g
Dietary Fibre ....0.9 g
Sodium ....5 mg
Potassium ....158 mg

SOURCE: USDA

Green Leaf Lettuce

General Information: There are four categories of lettuce: crisphead, butterhead, leaf and romaine. Leaf lettuce is distinguished from other varieties of lettuce in that it doesn't have a "head." Oak leaf, red leaf and green leaf are all leaf lettuces. They are crisp and flavorful, and are available year-round.

Selection & Storage: Avoid lettuce with leaf edges that are slimy or dark. Leaf lettuce lasts longer if washed when brought home. Soak in a sink full of cold water, swishing it to loosen dirt. Drain and then dry lettuce thoroughly in a salad spinner or blot with paper towels. Refrigerate, loosely wrapped in a paper towel inside a plastic bag, for up to 1 week.

Preparation & Cooking Tips: A green leaf salad with cut grapefruit sections, scallions, sliced cooked potatoes, crisp bacon and light-mustard vinaigrette makes a good luncheon served with warm French bread. Always add salad dressing right before serving.

Greens

Iceberg Lettuce

General Information: Pale-green iceberg lettuce has less vitamins than its darker-leafed cousins. But what would a taco be without crisp, shredded iceberg lettuce? Thai restaurants often use iceberg lettuce as a "wrapper" for their spicy appetizers such as larb and nam sod. Iceberg lettuce is available year-round in all supermarkets.

Selection & Storage: Choose firm, densely packed heads that are heavy for their size. Avoid any that have browning or slimy edges. Refrigerate, unwashed, in a sealed plastic bag for up to 2 weeks.

Preparation: Remove the core with a sharp knife or rap the core against the counter; then hold the core, twist it and lift out. Run water into the cavity until it flows up out of the leaves. Invert the lettuce head and drain. Rip lettuce leaves by hand, not with a knife, unless it is razor-sharp (duller knives will cause browning edges). Iceberg lettuce has enough texture to hold up to a creamy, thick dressing such as blue cheese.

Kale

General Information: Kale has blue-green leaves and a thick center stem. It is rich in vitamins A, B-complex and C, iron and calcium. Kale tastes like a mild cabbage. Cooked kale, usually made with bacon drippings, onions and vinegar, is a popular dish in the Southern United States. Kale is available year-round.

Selection & Storage: Choose richly colored, relatively small bunches of kale with fresh, strong leaves and no sign of limpness. Avoid those with yellow spots or browning. Refrigerate, unwashed, in a plastic bag for 2 to 3 days.

Preparation & Cooking Tips: With a sharp knife, cut the leaves away from the stem and thick center rib. Rinse well, but do not soak. Kale's C and B-complex vitamins are water-soluble. Remove excess water in a salad spinner. Remove the ribs if they are tough. Strips of kale are perfect for stir-frying. Kale may be prepared the same way as spinach. Small amounts make a nice addition to green salads.

Kohlrabi

General Information: Kohlrabi's flavor is similar to fresh broccoli stems with a mellow touch of radish. Kohlrabi is not a root, but a thickened, enlarged stem, with smaller, leafed stems shooting up from the top. The leaves are edible and, when cooked, taste like a combination of kale and collard greens. Its peak season is early summer.

Selection & Storage: Choose small or medium-sized kohlrabi with the smallest, smoothest ball and stems, free of cracks and fibers. Look for fresh, green leaves with no sign of yellowing. To store, separate the leaves from the stems. Wrap in plastic and store in the refrigerator. The leaves will last only 2 days; the stems will last 1 week.

Preparation & Cooking Tips: Wash the leaves in warm water. Strip the stems by folding the leaves in half, like a paper heart, and pull the stem away from the leaf. Cook as desired. The bulbous stems must be pared to remove the fibrous first layer under the skin. They can be peeled before or after cooking. Kohlrabi is good raw in slaws.

Mustard Greens

General Information: Mustard greens are sharply pungent, the strongest of the bitter greens. Mustard greens are most abundant from December through early March.

Selection & Storage: Look for bright-green mustard greens with no sign of yellowing. Avoid those with tough, thick stems. For salad, choose small leaves. For cooking, medium and large leaves are acceptable. Use as soon as possible after purchase. They will last 2 days wrapped tightly in plastic and refrigerated.

Preparation & Cooking Tips: Clean mustard greens in a sink full of lukewarm water. Swirl leaves around. Gently lift out and drain the sink. Repeat the process. Dry and remove the stems. Strip the stems by folding the leaves in half, like a paper heart, and pull the stem away from the leaf. For salads, combine mustard greens with Swiss chard and Bibb lettuce and top with a warm, sweet dressing. Do not cook mustard greens in aluminum or iron pans. Mustard greens also can be sautéed like spinach.

NUTRITION FACTS

UNITED STATES — Serving Size: ⅙ head
Calories 15; Protein 1 g; Fat 0 g; Carbohydrates 3 g; Dietary Fiber 1 g; Sodium 10 mg

CANADA — Serving Size: per 60 g (250 mL/1 cup)
Energy 8 cal/30 kJ; Protein 0.6 g; Fat 0.1 g; Carbohydrates 1.3 g; Dietary Fibre 0.8 g; Sodium 5 mg; Potassium 95 mg

UNITED STATES — Serving Size: 1 cup, chopped
Calories 33; Protein 2 g; Fat 0.5 g; Carbohydrates 7 g; Dietary Fiber 1 g; Sodium 30 mg

CANADA — Serving Size: per 56 g (250 mL)
Energy 28 cal/117 kJ; Protein 1.9 g; Fat 0.5 g; Carbohydrates 5.7 g; Dietary Fibre n/a; Sodium 24 mg; Potassium 250 mg

UNITED STATES — Serving Size: ½ cup, sliced
Calories 20; Protein 1 g; Fat 0 g; Carbohydrates 4 g; Dietary Fiber 3 g; Sodium 15 mg

CANADA — Serving Size: per 1 cup, raw
Energy 36 cal/152 kJ; Protein 2.2 g; Fat 0.1 g; Carbohydrates 8.3 g; Dietary Fibre 4.8 g; Sodium 27 mg; Potassium 472 mg

UNITED STATES — Serving Size: 1½ cups
Calories 20; Protein 2 g; Fat 0 g; Carbohydrates 4 g; Dietary Fiber 2 g; Sodium 20 mg

CANADA — Serving Size: per 90 g (375 mL/1½ cups)
Energy 23 cal/100 kJ; Protein 2.4 g; Fat 0.2 g; Carbohydrates 4.4 g; Dietary Fibre 1.8 g; Sodium 23 mg; Potassium 319 mg

SOURCE: USDA

Radicchio

General Information: Radicchio (rod-EEK-ee-o) is red-leafed chicory. Bittersweet and satiny, radicchio is a favorite of gourmets. Radicchio starts as a green-leafed plant, turns deeper green and then reddens when the weather cools. The deep-red leaves surround white ribs. Various varieties of radicchio are named after the regions where they are grown. Radicchio is available year-round.

Selection & Storage: Choose small heads. Turn the radicchio over and look at the white core for signs of browning or holes. Check radicchio leaves for browning as well. Radicchio leaves are closely wrapped and there is rarely any waste. Refrigerate unwashed radicchio, loosely wrapped in plastic, for up to 1 week.

Preparation & Cooking Tips: To prepare, remove the core with a sharp knife. Separate and trim the leaves, then wash and blot or spin dry. Radicchio is good with meat, beans, mushrooms, oranges, nuts, olives, cheese or game; or sauté the leaves briefly.

Rapini/Broccoli Raab

General Information: The Chinese and Italians revere rapini for its characteristic bitterness. The Italians fry, braise and steam rapini. The Chinese add it to their soups. Rapini is related to both the cabbage and turnip families. It is a source of vitamins A, C and K, as well as potassium. Rapini is available year-round, but its peak season is from fall to spring.

Selection & Storage: Choose rapini that is firm with relatively few buds and flowers. Wrap loosely in plastic and place in the vegetable-crisper section of the refrigerator for up to a few days.

Preparation & Cooking Tips: Rinse the rapini and shake off the water. Cut off the heavier stem bottoms. Rapini should be cooked. To lessen the intensity of rapini, blanch it in boiling, salted water for 1 minute. Drain and dry, then cook as usual. Rapini can be sautéed, stir-fried, steamed or boiled. It cooks very quickly. Rapini is especially good with sweet Italian sausage.

Red Leaf Lettuce

General Information: Times have changed since salad meant only one thing — iceberg lettuce with thick salad dressing. Today's cooks delight in mixing a wild assortment of lettuces and greens. Leaf lettuce is distinguished from other varieties of lettuce in that it doesn't have a "head." Oak leaf, red leaf and green leaf are all leaf lettuces. They are crisp and flavorful, but generally more perishable than head lettuces. Red leaf lettuce has a burgundy/bronze tint and a mild taste. Red leaf lettuce is available year-round.

Selection & Storage: Avoid lettuce with leaf edges that are slimy or dark. Lettuce lasts longer if washed when brought home. Soak lettuce in a sink full of cold water, hand-stirring to loosen dirt. Let sit a few minutes. Drain and then dry lettuce in a salad spinner or blot with paper towels. It must be dry. Refrigerate for up to 1 week, loosely wrapped in a paper towel inside a plastic bag.

Preparation & Cooking Tips: Mix textures, flavors, colors and food groups. Always add salad dressing right before serving.

Romaine

General Information: Romaine lettuce is the preferred green for the popular Caesar salad. Tall and cylindrical in shape, its taste is sweetly bitter with a good crunch. Romaine lettuce is available year-round.

Selection & Storage: Look for crisp leaves with no rust spots or browning edges. Romaine will last longer if it is washed before storing. Break off the bottom and separate the leaves. In a sink full of cold water, swirl the lettuce to remove dirt. Drain the lettuce and dry thoroughly. Refrigerate for up to 1 week, loosely wrapped in a paper towel inside a plastic bag.

Preparation & Cooking Tips: Try this no-egg recipe for a Caesar-dressing substitute: 3 tbsp. extra-virgin olive oil, 1 tbsp. fresh lemon juice and 1 tsp. each Dijon mustard and anchovy paste. Blend together. Crush 1 garlic clove and place in the dressing. Let sit 1 hour. Remove garlic. Whisk. Add 1 head of romaine torn into bite-size pieces. Toss, and enjoy!

NUTRITION FACTS

UNITED STATES
Serving Size: ¾ cup
Calories	5
Protein	0 g
Fat	0 g
Carbohydrates	1 g
Dietary Fiber	1 g
Sodium	51 mg

CANADA
Serving Size: per 50 g (300 mL/ 1¼ cups)
Energy	11 cal....50 kJ
Protein	0.7 g
Fat	0.1 g
Carbohydrates	2.2 g
Dietary Fibre	0.5 g
Sodium	11 mg
Potassium	151 mg

UNITED STATES

NUTRITION FACTS
NOT AVAILABLE

CANADA

NUTRITION FACTS
NOT AVAILABLE

UNITED STATES
Serving Size: 1½ cups
Calories	15
Protein	1 g
Fat	0 g
Carbohydrates	4 g
Dietary Fiber	2 g
Sodium	30 mg

CANADA
Serving Size: per 60 g (250 mL/1 cup)
Energy	11 cal....50 kJ
Protein	0.8 g
Fat	0.2 g
Carbohydrates	2.1 g
Dietary Fibre	0.9 g
Sodium	5 mg
Potassium	158 mg

UNITED STATES
Serving Size: 1½ cups
Calories	15
Protein	1 g
Fat	0 g
Carbohydrates	2 g
Fiber	2 g
Sodium	5 mg

CANADA
Serving Size: per 60 g (250 mL/1 cup)
Energy	9.6 cal....40 kJ
Protein	1.0 g
Fat	0.1 g
Carbohydrates	1.4 g
Dietary Fiber	1.0 g
Sodium	5 mg
Potassium	174 mg

SOURCE: USDA

Greens

Salad Savoy/Flowering Kale

General Information: Salad savoy is also known as flowering kale. The oldest member of the cabbage family, salad savoy combines beauty, form and function. It has a semi-crisp texture with a subtle bitterness. Salad savoy is unmistakable in its appearance. With its loose head of purple or cream-colored ruffled leaves tinged with pink and green, it looks like a huge flower. It is available from September through December.

Selection & Storage: Select fresh-looking salad savoy with crisp leaves and no browning or holes. Keep in a plastic bag in the refrigerator for up to 5 days.

Preparation & Cooking Tips: Remove the ribs if they are tough. Like regular kale, flowering kale can be cooked long and slowly. Its taste is relatively strong, so it should be paired with other strong flavors such as bacon, garlic, ginger or cheese. Strips of salad savoy are perfect for stir-frying.

NUTRITION FACTS

UNITED STATES
Serving Size: 1 cup, shredded
Calories 20
Protein............................1 g
Fat ....0 g
Carbohydrates ....4 g
Dietary Fiber ....2 g
Sodium ....20 mg

CANADA
Serving Size: per 70 g (250 mL/1 cup)
Energy.............20 cal.....80 kJ
Protein............................1.5 g
Fat ....0.1 g
Carbohydrates ....4.5 g
Dietary Fibre ....2.3 g
Sodium ....20 mg
Potassium ....170 mg

Spinach

General Information: Popeye was right: spinach is good for you. It's loaded with vitamins A, B and C, as well as calcium, potassium and iron. Spinach leaves are dark green and may be flat or curled, depending on the variety. Spinach is available year-round.

Selection & Storage: Choose crisp, dark-green leaves with no yellowing. If it is pre-bagged, open immediately and remove any rotted leaves. Refrigerate for up to 3 days, wrapped loosely in paper towels inside a plastic bag.

Preparation & Cooking Tips: Spinach has sand and grit tucked into every nook and cranny. Fill the sink with cold water and add spinach. Remove large stems. Lift out of water and drain the spinach. Refill sink and repeat. Dry leaves on paper towels or in a salad spinner. Never cook spinach in aluminum pans. Raw spinach is good in salads by itself or with mixed greens. Spinach is best cooked briefly over a high heat and topped with a touch of butter and freshly grated nutmeg.

UNITED STATES
Serving Size: 1 cup
Calories 20
Protein............................2 g
Fat ....0 g
Carbohydrates.....................3 g
Dietary Fiber ....2 g
Sodium ....65 mg

CANADA
Serving Size: per 90 g (375 mL/1½ cups)
Energy.............20 cal.....80 kJ
Protein............................2.6 g
Fat ....0.3 g
Carbohydrates ....3.2 g
Dietary Fibre ....2.3 g
Sodium ....71 mg
Potassium ....502 mg

Swiss Chard

General Information: Swiss chard is like two vegetables for the price of one. The ivory stalks can be cooked like asparagus spears and the dark leaves can be steamed or stir-fried. The two parts are often cooked separately and then tossed together and seasoned. Swiss chard's peak season is June through October.

Selection & Storage: Swiss chard is highly perishable. Look for crisp stalks and bright leaves. Separate leaves from stalks and store separately. Wrapped in plastic and refrigerated, the leaves will last 2 days and the stalks 4 days.

Preparation & Cooking Tips: Clean thoroughly. Remove any strings. Cut stalks into thick slices. Sauté in olive oil, covered, over low heat for 15 minutes or until tender. Add strips of chard leaves. Cook over medium heat until wilted. Sprinkle with lemon juice, golden raisins and pine nuts. Raw Swiss chard will dominate a dish; use sparingly.

UNITED STATES
Serving Size: 2 cups, chopped
Calories 15
Protein............................1 g
Fat ....0 g
Carbohydrates.....................3 g
Dietary Fiber ....1 g
Sodium ....150 mg

CANADA
Serving Size: per 75 g (500 mL/2 cups)
Energy.............14 cal.....60 kJ
Protein............................1.4 g
Fat ....0.2 g
Carbohydrates ....2.8 g
Dietary Fibre ....1.2 g
Sodium ....160 mg
Potassium ....284 mg

Turnip Greens

General Information: Turnip greens are deliciously aggressive to the palate, both in taste and texture, as the flavor is robust and the leaves are coarse. Turnip greens can be steamed when young, but after that they are too pungent. Turnip greens are available sporadically, with their peak season from November through March.

Selection & Storage: Turnip greens will not be attached to turnips. Look for relatively small leaves that are moist and cool. Keep turnip greens away from heat, which makes them tough and even more sharp. Do not buy any turnip greens with heavy stems or yellowing. Wrap them in damp paper towels; place inside a plastic bag and refrigerate for 2 to 3 days.

Preparation & Cooking Tips: Wash thoroughly. Dunk in a sink full of lukewarm water. Drain and repeat. Remove stems. Boil, cooking long and slowly in a non-reactive pan with fatback or bacon.

UNITED STATES
Serving Size: 1½ cups
Calories 20
Protein............................1 g
Fat ....0 g
Carbohydrates.....................5 g
Dietary Fiber ....2 g
Sodium ....35 mg

CANADA
Serving Size: per 100 g (1 cup)
Energy.............27 cal.....110 kJ
Protein............................1.5 g
Fat ....0.3 g
Carbohydrates ....5.7 g
Dietary Fibre ....2.4 g
Sodium ....40 mg
Potassium ....296 mg

SOURCE: USDA

Watercress

NUTRITION FACTS

UNITED STATES	
Serving Size: 2 cups	
Calories	5
Protein	2 g
Fat	0 g
Carbohydrates	1 g
Fiber	2 g
Sodium	30 mg

CANADA		
Serving Size: per 70 g (500 mL/2 cups)		
Energy	8 cal	30 kJ
Protein		1.6 g
Fat		0.1 g
Carbohydrates		1 g
Dietary Fiber		1.6 g
Sodium		29 mg
Potassium		231 mg

General Information: Watercress is a delicate green with a peppery bite. It grows wild in and alongside running water, hence the name. Watercress is a member of the mustard family. It has small, crisp, dark-green leaves and fragile stems. The watercress that comes to market here is cultivated, and is available year-round.

Selection & Storage: Watercress is sold in bunches. Look for fresh leaves with deep-green color. Do not buy if there is any yellowing, wilting or if they are bruised. Use watercress on the day of purchase, if possible. Store watercress wrapped in damp paper towels in a plastic bag; refrigerate for only a day or so.

Preparation & Cooking Tips: Cut off the tips of the stems and rinse thoroughly in a sink full of water. Pat dry between paper towels. The dime-sized leaves and edible stems of this peppery plant make it perfect for sandwiches, soups and salads. Watercress is delicious in scrambled eggs. It is a good garnish as well.

Incredible Mushrooms

Want a sure-fire way to enhance the flavor of cooked mushrooms? Add a little salt, a little sugar and a little soy sauce. Together, the three act as a magic flavor booster.

For a yummy appetizer, try this! Clean 10 large white mushrooms and remove stems. Place them cap-side-up in a glass dish. Insert a rolled anchovy fillet inside each mushroom cap. Cover with vented plastic and cook in the microwave on high for 2½ minutes.

For an Oriental twist, cook a pound of thinly sliced mushrooms in a tablespoon of sesame oil and a teaspoon of vegetable oil over moderate heat. Stir frequently. When mushrooms are golden, add 1 tablespoon of water and some sliced scallion greens. Cook for another minute.

This mushroom pâté is a tasty appetizer. Put chopped mushrooms (including stems) in a small, heavy pot with a little olive oil and 2 minced cloves of garlic. Cover and cook over low heat for 25 minutes. Add salt and pepper. Cook, uncovered, for 1 minute. Purée and spread on toasted French bread rounds.

Mushrooms

Button

NUTRITION FACTS

UNITED STATES	
Serving Size: 5 medium	
Calories	20
Protein	3 g
Fat	0 g
Carbohydrates	3 g
Dietary Fiber	1 g
Sodium	0 mg

CANADA		
Serving Size: per 90 g (5 medium)		
Energy	23 cal	90 kJ
Protein		1.9 g
Fat		0.4 g
Carbohydrates		4.2 g
Dietary Fibre		1.2 g
Sodium		4 mg
Potassium		333 mg

SOURCE: USDA

General Information: Button mushrooms are small, cultivated white mushrooms. When eaten raw, button mushrooms have a very mild, earthy taste. The flavor intensifies with cooking. They are available year-round.

Selection & Storage: Buy mushrooms that are firm, evenly colored and have tightly closed caps. If the gills underneath are visible, the mushroom is past its prime. For cooking purposes, buy those of similar size so they will cook evenly. Store in a single layer on a tray. Cover with a damp paper towel and refrigerate for up to 3 days.

Preparation & Cooking Tips: Never soak mushrooms, as they will absorb water and turn mushy. Either "sweep" with a soft brush or take a damp paper towel and remove dirt. Trim ¼ inch off the stem. When sautéing, be sure the pan and oil are hot. Mushrooms give off a lot of liquid; stir and cook until liquid evaporates. They are a good appetizer when dressed with vinaigrette and refrigerated for 2 days.

Chanterelle

General Information: Chanterelles have a delicate, sometimes nutty, sometimes fruity taste. Their texture is chewy. Most of the chanterelles that come to market have been picked in the wild. Look for them in summer and fall.

Selection & Storage: Gently stroke the frilled edges to make sure they are firm and plump. Avoid those with broken or shriveled caps. Scent is important: If it is intense, the taste will be as well; a lighter scent will result in a more delicate dish. Store chanterelles in a single layer in a basket covered by a piece of slightly damp cheesecloth. If in prime condition, they should last 1 week. Chanterelles freeze well, both raw and cooked (store with cooking juices).

Preparation & Cooking Tips: Brush dirt off with a soft brush. Trim ¼ inch from the stem. If large, slice into bite-size pieces. If small, leave whole. Chanterelles may be baked, broiled or stir-fried. A dish of sautéed black and gold chanterelles is a simple, yet elegant, appetizer.

NUTRITION FACTS

UNITED STATES

NUTRITION FACTS NOT AVAILABLE

CANADA

NUTRITION FACTS NOT AVAILABLE

Cremini/Italian Brown

General Information: Cremini mushrooms are cocoa brown and firmer with meatier flavor than the common white mushroom. They are also known as Italian brown or Roman brown mushrooms and are available year-round.

Selection & Storage: Choose creminis with evenly colored, firm caps. Place mushrooms in a single layer on a tray. Place a slightly damp paper towel or piece of cheesecloth over the mushrooms and refrigerate for up to 3 days. If mushrooms seem wet, blot dry. If dry, rewet cloth.

Preparation & Cooking Tips: Never soak mushrooms as they will absorb water and turn mushy. Either "sweep" with a soft brush or take a damp paper towel and remove dirt. Trim ¼ inch off the stem. Slice to desired thickness. Cremini mushrooms should be cooked to bring out their true flavor. When sautéing, be sure the pan and oil are hot. Mushrooms will give off a lot of liquid; stir and cook until liquid evaporates. Cremini mushrooms are delicious in soups, stews or casseroles.

UNITED STATES
Serving Size: 1 piece
Calories 3
Protein ....0 g
Fat ....0 g
Carbohydrates..................0 g
Dietary Fiber ....5 g
Sodium ....0 mg

CANADA
Serving Size: per 1 piece
Energy ....3 cal......12 kJ
Protein..........................0.3 g
Fat ....0.0 g
Carbohydrates ....0.5 g
Dietary Fibre ....0.0 g
Sodium ....0.8 mg
Potassium ....62.7 mg

Enoki

General Information: Enoki is a wild mushroom that has been successfully cultivated. Enoki mushrooms taste more like grapes than mushrooms and have a crisp texture. Enokis are quite odd-looking, like cooked spaghetti topped with tiny button-caps and joined at the base. Enoki mushrooms are available year-round.

Selection & Storage: Enokis are sold wrapped in plastic. Try to see the base of the mushrooms; it should be white or creamy beige. Do not buy if the base is brown or watery. Store in the refrigerator for up to 4 days.

Preparation & Cooking Tips: Cut off the spongy base. Trim 1 inch off the stems, then separate for use. Their crisp, lemony flavor makes enokis perfect for eating raw. Toss them into salads, tuck inside a sandwich or use as a garnish for soup. Cook very briefly. Prolonged heat will cause them to become stringy and tough.

UNITED STATES
Serving Size: 3 ounces
Calories 30
Protein...............................3 g
Fat ....0 g
Carbohydrates..................6 g
Fiber ....0 g
Sodium ....0 mg

CANADA
Serving Size: per 85 g (3 oz./17 large or 26 med.)
Energy...........29 cal.....120 kJ
Protein...........................2.0 g
Fat ....0.3 g
Carbohydrates ....3.6 g
Dietary Fibre ....2.2 g
Sodium ....9 mg
Potassium ....255 mg

Hen of the Woods

General Information: Hen-of-the-woods mushrooms are polypores, which means multiple mushroom caps grown from a single stem. As with all mushrooms, hen-of-the-woods mushrooms are 90 percent water, full of vitamins and minerals and low in calories. The caps are pearly white with ruffled, brown edges. They are available in the late spring and autumn.

Selection & Storage: Select hen-of-the-woods mushrooms that are plump, firm and fragrant with no sign of wetness. Refrigerate, unwashed, in a paper bag or in a single layer in a basket or tray. Cover with a slightly dampened towel. They will last 2 or 3 days.

Preparation & Cooking Tips: Trim the stem. Gently clean the mushrooms with a damp paper towel. Hen-of-the-woods mushrooms can be sautéed, stir-fried or simmered in soups. Add hen-of-the-woods mushrooms in the last 30 minutes of cooking time for soups or stews.

UNITED STATES

NUTRITION FACTS NOT AVAILABLE

CANADA

NUTRITION FACTS NOT AVAILABLE

SOURCE: USDA

Morel

General Information: Prized by gourmets for their earthy, smoky, nutty flavor, morel mushrooms are found in the wild. Morels are unusual looking with a cap that resembles a honeycomb that can be as small as a cherry tomato or as large as an avocado. They are available from early spring to July.

Selection & Storage: Choose morels that smell of sweet earth, avoiding those with a sour odor. Look for caps that are as clean as possible and springy and dry to the touch. Store in a single layer in a dish. If morels are dry, cover with a barely damp paper towel. If they are moist, cover with a dry paper towel. Refrigerate. Use within 2 or 3 days.

Preparation & Cooking Tips: Clean morels just before cooking. Wash quickly, as mushrooms will absorb water. Place them in a colander and run water over them. Shake to loosen dirt. Dry on paper towels. Trim thick end from stem, then slice or leave whole. Morels shine in simple sauces. Slowly simmer in cream or veal stock.

Oyster

General Information: Oyster mushrooms grow in the wild on trees, but are also cultivated, ensuring a year-round supply. They have a mild taste, silky texture, and come in a variety of hues.

Selection & Storage: Look for firm oyster mushrooms with a velvety feel. They should be dry, but not powdery, with no darkened areas. Wetness indicates spoilage. Oyster mushrooms are very perishable, so choose carefully. Try to use them right away, as they don't store well and absorb odors from other foods. Refrigerate in a dish covered with a barely damp towel for only a day or so.

Preparation & Cooking Tips: It is usually not necessary to wash oyster mushrooms. Trim the bottom of the stems. Simplicity is the key in cooking oyster mushrooms. Their taste is easily overpowered. They cook more rapidly than common mushrooms. Do not eat raw. Serve in soup, creamed, or lightly sautéed in butter. They are also good on pasta or polenta.

Porcini

General Information: Like morels and truffles, porcini (por-CHEE-nee) mushrooms are prized by gourmets for their rich, buttery taste and rarity. They are also known as boletes and cèpes. They resemble swollen common mushrooms with tan to brown tops and bulbous stems. On their undersides, porcini mushrooms do not have gills but a spongy mass of tubes. They are available in spring and fall.

Selection & Storage: Choose porcini whose caps are firm and 6 to 7 inches in diameter. Buy those with pale undersides. If the underside is brown and mushy, the mushroom is overmature. Refrigerate on a towel-covered tray up to 5 days; change towel daily.

Preparation & Cooking Tips: Trim bottom of stems. The stems are delicious, but more fibrous. You can save them for a separate dish or cook with caps. Porcini mushrooms are wonderful grilled with a garlic-flavored olive oil, or slowly braised.

Portabella

General Information: Meaty and delicious, portabella mushrooms are a vegetarian's dream. They are large, generally 4 to 6 inches wide. Their stems are thick and topped by a mottled brown cap with dark-brown gills. Portabellas are actually matured cremini mushrooms. They are available year-round.

Selection & Storage: Choose unbroken portabella mushrooms. Store in a dish covered with a barely damp paper towel in the refrigerator for up to 3 days.

Preparation & Cooking Tips: Portabella stems are woody and should be removed. Do not discard, but use to flavor stocks. Wipe cap with a damp paper towel to remove dirt. Portabella mushrooms are wonderful when grilled. Combine salt, pepper, minced garlic and parsley to taste. Sprinkle over the gill side. Top with 3 tablespoons of olive oil and grill for 2 to 3 minutes. Do not overcook.

NUTRITION FACTS

UNITED STATES

NUTRITION FACTS NOT AVAILABLE

CANADA

NUTRITION FACTS NOT AVAILABLE

UNITED STATES

Serving Size: 3.5 ounces
Calories 25
Protein ....2 g
Fat ....0 g
Carbohydrates.................5 g
Fiber...................................1 g
Sodium ....4 mg

CANADA

Serving Size: per 100g (3.5 oz.)
Energy.............25 cal.....90 kJ
Protein...........................2.1 g
Fat ....0.4 g
Carbohydrates ....4.6 g
Dietary Fibre ....1.3 g
Sodium ....4 mg
Potassium ....367 mg

UNITED STATES

NUTRITION FACTS NOT AVAILABLE

CANADA

NUTRITION FACTS NOT AVAILABLE

UNITED STATES

Serving Size: 28 g (1 oz.)
Calories 7
Protein..........................0.7 g
Fat ....0 g
Carbohydrates.................1 g
Dietary Fiber ....0.5 g
Sodium ....2 mg

CANADA

Serving Size: per 85 g (3 oz.)
Energy.............21 cal.....90 kJ
Protein...........................1.8 g
Fat ....0.4 g
Carbohydrates ....4.0 g
Dietary Fibre ....1.1 g
Sodium ....3 mg
Potassium ....315 mg

SOURCE: USDA

Mushrooms

Shiitake

General Information: Shiitakes are popular with gourmets, who enjoy their rich flavor and garlic-pine aroma. They can be as large as 10 inches across, but most are 3 to 6 inches wide. Shiitakes are available year-round, but are most plentiful in spring and autumn.

Selection & Storage: If shiitakes are odorless, they are not fresh. Look for those with domed and dappled caps with their edges turned under. Choose shiitakes with a dry surface, and firm and fairly meaty texture. Shiitakes can lose their lush texture easily. Place shiitakes in a single layer in a dish. Cover with a barely damp paper towel and refrigerate. Check daily and sprinkle water on the towel if mushrooms seem dry.

Preparation & Cooking Tips: Trim the base of the stems. Clean caps with a damp paper towel. Too much heat or oil detracts from the delicate flavor. Shiitakes are best when braised or sautéed. Do not eat raw.

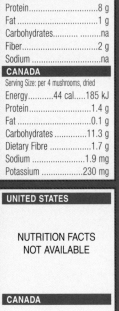

NUTRITION FACTS

UNITED STATES	
Serving Size: 3.5 ounces	
Calories	170
Protein	8 g
Fat	1 g
Carbohydrates	na
Fiber	2 g
Sodium	na

CANADA	
Serving Size: per 4 mushrooms, dried	
Energy	44 cal....185 kJ
Protein	1.4 g
Fat	0.1 g
Carbohydrates	11.3 g
Dietary Fibre	1.7 g
Sodium	1.9 mg
Potassium	230 mg

Wood Ear

General Information: Wood ear mushrooms are prized for their consistency, which has been variously described as springy-soft, and gelatinous with a crunch. Wood ear mushrooms grow in clusters and do resemble the shape of ears, with curled edges around flat caps. They vary in size from a large button to teacup saucer. Glossy brown or black, wood ears have a mild flavor. They are often sold dried. When soaked in hot water, they expand to 6 times their size.

Selection & Storage: Wet-looking wood ears are fine, but avoid those that look mushy. Store in the refrigerator and use within 1 week.

Preparation & Cooking Tips: Rinse vigorously under running water; pat dry with paper towels. Discard any mushy pieces. Wood ear mushrooms are best used as an accent to other foods. Wood ears go well with noodles, beef, poultry, seafood and other vegetables. They are also good in stir-fries and casseroles.

UNITED STATES
NUTRITION FACTS NOT AVAILABLE

CANADA
NUTRITION FACTS NOT AVAILABLE

Onions for all Seasons

Onions are a good source of vitamin C. They are fat, sodium and cholesterol free, and low in calories. They add a taste sensation to many preparations. In order to enjoy all varieties during all seasons, onions can be frozen or dried.

In the freezer: For long-term storage, sweet onions can be frozen, but their texture changes so they should be used only for cooking. Chop and place on a cookie sheet and place in the freezer. When frozen, store in freezer containers or bags. To store whole onions: peel, wash, core and freeze in a freezer-proof container or bag.

Drying: Chop and dry in the oven, using the lowest setting. Remove when thoroughly dry, but not brown. Store at room temperature in an airtight container.

Onions

Boiler

General Information: Boiler onions are white, small and round, about 1 inch to 1½ inches in diameter. As their name suggests, they are used primarily as boiling onions. Boiler onions have a mild flavor, and are available year-round.

Selection & Storage: Choose boiler onions that are heavy for their size and have dry, papery skins with no sign of moisture. Avoid any onions with soft spots or green sprouts. Humidity breeds spoilage in onions. Store up to 1 month in a well-ventilated bag, basket or crate in a cool, dark place (50°F to 55°F). Never store onions with potatoes; they speed each other's decay. Once cut, wrap tightly, refrigerate and use within 4 days.

Preparation & Cooking Tips: To peel, drop into boiling water for 10 seconds. Remove and cool immediately under cold running water. Drain and peel with a small knife. Boiler onions are great in casseroles, soups or creamed dishes.

NUTRITION FACTS

UNITED STATES	
Serving Size: 1 cup boiled	
Calories	92
Protein	3 g
Fat	0 g
Carbohydrates	21 g
Fiber	2 g
Sodium	6 mg

CANADA	
Serving Size: per 85 g (125 mL/½ cup)	
Energy	32 cal....140 kJ
Protein	1.0 g
Fat	0.1 g
Carbohydrates	7.3 g
Dietary Fibre	1.4 g
Sodium	3 mg
Potassium	133 mg

SOURCE: USDA

Dry

General Information: Onions are divided into two categories: green onions (scallions, leeks) and dry onions. Dry onions have been cured, which causes them to form dry, brittle skins. The most commonly used dry onion is the yellow onion. Onions are available year-round.

Selection & Storage: Choose firm onions that feel heavy for their size. Avoid those with green sprouts or soft spots. Keep in a cool, dark and well-ventilated place for up to 2 weeks. Once cut, onions may be kept in a tightly sealed glass jar in the refrigerator for 2 to 3 days.

Preparation & Cooking Tips: Slice off root and stem ends. Remove papery skin and outer layer. Cut to desired size. Browning an onion slowly over low heat (called caramelizing) brings out a sweet, mild flavor; over medium heat, a stronger taste emerges. If cooked quickly in very hot oil, a more jagged flavor develops. All methods are called "browning an onion," but each produces a big difference in the taste of a dish.

Green/Scallions

General Information: Green onions have a white base that has not fully developed into a bulb and long, straight, green leaves. True scallions have a flat base. Green onions have a rounded base, indicating the beginning of a bulb. Scallions and green onions can be used interchangeably, but scallions are milder than green onions.

Selection & Storage: Look for green onions and scallions with bright-green, crisp tops and firm white bases. Select those with the most white up the stem. Refrigerate, wrapped in a plastic bag, for up to 5 days.

Preparation & Cooking Tips: Most of this vegetable is edible. Slice off the white roots at the base and then slice as desired. Many recipes will specify white part only, or white and 3 inches of the green. Scallions and green onions are good in salads, and they can be braised like baby leeks in butter and stock.

Knob

General Information: Knob onions have thick green stems, like leeks, and rounded white bulb bottoms. Sold with their long green tops attached, knob onions belong to the sweet onion family. Other names for the knob onion include bald onion and Florida sweet onion. They are occasionally mislabeled as boiling onions. They are available year-round, with their peak in late spring and summer.

Selection & Storage: Knob onions are sold in bunches. Look for those with fresh green leaves, beige roots and bright-white bulbs with firmLy attached stems. Avoid any with spotted or yellowing greens. Refrigerate, unwashed, in a plastic bag for up to 5 days.

Preparation & Cooking Tips: Slice off the roots and then cut where the onions end and the stems begin. The green stem, up to where the leaves start, can be used in stir-fries and braised dishes. The bulb buttoms may be steamed whole or sliced for use in stir-fries. Knob onions are particularly good sliced, sautéed in butter and served on dark bread.

Leeks

General Information: Leeks resemble oversized scallions, but their flavor is milder with a sweet nuttiness. They are the sweetest member of the onion family. Leeks are available year-round.

Selection & Storage: Choose leeks with bright-green leaves and white bulbs. Avoid those with yellowing or spotted leaves. Refrigerate, unwashed, in a plastic bag for no more than 5 days.

Preparation & Cooking Tips: Leeks must be well cleaned, as they are laden with sand. If using whole leeks, cut off roots, make an "X" in the bulbs and soak in a mixture of water and 1 tbsp. of vinegar for 30 minutes. If using sliced leeks, first slice in half lengthwise and put each leaf under cold running water to remove grit. Only eat the white and pale-green parts of a leek. Leeks may be shredded raw and eaten in salads, but their special flavor is enhanced when sautéed or braised. They are used in the classic soup, vichyssoise.

NUTRITION FACTS

UNITED STATES
Serving Size: 1 medium
Calories 60
Protein.............................2 g
Fat ....0 g
Carbohydrates............ ....14 g
Fiber.................................3 g
Sodium ....0 mg

CANADA
Serving Size: per 85 g (125 mL/½ cup)
Energy..........32 cal.....140 kJ
Protein.............................1.0 g
Fat ....0.1 g
Carbohydrates ....7.3 g
Dietary Fibre ....1.4 g
Sodium ....3 mg
Potassium ....133 mg

UNITED STATES
Serving Size: 1 medium
Calories 10
Protein...............................0 g
Fat ....0.1 g
Carbohydrates.................2 g
Fiber.................................1 g
Sodium ....5 mg

CANADA
Serving Size: per 25 g (60 mL/¼ cup)
Energy.............8.0 cal.....30 kJ
Protein.............................0.5 g
Fat ....0.1 g
Carbohydrates ....1.8 g
Dietary Fibre ....0.6 g
Sodium ....4 mg
Potassium ....69 mg

UNITED STATES

NUTRITION FACTS
NOT AVAILABLE

CANADA

NUTRITION FACTS
NOT AVAILABLE

UNITED STATES
Serving Size: 1 medium
Calories 80
Protein.............................2 g
Fat ....0 g
Carbohydrates............18 g
Fiber..............................2 g
Sodium ....25 mg

CANADA
Serving Size: per 75 g (125 mL/1/2 cup)
Energy..........46 cal.....190 kJ
Protein.............................1.1 g
Fat ....0.2 g
Carbohydrates ....11 g
Dietary Fibre ....1.4 g
Sodium ....15 mg
Potassium ....135 mg

SOURCE: USDA

Onions

Pearl

General Information: True pearl onions are never more than 1 inch in diameter. They are sweet and tangy nuggets of taste, available year-round.

Selection & Storage: Choose pearl onions that are firm with dry, papery scales and small necks. Avoid any pearl onions with green spots, blackish decayed areas or moldy spots. Do not buy if they are sprouting green tips. Store in a well-ventilated bag, basket or crate in a cool, dark place (50°F to 55°F). Pearl onions will keep about 1 month.

Preparation & Cooking Tips: Pearl onions are rarely eaten raw. To skin pearl onions, drop them in boiling water. Cook for 1 minute. Drain pearl onions and run under cold water. Pinch the root end. The skin will slip off easily; or place pearl onions with ¼ cup water in a covered casserole in microwave. Cook on high for 3½ minutes, turning once. Drain and place onions in ice. Pearl onions are perfect for stews and dishes cooked *en papillote* (in parchment paper).

Shallots

General Information: Shallots are a member of the onion family but are shaped more like cloves of garlic, with a head composed of multiple cloves. Each clove is covered with a thin, papery skin. The flesh is tinged with purple or green between the layers. Fresh green shallots are sold in the spring, but dried shallots (with moist flesh) are available year-round.

Selection & Storage: Choose dry shallots that do not yield to pressure and are plump and firm. Avoid those that have sprouted. If possible, buy loose, not boxed, shallots. Store dried shallots for up to a month in a well-ventilated, cool, dark place (50°F to 55°F). Fresh, wrapped shallots can be kept in the refrigerator for up to 1 week.

Preparation & Cooking Tips: Slice off the roots. Remove papery skin and mince like an onion. Use to impart a subtle hint of onion and garlic to dishes. Shallots go with just about everything: meat, poultry, eggs, fish, vegetables, salads and cream sauces.

Spanish

General Information: Onions are a universal seasoning, grown and consumed throughout the world. Spanish onions are globe shaped and come in yellow, red and white varieties. Their taste is milder than regular onions, but not as mild as sweet onions. The Spanish onion is an excellent choice to add the flavor of an onion without overpowering the dish. They are available August through March.

Selection & Storage: Look for onions that are dry and firm with no decay. Necks should be tightly closed with no sprouting. Avoid those with green sprouts or soft spots. Keep in a cool, dry and well-ventilated area. Once cut, onions may be kept in a tightly sealed containers in the refrigerator for 2 to 3 days.

Preparation & Cooking Tips: Slice off root and stem ends. Remove papery skin and outer layer. Cut to desired size. Cutting onions releases a tear-provoking substance. To minimize watery eyes, try lighting a candle and place it next to the onion while chopping. Never chop onions in a food processor; they won't cook properly.

Spring Onions/Sweets

General Information: Vidalia™ (VIE-dale-yah) is the best known of the fairly recent, sweet hybrids. Sweet onions are mild and creamy. The name Vidalia™ onions is protected under Georgia law; only onions grown in 19 specified Georgia counties can be called Vidalia™ onions. Some of the sweet domestic onion names are Vidalia™, Texas 1015, Super Sweets, Walla Walla, Imperial, Grand Canyon and Maui. Sweet onions are available March through September, and in limited supply in December.

Selection & Storage: Due to their high moisture content, Vidalia™ onions are highly perishable. Buy those that are absolutely dry and shiny-smooth. Vidalia™ onions are best used as soon as possible. To store, place onions in an old stocking and tie knots between each. Hang in a cool, dry area.

Preparation & Cooking Tips: Sweet onions are great raw, on sandwiches, burgers and salads. They also make delicious onion rings. Roasted and grilled sweet onions lose none of their sweet juiciness.

NUTRITION FACTS

Pearl

UNITED STATES
Serving Size: ¼ cup
Calories	11
Protein	0 g
Fat	0 g
Carbohydrates	3 g
Fiber	0 g
Sodium	3 mg

CANADA
Serving Size: per 30 g (60 mL/¼ cup)
Energy	11 cal.....50 kJ
Protein	0.4 g
Fat	0.1 g
Carbohydrates	2.6 g
Dietary Fibre	0.5 g
Sodium	1 mg
Potassium	47 mg

Shallots

UNITED STATES
Serving Size: 4 tablespoons
Calories	30
Protein	1 g
Fat	0 g
Carbohydrates	7 g
Fiber	0 g
Sodium	0 mg

CANADA
Serving Size: per 35 g (50 mL/4 tbsp.)
Energy	25 cal.....110 kJ
Protein	0.9 g
Fat	0 g
Carbohydrates	5.9 g
Dietary Fibre	n/a
Sodium	4 mg
Potassium	117 mg

Spanish

UNITED STATES
Serving Size: 1 medium
Calories	60
Protein	1 g
Fat	0 g
Carbohydrates	16 g
Fiber	3 g
Sodium	5 mg

CANADA
Serving Size: per 85 g (125 mL/½ cup)
Energy	32 cal.....140 kJ
Protein	1.0 g
Fat	0.1 g
Carbohydrates	7.3 g
Dietary Fibre	1.4 g
Sodium	3 mg
Potassium	133 mg

Spring Onions/Sweets

UNITED STATES
Serving Size: 1 medium
Calories	60
Protein	1 g
Fat	0 g
Carbohydrates	16 g
Fiber	3 g
Sodium	5 mg

CANADA
Serving Size: per 85 g (125 mL/½ cup)
Energy	32 cal.....140 kJ
Protein	1.0 g
Fat	0.1 g
Carbohydrates	7.3 g
Dietary Fibre	1.4 g
Sodium	3 mg
Potassium	133 mg

SOURCE: USDA

Peppers

Anaheim

General Information: Anaheim chilies got their name from the area (Anaheim, California) where they were grown at the turn of the century. In general, the smaller the chili pepper, the hotter the bite. The Anaheim is a large pepper and mild in flavor. The green Anaheim is about 6 inches long and 2 inches in diameter, making it an ideal stuffing pepper. The red Anaheim is the ripened chili and is known as chili Colorado. Both are available year-round.

Selection & Storage: Look for peppers of deep color with no soft spots or withering. Refrigerate, wrapped in a paper towel, for up to 2 weeks.

Preparation & Cooking Tips: Since Anaheims are mild, it is not necessary to take the usual precautions when handling hot chilies, such as wearing rubber gloves. Anaheim chili peppers, both red and green, are good in fruit salsas. Chili rellenos (stuffed peppers) are made with Anaheims. Red Anaheims are also good pickled (en escabeche), or roasted on a grill.

Banana

General Information: True to their name, banana peppers resemble bananas in shape and color. They are mild and sweet in flavor.

Selection & Storage: Sometimes labeled as "yellow wax" peppers in grocery stores, along with their far hotter twin — the Hungarian wax pepper — be sure to ask your grocer which variety is on display. Look for banana peppers with taut, glossy, unbroken skin and green, well-attached caps. Refrigerate, unwashed, in a plastic bag for up to 1 week.

Preparation & Cooking Tips: Banana peppers are delicious sliced raw and tossed in salads or layered in sandwiches. They can also be chopped and added to soups, stews and sauces.

Bell

General Information: Bell peppers are sweet peppers. Chunky in shape, but nearly hollow inside, bell peppers wear many colors: deep green, blond, bright yellow, orange, fire-truck red and purple-black. Green bell peppers are available year-round.

Selection & Storage: Look for firm, vividly colored peppers with smooth and shiny skin. Check for soft spots. Refrigerate, wrapped in plastic, for up to 2 weeks.

Preparation & Cooking Tips: Wash bell peppers well. With a paring knife, slice around the edge of the stem. Remove stem. Cut pepper in half; remove remaining seeds. Bell peppers can be stuffed or used in salads and casseroles. They can be baked or grilled. Roasted red bell peppers are excellent. Under a broiler or over a grill, char whole peppers on all sides. Place blackened peppers in a bowl and cover. Let steam 20 minutes. When cool, peel off the black skin. Remove seeds. Place strips of pepper in a bowl with a little olive oil, a crushed garlic clove and balsamic vinegar.

Cherry

General Information: The cherry pepper is also known as the Hungarian cherry pepper. Cherry peppers are slightly sweet with moderate heat. They are available year-round.

Selection & Storage: Look for firm, unblemished peppers. Refrigerate, wrapped in a paper towel, for up to 2 weeks.

Preparation & Cooking Tips: To avoid being burned, care must be taken when handling cherry peppers. Eighty percent of a pepper's heat comes from its ribs and seeds, where capsaicin oil resides. Capsaicin is a fiery substance that can burn the skin for 12 hours. (Soap will not remove the burn.) Always wear rubber gloves and keep hands away from face and nose. Slice stem off and cut in half lengthwise. Carefully remove seeds and ribs (for milder flavor), and discard. Two peppers from the same plant can have different heat intensity. Test each pepper. Drink milk — not water — or eat starchy foods if the heat is too intense.

NUTRITION FACTS

UNITED STATES
NUTRITION FACTS NOT AVAILABLE

CANADA
NUTRITION FACTS NOT AVAILABLE

UNITED STATES	
Serving Size: 1 medium, raw	
Calories	12
Protein	0.7 g
Fat	0.2 g
Carbohydrates	2 g
Fiber	1.5 g
Sodium	6 mg

CANADA		
Serving Size: per 1 medium, raw		
Energy	12 cal	51 kJ
Protein		0.7 g
Fat		0.2 g
Carbohydrates		2.4 g
Dietary Fibre		1.5 g
Sodium		5.9 mg
Potassium		117 mg

UNITED STATES	
Serving Size: 119g (1 medium, raw)	
Calories	30
Protein	1 g
Fat	0 g
Carbohydrates	7 g
Fiber	2 g
Sodium	2 mg

CANADA		
Serving Size: per 120 g (1 medium)		
Energy	32 cal	134 kJ
Protein		1 g
Fat		0.2 g
Carbohydrates		7.7 g
Dietary Fibre		1.1 g
Sodium		2.4 mg
Potassium		425 mg

UNITED STATES
NUTRITION FACTS NOT AVAILABLE

CANADA
NUTRITION FACTS NOT AVAILABLE

SOURCE: USDA

Peppers

Cubanelle

General Information: Cubanelle peppers are sweet and mild. A cubanelle looks like an elongated bell pepper and is pale green to yellow. Red cubanelles, which are just a fully matured pepper, are occasionally available. Cubanelle peppers are similar to banana peppers, and are an acceptable substitute for recipes calling for Anaheim peppers. Cubanelle peppers are available during the summer.

Selection & Storage: Select firm, smooth and glossy cubanelles with green stems. Avoid any with soft spots or cracks. If the skin is wrinkled, the pepper is past its prime. Refrigerate green cubanelles, unwashed, in a plastic bag for up to 1 week. Red cubanelles will keep only a few days.

Preparation & Cooking Tips: With a paring knife, slice around the edge of the stem. Remove stem (most of the seeds should be attached). Slice pepper in half and remove remaining seeds. Cubanelle peppers can be stuffed or used in salads and casseroles. Cubanelles are also good on top of pizzas or in sub sandwiches.

Fresno

General Information: The Fresno chili pepper, sometimes referred to as chili caribe, is often mistaken as a red jalapeño. The Fresno is broader at the top and is hotter than the jalapeño. They are available in the late fall.

Selection & Storage: Look for Fresno peppers that are firm and without soft spots. Refrigerate, wrapped in a paper towel, for up to 2 weeks.

Preparation & Cooking Tips: Eighty percent of a pepper's heat comes from its ribs and seeds, where capsaicin oil resides. Capsaicin is a fiery substance that can burn the skin for 12 hours. (Soap will not remove the burn.) Always wear rubber gloves when working with hot peppers, and keep hands away from eyes and nose. Slice stem off the chili and cut in half lengthwise, carefully remove seeds and ribs (for milder flavor), and discard. Two peppers from the same plant can have different heat intensity. Test each pepper. Drink milk — not water— or eat starchy foods if the heat is too intense.

Habañero

General Information: The habañero is the hottest of the hot chilies and is 1,000 times hotter than the jalapeño! Habañero chilies are green to orangish-red and shaped like a small lumpy square. For people who can handle the heat, habañeros have a distinct flavor reminiscent of tropical fruits.

Selection & Storage: Choose peppers with shiny skins. Refrigerate, wrapped in a paper towel, for up to 2 weeks.

Preparation & Cooking Tips: To avoid being burned, care must be taken when handling chili peppers. (Soap will not remove the burn.) Always wear rubber gloves when working with hot pepers, and keep hands away from eyes and nose. Slice stem off the chili and cut in half lengthwise. Carefully remove seeds and ribs (for milder flavor), and discard. Two peppers from the same plant can have different heat intensity. Test each pepper. Drink milk — not water — or eat starchy foods if the heat is too intense.

Hungarian Wax

General Information: Shaped like an elongated bell pepper, Hungarian wax chilies are warm to moderately hot. Most Hungarian wax chilies in the market are yellow and are sometimes labeled yellow wax chilies. Unfortunately, mild banana peppers, which look like Hungarian wax chilies, are marketed under the same label. Taste before using. They are available from June to March.

Selection & Storage: Look for firm, glossy peppers without blemishes. Refrigerate in a paper bag for 1 week.

Preparation & Cooking Tips: To avoid being burned, care must be taken when handling chili peppers. (Soap will not remove the burn.) Always wear rubber gloves when working with hot peppers, and keep hands away from eyes and nose. Slice stem off the chili and cut in half lengthwise. Carefully remove seeds and ribs (for milder flavor), and discard. Two peppers from the same plant can have different heat intensity. Test each pepper. Drink milk — not water — or eat starchy foods if the heat is too intense.

NUTRITION FACTS

UNITED STATES

NUTRITION FACTS NOT AVAILABLE

CANADA

NUTRITION FACTS NOT AVAILABLE

UNITED STATES

NUTRITION FACTS NOT AVAILABLE

CANADA

NUTRITION FACTS NOT AVAILABLE

UNITED STATES

NUTRITION FACTS NOT AVAILABLE

CANADA

NUTRITION FACTS NOT AVAILABLE

UNITED STATES

NUTRITION FACTS NOT AVAILABLE

CANADA

NUTRITION FACTS NOT AVAILABLE

SOURCE: USDA

Vegetables

NUTRITION FACTS

UNITED STATES	
Serving Size: 1 medium with skin	
Calories	18
Protein	1 g
Fat	0 g
Carbohydrates	4 g
Dietary Fiber	1 g
Sodium	3 mg

CANADA	
Serving Size: per 45 g (1 medium)	
Energy	18 cal....80 kJ
Protein	0.9 g
Fat	0.1 g
Carbohydrates	4.3 g
Dietary Fibre	0.7 g
Sodium	3 mg
Potassium	153 mg

UNITED STATES
NUTRITION FACTS NOT AVAILABLE

CANADA
NUTRITION FACTS NOT AVAILABLE

UNITED STATES	
Serving Size: per 45 g (1 pepper)	
Calories	18
Protein	1 g
Fat	0 g
Carbohydrates	4.28 g
Dietary Fiber	0.5 g
Sodium	3 mg

CANADA	
Serving Size: per 84 g (2 peppers)	
Energy	34 cal....50 kJ
Protein	2 g
Fat	0 g
Carbohydrates	7.98 g
Dietary Fibre	1 g
Sodium	6 mg
Potassium	286 mg

UNITED STATES
NUTRITION FACTS NOT AVAILABLE

CANADA
NUTRITION FACTS NOT AVAILABLE

SOURCE: USDA

Jalapeño

General Information: Jalapeño peppers are the most common hot chili pepper in the American marketplace. Tapered, deep green and about 2 inches long, jalapeño peppers pack a punch. Occasionally, mature red jalapeño peppers are available. (They are often mistaken for Fresno chile peppers.) They are available year-round.

Selection & Storage: Jalapeño peppers often have beige lines running down from the stem. This does not affect their flavor. Refrigerate jalapeños in a paper bag for up to 10 days.

Preparation & Cooking Tips: To avoid being burned, care must be taken when handling chili peppers. (Soap will not remove the burn.) Always wear rubber gloves when working with hot peppers, and keep hands away from eyes and nose. Slice stem off the chili and cut in half lengthwise. Carefully remove seeds and ribs (for milder flavor), and discard. Two peppers from the same plant can have different heat intensity. Test each pepper. Drink milk — not water — or eat starchy foods if the heat is too intense.

Korean

General Information: Curved, long, thin and dark green, Korean chilies are hot and often used in marinades. They are also a key ingredient in kim chee, a Korean dish.

Selection & Storage: Look for unblemished, evenly colored glossy peppers. Refrigerate, wrapped in a paper towel, for up to 1 week.

Preparation & Cooking Tips: To avoid being burned, care must be taken when handling chili peppers. Eighty percent of a pepper's heat comes from its ribs and seeds, where most of the capsaicin oil resides. Capsaicin is a fiery substance that can burn the skin for 12 hours. (Soap will not remove the burn.) Always wear rubber gloves when working with hot peppers, and keep hands away from face and nose. Slice stem off the chili and cut in half lengthwise. Carefully remove seeds and ribs (for milder flavor), and discard. Two peppers from the same plant can have different heat intensity. Test each pepper. Drink milk — not water — or eat starchy foods if the heat is too intense.

Pasilla

General Information: Moderately hot, pasilla peppers — also known as chili negro — are actually the dried version of the chilaca chili. Pasillas are dark blackish-brown and elongated in shape.

Selection & Storage: Look for richly colored, fragrant pasilla peppers that are whole and unbroken. Store them in an airtight container in a cool, dry, dark place for 6 months or more.

Preparation & Cooking Tips: To reconstitute pasillas, remove stem and seeds and place chilies in a pot of water on the verge of boiling. Remove pan from heat and allow chilies to soak for a half-hour or until tender. To use, chop or place in a food processor or blender. Pasilla peppers are excellent for use in sauces, Spanish mole and for flavoring seafood and vegetables.

Poblano

General Information: Both fresh and dried poblano chilies are very important to Mexican cuisine. Dark green with a purplish tint, the poblano varies in intensity from medium to hot. The green poblano is never eaten raw. Roasting poblanos gives them a lovely smoky flavor. When fully mature, a poblano chili turns red and becomes sweeter. Dried poblano chilies are called ancho chilies. Their flavor hints at plum and raisin. Smoked and dried poblanos are called mulato chilies, and are available year-round.

Selection & Storage: Look for firm poblanos with smooth, unwrinkled skin. The darkest poblanos have the richest flavor. Refrigerate, loosely wrapped in a paper towel, for up to 1 week. Store dried ancho and mulato chilies in a cool, dry place.

Preparation & Cooking Tips: Very hot poblanos should be seeded and deveined before cooking. Poblano chilies are excellent stuffing peppers and are also good roasted, peeled and cut into strips.

Peppers

Serrano

General Information: Hotter than the jalapeño chilies, there is nothing subtle about a serrano chili. Small and tapered, serrano chilies are dark green or scarlet red when ripe.

Selection & Storage: Look for firm serrano peppers. Store in a paper bag in the refrigerator for up to 1 week.

Preparation & Cooking Tips: To avoid being burned, extreme care must be taken when handling serrano chilies. Eighty percent of a pepper's heat comes from its ribs and seeds, where capsaicin oil resides. It can burn the skin for 12 hours. (Soap will not remove the burn.) Always wear rubber gloves, and keep hands away from eyes and nose. Slice stem off the chili and cut in half lengthwise. Carefully remove seeds and ribs   (for milder flavor), and discard. Two peppers from the same plant can be different heat intensity. Test each pepper. Drink milk — not water — or eat starchy foods if the heat is too intense.

NUTRITION FACTS	
UNITED STATES	
Serving Size: 1 pepper	
Calories	2
Protein	0 g
Fat	0 g
Carbohydrates	0 g
Dietary Fiber	0 g
Sodium	1 mg
CANADA	
Serving Size: per 1 pepper	
Energy	1.9 cal.....8.1 kJ
Protein	0.1 g
Fat	0.0 g
Carbohydrates	0.4 g
Dietary Fibre	0.2 g
Sodium	0.6 mg
Potassium	18.6 mg

Thai

General Information: One Thai chili packs the heat of 3 serrano chilies; the heat does not diminish when cooked. Thin and elongated, Thai chilies are green and, when fully ripe, red. They are available year-round.

Selection & Storage: Look for firm chilies without spots. Store in a paper bag in the refrigerator for 1 week.

Preparation & Cooking Tips: To avoid being burned, extreme care must be taken when handling Thai chilies. Capsaicin, the fiery substance that gives chilies heat, can burn the skin for 12 hours. (Soap will not remove the burn.) Thai chilies are so thin that it is difficult to slice them to remove the heat-bearing seeds and ribs. Generally, they are used whole. Just cut off the stem. Always wear rubber gloves and keep hands away from face and nose. Two peppers from the same plant can have different heat intensity. Test each pepper. Drink milk — not water — or eat starchy foods if the heat is too intense.

UNITED STATES
NUTRITION FACTS NOT AVAILABLE
CANADA
NUTRITION FACTS NOT AVAILABLE

Tasty Ideas for Potatoes

The potato is one of nature's most versatile vegetables.

Mashed: For best results, place a quarter of a lemon in the cooking water and cook them in their skins to prevent water logging. Remove skin. While mashing, gradually add warm milk to potatoes to desired consistency.

Microwaved: Wash, scrub, and dry potatoes; prick with a fork and then wrap in a paper towel, placing 1" apart on a microwave rack. Follow your oven's cooking guidelines.

Baked: Scrub potatoes for baking and prick the skin several times with a fork. Place potatoes directly on the oven rack at 450°F for 50 minutes. For a crispier skin, rub with olive oil.

Potatoes

Red

General Information: Red potatoes are boiling potatoes. Red potatoes have a rosy red, thin skin and white flesh. When red potatoes are small and newly harvested, they are called "new potatoes." They are available year-round.

Selection & Storage: Avoid potatoes with cracks, withering or soft spots. If they will be served with the skin on, avoid any with a greenish tinge. This comes from too much exposure to bright light and can be toxic. Store red potatoes for up to 2 weeks in a cool, dark place (50°F to 55°F). Refrigeration is not recommended.

Preparation & Cooking Tips: Rub thin-skinned red potatoes gently with a sponge; peeling is not necessary, but rinse them well after peeling. Red potatoes are a good choice for low-fat oven fries. Cut medium red potatoes (unpeeled) into bite-size pieces. Place in a bowl. Drizzle 1 tablespoon of olive oil over potatoes. Toss potatoes to coat. In a 400°F oven, bake for 30 to 40 minutes, turning once.

NUTRITION FACTS	
UNITED STATES	
Serving Size: 1 medium	
Calories	81
Protein	3 g
Fat	0 g
Carbohydrates	27 g
Dietary Fiber	2 g
Sodium	5 mg
CANADA	
Serving Size: per 110 g (1 medium)	
Energy	87 cal....360 kJ
Protein	2.3 g
Fat	0.1 g
Carbohydrates	20 g
Dietary Fibre	1.7 g
Sodium	7 mg
Potassium	597 mg

SOURCE: USDA

NUTRITION FACTS

UNITED STATES
Serving Size: 1 medium
Calories	87
Protein	3 g
Fat	0 g
Carbohydrates	27 g
Fiber	2 g
Sodium	5 mg

CANADA
Serving Size: per 110 g (1 medium)
Energy	87 cal.....360 kJ
Protein	2.3 g
Fat	0.1 g
Carbohydrates	20 g
Dietary Fibre	1.7 g
Sodium	7 mg
Potassium	547 mg

UNITED STATES
Serving Size: 1 medium
Calories	136
Protein	2 g
Fat	0 g
Carbohydrates	33 g
Fiber	4 g
Sodium	17 mg

CANADA
Serving Size: per 56 g
Energy	131 cal.....125 kJ
Protein	2.0 g
Fat	0.4 g
Carbohydrates	30.1 g
Dietary Fibre	n/a
Sodium	16.3 mg
Potassium	255 mg

UNITED STATES
Serving Size: 1 medium
Calories	100
Protein	4 g
Fat	0 g
Carbohydrates	26 g
Fiber	3 g
Sodium	0 mg

CANADA
Serving Size: per 110 g (1 medium)
Energy	87 cal.....360 kJ
Protein	2.3 g
Fat	0.1 g
Carbohydrates	20 g
Dietary Fibre	1.7 g
Sodium	7 mg
Potassium	597 mg

UNITED STATES
Serving Size: 1 cup, cubed, raw
Calories	177
Protein	2 g
Fat	0.2 g
Carbohydrates	42 g
Fiber	6 g
Sodium	13.5 mg

CANADA
Serving Size: 1 cup, cubed, raw
Energy	177 cal....741 kJ
Protein	2.2 g
Fat	0.2 g
Carbohydrates	41.8 g
Dietary Fibre	6.1 g
Sodium	13.5 mg
Potassium	1224 mg

SOURCE: USDA

Russet

General Information: Russet, brown, potatoes have a low moisture but high starch content, which results in a lovely floury texture when baked. Typical varieties include Burbank and Norkotah; only potatoes grown in Idaho can be called "Idaho potatoes." Russet, brown potatoes are available year-round.

Selection & Storage: Check the potato for soft spots, cracks or withering. Be sure the "eyes" have not sprouted. If the skin has a greenish tinge, do not buy it. Greenish skin means the potato was exposed to bright light too long. Store for up to 2 weeks in a cool, dark place (50°F to 55°F).

Preparation & Cooking Tips: Scrub well with a vegetable brush. Prick each potato with a fork several times. Contrary to popular practice, potatoes should not be wrapped in foil before baking; this prevents them from becoming fluffy. Cook, unwrapped, at 400°F for 45 to 60 minutes. Serve with herbed butter, sour cream, salsa or grated cheddar cheese.

Sweet

General Information: Sweet potatoes are often called yams, but they are not related. However, in the Southern United States, a sweet potato is called a yam. To further the confusion, canned sweet potatoes are often called yams. There are two varieties of sweet potatoes sold: The pale sweet potato (boniato) has thin, light-yellow skin and pale-yellow flesh. The darker sweet potato has a thicker, rusty-colored skin and a deep-orange flesh. Sweet potatoes are generally available year-round.

Selection & Storage: Choose small to medium sweet potatoes without cracks, soft spots or blemishes. Avoid those with a greenish tinge. Do not refrigerate sweet potatoes, but store them in a cool, dark place (50°F to 55°F).

Preparation & Cooking Tips: Wash well. Sweet potatoes are more nutritious if cooked in their skins and are easier to peel after they have been cooked. Prick skin with fork. Cook until tender in a 375°F oven, about 45 minutes.

White

General Information: There are two types of white potatoes: the long whites and the round whites. The long white is an "all-purpose" potato with a medium starch content. Round whites are known as "boiling potatoes" because they have a low starch content. Round whites are delicious mashed, and are perfect for salads and any dishes in which the potato slices must retain their shape. White potatoes are available year-round.

Selection & Storage: Look for unblemished white potatoes with no withering, cracking or sprouting of "eyes." Store for up to 2 weeks in a cool, dark place (50°F to 55°F). Refrigerated potatoes tend to sweeten and turn dark when cooked.

Preparation & Cooking Tips: Upon peeling, if the flesh has a greenish tinge, cut that part off. Greenish flesh means the potato was exposed to light too long. If eaten in quantity, the greenish flesh can be toxic. The remaining potato can be used safely.

Yam

General Information: Although sweet potatoes are sometimes mistakenly called yams, true yams are an entirely different kind of tuber. Grown primarily in Africa and Asia, and a staple in many countries, the yam can be used like a potato. They are an excellent source of potassium.

Selection & Storage: Look for yams with unbroken skin with no cracks or soft spots. The skin can be coarse or downy, and the flesh ranges from white to yellow and even pink. Store in a cool, dry, well-ventilated place for up to 1 month. Do not store in plastic bags.

Preparation & Cooking Tips: Peel and cut into pieces, then blanch in boiling salted water. Yams can be used in place of potatoes and sweet potatoes in most recipes, particularly soups and stews.

Radishes

Black

General Information: Black radishes look more like black turnips, ranging from 2 to 6 inches across. The flavor of their crisp, white flesh is also turnip-like. One of the popular ways to serve black radish is to grate and salt it, bind it together with sour cream or chicken fat, and slather mixture on black bread. Black radishes are available primarily in the winter.

Selection & Storage: Look for firm black radishes that have had their leaves and roots removed. Refrigerate black radishes in a perforated plastic bag. They will keep for at least 1 month and their flavor will mellow.

Preparation & Cooking Tips: Scrub clean. Black radishes need to be salted to tame their flavor. Put sliced, grated or shredded black radish in a colander. Sprinkle with salt, toss and let sit for 1 hour. Rinse, press out all the liquid and blot dry. Black radishes maintain their skin color while cooking. Make a dramatic black and white radish by peeling stripes with a vegetable peeler.

Daikon

General Information: The daikon is a large Asian radish with a peppery, but sweet, fresh flavor. Daikons look like enormous white carrots (they can grow to 18 inches). Once a stranger to the North American market, daikons have gained popularity. As an added advantage, daikons contain diastatse, an enzyme that aids digestion. They are available year-round.

Selection & Storage: Choose firm, smooth roots with a luminous white gleam. If they are an opaque, flat white, they have been stored too long. As daikon does not store well, it is best eaten the day of purchase. Remove any attached greens, wrap in plastic and refrigerate for up to 3 days.

Preparation & Cooking Tips: The skin is thin and generally does not need to be peeled. Daikon can be cut in cubes or strips and stir-fried. Use daikon in soups and salads or with a dip. Daikon is also good braised in butter and stock.

Red

General Information: Red radishes are round, oval or elongated. Inside their red skin, their flesh is a crisp white. Their size ranges from that of a cherry tomato to that of a small orange. The flavor varies from mildly peppery to pungently fiery. Red radishes are available year-round.

Selection & Storage: Look for smooth, firm, red radishes with a minimum of surface pits; do not buy if they have black spots, are wilted or feel spongy. If a radish yields to pressure, the inside will be pithy, not crisp. Any attached leaves should be green and crisp. Remove leaves. Refrigerate in a plastic bag for up to 1 week.

Preparation & Cooking Tips: Wash radishes and trim roots just before using. Do not peel red radishes, as the color is what makes them distinctive. Dip red radishes in ice water for 1 hour to crisp before serving. Radishes are usually grated or sliced in salads, or used as a garnish. Try cooking thinly sliced radishes in butter until just tender. Sprinkle with sugar, salt and pepper.

White

General Information: Radishes are an ancient species that probably originated in Asia. Egyptians grew radishes for their seeds, which they pressed for the oil. (This was before the advent of the olive in Egypt.) White radishes can be round or carrot-shaped with a creamy white skin. The taste of a white radish is similar to the red radish, which varies from mild to pungent. They are known in some markets as "white icicles" and are available year-round.

Selection & Storage: Look for smooth, firm, white radishes with a minimum of surface pits; do not buy if they have black spots, are wilted or feel spongy. If a radish yields to pressure, the inside will be pithy, not crisp. Any attached leaves should be green and crisp. Remove leaves. Refrigerate in a plastic bag for up to 1 week.

Preparation & Cooking Tips: Wash radishes and trim roots just before using. Use sliced in salads or grated in stir-fries. If serving as an appetizer, place radishes in ice water for 1 hour to crisp.

NUTRITION FACTS

UNITED STATES

NUTRITION FACTS NOT AVAILABLE

CANADA

NUTRITION FACTS NOT AVAILABLE

UNITED STATES
Serving Size: 1 cup, sliced
Calories	15
Protein	1 g
Fat	0 g
Carbohydrates	4 g
Fiber	1 g
Sodium	20 mg

CANADA
Serving Size: per 90 g (250 mL/1 cup)
Energy	16 cal....70 kJ
Protein	0.5 g
Fat	0.1 g
Carbohydrates	3.7 g
Dietary Fibre	2.0 g
Sodium	19 mg
Potassium	204 mg

UNITED STATES
Serving Size: 7 medium
Calories	15
Protein	1 g
Fat	0 g
Carbohydrates	3 g
Fiber	0 g
Sodium	25 mg

CANADA
Serving Size: per 70 g (7 medium)
Energy	12 cal....50 kJ
Protein	0.4 g
Fat	0.4 g
Carbohydrates	2.5 g
Dietary Fibre	1.5 g
Sodium	17 mg
Potassium	162 mg

UNITED STATES
Serving Size: ¾ cup, sliced
Calories	10
Protein	1 g
Fat	0 g
Carbohydrates	2 g
Fiber	0 g
Sodium	10 mg

CANADA
Serving Size: per 75 g (174 mL/¾ cup)
Energy	11 cal....40 kJ
Protein	0.8 g
Fat	0.1 g
Carbohydrates	2.0 g
Dietary Fibre	1.1 g
Sodium	12 mg
Potassium	210 mg

SOURCE: USDA

Acorn

General Information: Acorn squash is a type of hard-skinned winter squash. It is generally oval, with deep furrows. The skin is dark green blushed with orange or gold. The flesh is orange and tasty. It is available year-round.

Selection & Storage: Look for dull, not shiny, skin with an orange blush on dark green. Avoid those with bruises, cracks or dents. Do not refrigerate; store in a cool, dark place for up to 1 month.

Preparation & Cooking Tips: Wash and scrub well. The skin and flesh of an acorn squash are very tough, so care must be taken when cutting. Using a large, heavy knife, work slowly, gently rocking the knife or the squash while cutting. For squash that is to be sliced, first cut off the top stem end and the bottom. With a spoon, scrape all seeds and strings from the center cavity. Acorn squash goes well with a variety of flavors. Bake it with butter, cinnamon and maple syrup in the center cavity. Or, try onions and thyme, cheese and bacon, or cranberries.

Australian Blue

General Information: The Australian blue squash, also known as the Queensland pumpkin, is commonly served in a soup Down Under. When cooked, the flesh of this winter squash is soft, with a mild pumpkin flavor. The Australian blue squash has amazing recuperative powers. If a bad spot in the skin is cut away, the squash naturally seals itself. They weigh about 8 to 9 pounds. Now grown in California, they are available from July to March.

Selection & Storage: Look for firm Australian blue squash. If there are unusual divots, do not be alarmed, as the squash seals itself. Store for 3 to 6 months in a cool, dark place (50°F to 55°F).

Preparation & Cooking Tips: Wash and scrub well. The skin and flesh of the Australian blue squash are very tough, so care must be taken when cutting. Using a large, heavy knife, work slowly, gently rocking the knife or the squash while cutting. Cut into sections to make it easier to remove the seeds. Remove skin before or after cooking.

Bitter Melon

General Information: Those who like endive or chicory should try bitter melon. Bitter melon looks like no other squash. Roughly the size of zucchini but tapered at both ends, the bitter melon is covered with a bumpy, green skin. A native of India, it is now grown in other southern climates. The bitter melon is picked green, when it is at its most mild. Once it turns yellow, the taste intensifies. Bitter melon is available year-round.

Selection & Storage: Choose those with light-green, shiny skin. Refrigerate, tightly wrapped, for up to 1 week.

Preparation & Cooking Tips: Bitter melon must be salted to reduce the bitterness. Cut off both ends. Slice lengthwise. Remove all seeds. Slice into ¼-inch-thick, half-moon slices. Spread them out in a colander and sprinkle lightly with salt. Let sit 1 hour. Rinse and pat dry. The Chinese use bitter melon in meat stir-fries with lots of other vegetables. Others recommend stuffing bitter melons with pork or seafood and then topping them with oyster sauce.

Buttercup

General Information: Buttercup is a winter squash with a distinctive look. Shaped like a small, dark-green pumpkin with narrow stripes of bluish-gray, the buttercup sports a "cap" on its blossom end. The orange flesh is finely textured, creamy and mild. When cooked, the taste is similar to sweet potato. Look for it from late summer through winter.

Selection & Storage: Always buy buttercup squash with the stem attached. If the stem is blackened or greenish, the squash will be tasteless. Look for hard shells with no dents or soft spots. Do not refrigerate; store for 3 to 6 months in a cool, dark place (50°F to 55°F).

Preparation & Cooking Tips: Most buttercups will cut like other winter squashes, but for a particularly hard rind, position a cleaver or large knife to the right of the stem. With a mallet or rolling pin, gently pound where the blade joins the handle. Continue until the squash is split in half. Discard seeds and strings. Peel after cooking. Buttercups can be baked, steamed or simmered.

NUTRITION FACTS

UNITED STATES
Serving Size: ¼ medium
Calories 45
Protein..............1 g
Fat ....0 g
Carbohydrates...........11 g
Fiber...............2 g
Sodium ....0 mg

CANADA
Serving Size: per 100 g (¼ med./175 mL/¾ cup)
Energy..........40 cal.....170 kJ
Protein.............0.8 g
Fat ....0.1 g
Carbohydrates ....10 g
Dietary Fibre ....1.8 g
Sodium ....3 mg
Potassium ....347 mg

UNITED STATES

NUTRITION FACTS NOT AVAILABLE

CANADA

NUTRITION FACTS NOT AVAILABLE

UNITED STATES

NUTRITION FACTS NOT AVAILABLE

CANADA

NUTRITION FACTS NOT AVAILABLE

UNITED STATES
Serving Size: ¼ medium
Calories 49
Protein.............0 g
Fat ....0 g
Carbohydrates...........11 g
Fiber...............2 g
Sodium ....0 mg

CANADA
Serving Size: per 85 g (175 mL/¾ cup)
Energy..........32 cal.....130 kJ
Protein.............1.3 g
Fat ....0.2 g
Carbohydrates ....7.5 g
Dietary Fibre ....1.5 g
Sodium ....3 mg
Potassium ....298 mg

SOURCE: USDA

Squash

Butternut

General Information: Butternut is one of the commonly available winter squashes. Winter squashes have hard skins, firmer flesh and larger seeds than summer squashes. Butternut squash is 8 to 12 inches long and tan in color. Two-thirds of its body is cylindrical, then it broadens into a bulbous shape. It's nicknamed the African bell. The orange flesh has a rich squash flavor. It is available year-round.

Selection & Storage: Select smooth-skinned squashes without soft spots or splits that are heavy for their size. Do not store in the refrigerator. Store for 3 to 6 months in a cool, dark place (50°F to 55°F).

Preparation & Cooking Tips: Slice off the stem end and cut squash down the middle. Remove all seeds and fibrous strings. Cut into large chunks. It will be easier to peel a butternut squash after it has been cooked. One pound of butternut squash yields about 2 cups of cooked pieces. Butternut squash is good steamed, baked or simmered. It goes well with pork.

NUTRITION FACTS

UNITED STATES
Serving Size: ½ medium
Calories	30
Protein	1 g
Fat	0 g
Carbohydrates	0 g
Fiber	1 g
Sodium	0 mg

CANADA
Serving Size: per 100 g (175 mL/¾ cup)
Energy	45 cal.....190 kJ
Protein	1.0 g
Fat	0.1 g
Carbohydrates	12 g
Dietary Fibre	1.8 g
Sodium	4 mg
Potassium	352 mg

Chayote

General Information: Chayote (chay-O-tay) is a squash-like vegetable. Its flesh is firm and extremely mild. Some say it tastes like cucumber or zucchini. Chayote's color can vary, but the color most often found is pale green. Chayote has one large seed that is soft and edible. Cooked, the seed tastes like a cross between a lima bean and an almond. Chayote is available year-round.

Selection & Storage: Look for firm, unblemished chayotes. Smaller chayotes are more tender. Wrap lightly in plastic and refrigerate. Chayotes will last several weeks.

Preparation & Cooking Tips: Simmer chayote whole in lightly salted water until just tender. Slice in half lengthwise to remove the edible "pit." Drizzle a little olive oil over the chayote and bake in a hot oven until lightly browned. The skin may be tough; peel after cooking. To peel it before cooking, do so under running water, as some skin is irritated by the slippery juice. Try chayotes for dessert as well, poaching them like pears in a sweet syrup.

UNITED STATES
Serving Size: ½ medium
Calories	25
Protein	1 g
Fat	0 g
Carbohydrates	5 g
Fiber	3 g
Sodium	0 mg

CANADA
Serving Size: per 100 g (175 mL/½ cup)
Energy	24 cal.....100 kJ
Protein	0.9 g
Fat	0.3 g
Carbohydrates	5.4 g
Dietary Fibre	3.0 g
Sodium	4 mg
Potassium	150 mg

Golden Nugget

General Information: Golden nugget squashes are small, weighing on average about 1 pound. Both the skin and the flesh are orange. The flesh of a golden nugget can be sweet, but it will be bland if not mature. It is available from late summer through early winter.

Selection & Storage: Choose golden nuggets with intact stems that look like brown cork. If the stem is blackened or green, do not buy the squash. Look for hard rinds that are a dull, flat orange color without soft spots or dents. Do not refrigerate. Keep for up to 2 months in a cool, dark place (50°F to 55°F).

Preparation & Cooking Tips: Do not eat raw. The rind of the golden nugget squash is so tough it is nearly impenetrable, even with a sharp knife. Steam or bake whole until fork-tender. Slice in half lengthwise. Scoop out seeds and fibers. Serve squash in halves with butter and seasoning, or stuffed with sausage. Or, scoop out the pulp and mash with orange juice, butter and brown sugar.

UNITED STATES

NUTRITION FACTS
NOT AVAILABLE

CANADA

NUTRITION FACTS
NOT AVAILABLE

Hubbard

General Information: Hubbard squash is one of the larger winter squashes — often growing to 25 pounds — so it is frequently sold in chunks. The skin is tough and bumpy and can be orange, gray-blue or green. They are available from early September through March.

Selection & Storage: Look for firm squashes with no dents or cracks. Choose those with evenly colored skin that is free from blemishes. Store for up to 6 months in a cold area (under 50°F).

Preparation & Cooking Tips: Hubbard squash is generally boiled or baked and then mashed or puréed. Its texture is drier than other winter squashes. Cut into chunks; place cut side down on a buttered baking dish. Cook in a 400°F oven for 1 hour or until fork-tender. Scoop out the warm flesh and put it in the bowl of a food processor. Pulse until smooth. Gradually add liquid such as apple juice, chicken stock or cream. While machine is running, season with a pat of butter, salt and pepper.

UNITED STATES
Serving Size: 1 cup, cubed
Calories	46
Protein	2 g
Fat	0.5 g
Carbohydrates	10 g
Fiber	2 g
Sodium	8 mg

CANADA
Serving Size: per 100 g (175 mL/¾ cup)
Energy	34 cal.....140 kJ
Protein	1.7 g
Fat	0.4 g
Carbohydrates	7.4 g
Dietary Fibre	1.5 g
Sodium	6 mg
Potassium	272 mg

SOURCE: USDA

Kabocha

General Information: Kabocha (kah-BOW-cha) squash is dark green with uneven, pale-green stripes. The flesh is fine-grained (almost fiberless), sweet and yellowish-orange. Although they are grown in the United States, most of the crop goes to Japan. They are available nearly year-round.

Selection & Storage: Choose kabochas with intact stems that look like brown cork, not blackened or green. Choose hard rinds without soft spots or dents. Store for up to 1 month in a cool, dark place (50°F to 55°F).

Preparation & Cooking Tips: Wash and scrub well. The rind of the kabocha squash is very tough. If you come across a particularly hard rind, position a cleaver or large knife to the right of the stem. With a mallet or rolling pin, gently pound where the blade joins the handle. Continue until the squash is split in half. Discard all seeds. Bake with butter, brown sugar and grated ginger in the center cavity. Or, dress baked slices with ginger, sherry, soy sauce, sugar and lemon juice.

Opo

General Information: Opo, also known as long melon, is actually a variety of squash from the cucumber family that originated in the tropical areas of Southeast Asia. In shape, the opo resembles the zucchini. Its skin is a smooth, yellowy green. Opo squash also goes by the names pul qua and bottle gourd. Opo is available year-round in Asian and specialty produce markets. Its peak season is summer and early fall.

Selection & Storage: Select small and immature opos with attached stems. (As the opo matures, its flavor becomes more bitter.) Choose opos that are firm and without blemishes. Check for soft spots, especially at the ends. Refrigerate in a plastic bag for up to 1 week.

Preparation & Cooking Tips: Slice opo in half lengthwise. With a spoon, remove the seeds. Peel the squash. Opo can then be cut according to the recipe's directions. Opo is often stuffed with seafood, cooked in stews, or stir-fried.

Patty Pan

General Information: Patty pans are petite, as small as 1 inch in diameter. Patty pans are sometimes called scalloped squash. Their skin is thin and their flesh is mild. When small, they are pale green. Patty pans become even paler as they mature. Some bright-yellow varieties are also called patty pans. They are available throughout summer and early fall.

Selection & Storage: Select the smallest patty pans available; 1 to 3 inches in diameter is ideal. Anything larger will have a watery texture. Pick those without blemishes. Choose squash of equal size for even cooking. Handle carefully. Refrigerate, unwashed, in a plastic bag for up to 5 days.

Preparation & Cooking Tips: Patty pans are cooked whole. To prepare, simply wash well. They are best steamed, or when very small, sautéed in butter. Place patty pans in a steamer basket over 1 inch of boiling water and steam until fork-tender, about 5 minutes. Toss with butter, Parmesan cheese, salt and pepper.

Pumpkin

General Information: The variety of pumpkin that are carved for jack-o'-lanterns isn't the type used for cooking; sugar pumpkins are smaller and sweeter than their Halloween cousins. They are available in the fall and early winter.

Selection & Storage: Generally, the smaller the pumpkin, the better the flavor. Look for pumpkins that are heavy for their size with smooth, dry rinds, free of cracks and soft spots. The rind should be dull, not shiny, which is a sign the pumpkin was picked too soon. Store in a cool, dry place for up to 1 month.

Preparation & Cooking Tips: Wash rind thoroughly, then cut open with a large kitchen knife or cleaver. Scoop out the seeds and stringy fibers, then cut into smaller chunks. Pumpkin can be baked, boiled, microwaved, sautéed or steamed, or puréed and made into that autumn favorite — pumpkin pie.

NUTRITION FACTS

UNITED STATES

NUTRITION FACTS NOT AVAILABLE

CANADA

NUTRITION FACTS NOT AVAILABLE

UNITED STATES

NUTRITION FACTS NOT AVAILABLE

CANADA

NUTRITION FACTS NOT AVAILABLE

UNITED STATES

Serving Size: 1 cup, steamed

Calories	29
Protein	2 g
Fat	1 g
Carbohydrates	8 g
Fiber	3 g
Sodium	2 mg

CANADA

Serving Size: per 70 g (125 mL/½ cup)

Energy	14 cal...60 kJ
Protein	0.8 g
Fat	0.2 g
Carbohydrates	3.1 g
Dietary Fibre	1.2 g
Sodium	1 mg
Potassium	237 mg

UNITED STATES

Serving Size: 1 cup, cubed

Calories	30
Protein	1.1 g
Fat	0.1 g
Carbohydrates	7.5 g
Fiber	0.5 g
Sodium	1.2 mg

CANADA

Serving Size: per 100 g (175 mL/¾ cup)

Energy	22 cal...90 kJ
Protein	0.9 g
Fat	0.1 g
Carbohydrates	5.5 g
Dietary Fibre	1.3 g
Sodium	1 mg
Potassium	289 mg

SOURCE: USDA

Squash

Spaghetti

General Information: Spaghetti squash is fun. It is unlike any other summer squash in its texture. When cooked, the flesh separates quite naturally into long spaghetti-like strands. It is low in calories and serves as a ready substitute for pasta. Spaghetti squash is large, oblong and yellow. It is available year-round.

Selection & Storage: Choose spaghetti squashes that are a creamy to deep-yellow hue. Avoid any that are tinged with green, as they are not mature. Look for a hard-skinned, evenly colored squash without blemishes or ridges. Store at room temperature for several weeks.

Preparation & Cooking Tips: Rinse the skin and prick with a fork several times. Cook in a 350°F oven until it is fork-tender, about 45 minutes to 1 hour for a 2½-pound squash. To stop it from overcooking, cut in half at once. Overcooked squash becomes watery and loses its sweetness. Let cool briefly. Discard seeds. Rake the strands with a fork down to the skin. Serve with pasta sauce.

Turban

General Information: Turban squashes have a bright-orange, flattened, round base. On top of this is a striped cap of three large lumps. It has firm, dry, sweet, deep-orange flesh that makes it one of the tastiest of the winter squashes. It is available from June through January.

Selection & Storage: The skin of a turban squash will often be bumpy, but check for dents, bruises and cracks. Do not refrigerate. Store for up to 3 months in a cool, dark place (50°F to 55°F).

Preparation & Cooking Tips: Wrap a 3½ lb. turban squash in a double layer of foil. Place on a baking sheet and cook at 350°F for 2 hours. Let cool in foil. While still warm, unwrap the foil. Cut around the cap and lift off. Scoop out seeds. Discard. Scoop out flesh and combine with ¼ cup chicken stock, ½ cup shredded cheddar cheese, 1 teaspoon salt, 1 small minced onion and pepper. When smooth, put mixture back in the squash. Replace cap and bake 30 minutes at 350°F. Serve in shell.

Winter Melon

General Information: Winter melon is a huge muskmelon that is used as a squash. Most winter melons range from 1 to 2 feet across. The skin of a winter melon is the color of honeydew, but with a white dusting that looks like snow. In shape, the winter melon looks like a pumpkin. Although it is a muskmelon, winter melon does not have sweet flesh. Its snowy-white interior tastes like zucchini. It is most famous for winter melon soup and is available year-round.

Selection & Storage: Given its heft, winter melon is often sold in pieces. Choose whole winter melons without dents or blemishes. Whole winter melons will keep for a few weeks in a cool, dark place (50°F to 55°F). Refrigerate cut winter melons, wrapped in plastic, for only a few days.

Preparation & Cooking Tips: Before cooking, remove seeds. Peeled winter melon can be cooked like summer squash or it can be stir-fried. It is a good side dish for spicy foods.

Yellow

General Information: Yellow squashes come with either a crookneck and a bulging end, or are simply cylindrical. Yellow squash is the mildest of the edible-skinned summer squashes; its flesh is sweet. The crookneck variety has a bumpy skin. Six to 8 inches is the standard length. (Anything over 8 inches is overgrown and will be watery.) It is available year-round.

Selection & Storage: Look for yellow squash with glossy skin. Dull skin indicates it's past its prime. The smaller the squash, the more tasty it will be. Be sure the squash is firm, not spongy. Refrigerate, unwashed, in a plastic bag for up to 5 days.

Preparation & Cooking Tips: Do not peel before cooking. Wash, trim ends and cut to desired size. "Coins" of yellow squash are good sautéed in olive oil, garnished with fresh basil and grated Parmesan cheese. Yellow squash is a popular item for a raw vegetable tray. Its sweet, mild taste and gentle crunch make it a natural for dips.

NUTRITION FACTS

UNITED STATES — Serving Size: 1 cup
Calories 35; Protein 1 g; Fat 0.5 g; Carbohydrates 7 g; Fiber 1 g; Sodium 15 mg

CANADA — Serving Size: per 100 g (250 mL/1 cup)
Energy 33 cal / 140 kJ; Protein 0.6 g; Fat 0.6 g; Carbohydrates 6.9 g; Dietary Fibre 1.8 g; Sodium 17 mg; Potassium 108 mg

UNITED STATES — NUTRITION FACTS NOT AVAILABLE
CANADA — NUTRITION FACTS NOT AVAILABLE

UNITED STATES — NUTRITION FACTS NOT AVAILABLE
CANADA — NUTRITION FACTS NOT AVAILABLE

UNITED STATES — Serving Size: ½ medium
Calories 20; Protein 1 g; Fat 0 g; Carbohydrates 4 g; Fiber 2 g; Sodium 0 mg

CANADA — Serving Size: per 95 g (175 mL/¾ cup)
Energy 18 cal / 80 kJ; Protein 0.9 g; Fat 0.2 g; Carbohydrates 3.8 g; Dietary Fibre 1.6 g; Sodium 2 mg; Potassium 201 mg

SOURCE: USDA

Zucchini

NUTRITION FACTS

UNITED STATES	
Serving Size: ⅔ cup, sliced	
Calories	15
Protein	1 g
Fat	0 g
Carbohydrates	3 g
Fiber	1 g
Sodium	0 mg

CANADA	
Serving Size: per 85 g (150 mL/⅝ cup)	
Energy	12 cal....50 kJ
Protein	1.0 g
Fat	0.1 g
Carbohydrates	2.5 g
Dietary Fibre	1.5 g
Sodium	3 mg
Potassium	211 mg

General Information: The name zucchini comes from zucchino, the Italian word for "small squash." Some of these small squashes grow to 18 inches! With its mild taste, zucchini is enormously versatile. Oversized, mature zucchinis are best when stuffed and baked. They are available year-round.

Selection & Storage: The best zucchinis are the small tender ones (5 inches and under); anything over 8 inches is fit only for stuffing. Look for smooth, unblemished, deep-green skins with faint stripes or specks of gold, and no withering at either end. Refrigerate in plastic bag for up to 4 days. Be sure there is no moisture in the bag.

Preparation & Cooking Tips: To clean, scrub zucchini gently with a soft brush under running water. Slice off both ends. Do not peel the edible skin. Zucchinis can be baked, boiled, grilled or stir-fried. Tiny zucchinis are good raw, with just a drizzle of olive oil.

Basic Tomato Preparation

To stuff: Cut off stem end and scoop out seeds and pulp, but do not puncture skin. Sprinkle lightly with salt and drain upside down on a paper towel.

To stew: Place peeled whole or cut-up tomatoes in a saucepan without water. Season with salt, pepper and a pinch of sugar; add diced onion or green pepper, if desired. Simmer, tightly covered, over low heat until done, 10 to 15 minutes, stirring occasionally.

To roast: Slice tomatoes in thick slices and rub with olive oil. Arrange in a single layer on a prepared baking sheet. Sprinkle with salt, pepper and a pinch of sugar.

Tomatoes

NUTRITION FACTS

UNITED STATES	
Serving Size: 1 medium	
Calories	35
Protein	1 g
Fat	0.5 g
Carbohydrates	7 g
Fiber	1 g
Sodium	0 mg

CANADA	
Serving Size: per 100 g (1 small)	
Energy	21 cal....90 kJ
Protein	0.9 g
Fat	0.3 g
Carbohydrates	4.6 g
Dietary Fibre	1.2 g
Sodium	9 mg
Potassium	222 mg

Beefsteak/Vine Ripe

General Information: Beefsteak tomatoes are among the most popular tomatoes grown today. They are big, red and juicy, with slightly flattened tops and bottoms. Vine-ripened tomatoes are succulent and flavorful. Beefsteak tomatoes are available year-round, but are at their peak in summer and early fall.

Selection & Storage: Choose firm, ripe tomatoes without blemishes. Ripe tomatoes give slightly to gentle palm pressure and are fragrant and deeply colored; store for only a day or 2. Do not refrigerate, or set in the sun.

Preparation & Cooking Tips: Beefsteak tomatoes are great whether eaten raw or cooked. Their meatiness gives a richness to soups and stews. Peel tomatoes if they are to be cooked. With a sharp knife, cut an "X" into the bottom of the tomato. Dip tomato in boiling water for 20 seconds. Rinse under cold water and peel with your fingers. To seed, cut tomato in half crosswise. Squeeze in your palm, cut side down.

UNITED STATES	
Serving Size: 6 tomatoes	
Calories	21
Protein	1 g
Fat	0 g
Carbohydrates	5 g
Fiber	1 g
Sodium	9 mg

CANADA	
Serving Size: per 90 g (6 tomatoes)	
Energy	19 cal....80 kJ
Protein	0.8 g
Fat	0.3 g
Carbohydrates	4.2 g
Dietary Fibre	1.1 g
Sodium	8 mg
Potassium	200 mg

Cherry

General Information: Cherry tomatoes are very popular, especially in salad bars. The cherry tomato can be deep red or bright yellow. Both are used in salads and as a garnish. The yellow cherry tomato is less acidic than the red cherry tomato, which makes it less flavorful. Both are available year-round.

Selection & Storage: Cherry tomatoes come in small plastic cartons. Choose those that are of a uniform, bright color, with no split skins. Sniff for fresh aroma. Do not refrigerate, as the flavor will deteriorate in the cold. Store at room temperature out of the sun for only a day or 2 after ripening.

Preparation & Cooking Tips: Rinse cherry tomatoes well. Remove stems. Slice tomatoes in half, lengthwise. Cherry tomatoes are good in green, macaroni and vegetable salads. They are also delicious cooked. Quickly sauté halved tomatoes in a little olive oil with fresh herbs. Or, stuff as an appetizer: halve, scoop out flesh and stuff with smoked oysters or guacamole.

SOURCE: USDA

Vegetables

Plum Roma

General Information: Plum tomatoes are the ideal cooking tomato. With their thick, meaty walls and small seeds, they adapt well to heat. Plum tomatoes are narrow and elongated. Most plum tomatoes are red, but some are yellow. They are available year-round.

Selection & Storage: Choose deeply colored plum tomatoes that are firmly plump with taut skin. Ripe plum tomatoes yield to slight pressure, but don't buy any that are soft. Do not refrigerate; store at room temperature for only a day or 2 after ripening.

Preparation & Cooking Tips: Plum tomatoes are among the easiest tomatoes to use. To seed, slice off the top, hold upside down and squeeze over a bowl. Plum tomatoes are wonderful in an uncooked tomato pasta sauce. Seed tomatoes, halve lengthwise and then dice. Add olive oil, red wine vinegar, salt and pepper, a fresh herb such as arugula or basil, and cubed fontina cheese. Serve on hot pasta garnished with toasted pinenuts. Sliced plum tomatoes are also good on pizzas.

Slicing

General Information: Slicing tomatoes, also known as globe tomatoes, the most commonly available tomato. They are good cooked, but are best when sliced or quartered for salads. Slicing tomatoes are ripened off the vine in a special warming room. (Ripe tomatoes are too soft to handle packing and shipping.) They are available year-round.

Selection & Storage: Choose firm (not hard) tomatoes without blemishes. The hue should be uniform and deeply colored. Ripe tomatoes are fragrant and give slightly to gentle palm pressure. Do not refrigerate or set in the sun. Store stem-end down at room temperature for only a day or 2 after ripening. To ripen quickly, place in a paper bag.

Preparation & Cooking Tips: With a sharp knife, remove the white core of the tomato around the stem. Slice or quarter as desired. Sliced tomatoes are delicious when paired with mozzarella cheese. Alternate slices, drizzle with extra-virgin olive oil and garnish with fresh basil leaves.

Sun-Dried

General Information: Sun-dried tomatoes are nuggets of intense flavor. Sun drying is an age-old Mediterranean tradition that has recently become vogue in North America. (Many of the sun-dried tomatoes on the market today are actually oven-dried in California.) Tomatoes are reduced to a leathery pouch and then left, as-is, or packed in olive oil. They are available year-round.

Selection & Storage: Sun-dried tomatoes in olive oil are more costly than other sun-dried tomatoes. If buying them non-oil packed, choose tomatoes that are pliable, not brittle. Dried tomatoes will last in an airtight container for 1 year.

Preparation & Cooking Tips: Sun-dried tomatoes are easily revitalized; 3 ounces of dried tomatoes will plump up to 2 cups if placed in boiling water for 2 minutes. Diced sun-dried tomatoes add pizzazz to soups, stews and casseroles, and are an excellent topping for pizzas. Add them to tomato-based dishes to get an extra flavor burst.

Tamarillo

General Information: Once known as tree tomatoes, tamarillos are an unusual fruit. It's hard to decide if it's a sweet vegetable or a bitter fruit. It is a bit of both. The bitter, inedible skin can be golden-orange or purple-red. (The yellow is milder than the red.) Inside, golden-pink flesh surrounds two purple seed pouches. (The red seeds leave an indelible purple stain). Tamarillos are available from early summer through late fall.

Selection & Storage: Select firm, heavy tamarillos. Let ripen at room temperature. They will be fragrant and yield to slight pressure. Refrigerate for up to 1 week.

Preparation & Cooking Tips: A tamarillo must be peeled. Use a vegetable peeler, or blanch in boiling water for 1 minute, then peel. To eat raw, slice peeled fruit. Sprinkle with lime juice and sugar and let sit (macerate) a few hours. Tamarillos can be baked, simmered in simple syrup, or made into jams and chutneys. Tamarillos are good in combination with other fruits, but use sparingly.

NUTRITION FACTS

UNITED STATES
Serving Size: 2 medium

Calories	35
Protein	1 g
Fat	0.5 g
Carbohydrates	7 g
Fiber	1 g
Sodium	0 mg

CANADA
Serving Size: per 100 g (2 small)

Energy	21 cal.....90 kJ
Protein	0.9 g
Fat	0.3 g
Carbohydrates	4.6 g
Dietary Fibre	1.2 g
Sodium	9 mg
Potassium	222 mg

UNITED STATES
Serving Size: 1 medium

Calories	35
Protein	1 g
Fat	0.5 g
Carbohydrates	7 g
Fiber	1 g
Sodium	0 mg

CANADA
Serving Size: per 100 g (1 medium)

Energy	21 cal.....90 kJ
Protein	0.9 g
Fat	0.3 g
Carbohydrates	4.6 g
Dietary Fibre	1.2 g
Sodium	9 mg
Potassium	222 mg

UNITED STATES
Serving Size: 1 ounce

Calories	80
Protein	4 g
Fat	1 g
Carbohydrates	17 g
Fiber	4 g
Sodium	630 mg

CANADA
Serving Size: per 30 g (1 oz. or 125 mL)

Energy	73 cal.....310 kJ
Protein	4.0 g
Fat	0.8 g
Carbohydrates	16 g
Dietary Fibre	3.5 g
Sodium	594 mg
Potassium	972 mg

UNITED STATES
Serving Size: 3.5 ounces

Calories	36
Protein	2 g
Fat	1 g
Carbohydrates	5 g
Fiber	4 g
Sodium	2 mg

CANADA

NUTRITION FACTS
NOT AVAILABLE

SOURCE: USDA

Teardrop

General Information: The teardrop tomato is downright cute. Shaped like a petite pear, teardrop tomatoes are also called pear tomatoes. Teardrop tomatos can be red or bright yellow. Their taste is like that of cherry tomatos. Yellow teardrop tomatos are less acidic than red teardrop tomatoes. They are sweet and juicy. Teardrop tomatoes are slightly smaller than cherry tomatoes.

Selection & Storage: Teardrop tomatoes come in small plastic cartons. Choose those that are of a uniform, bright color, with no split skins. Sniff for a fresh aroma. Do not refrigerate, as the flavor will deteriorate in the cold. Store at room temperature out of the sun for only a day or 2 after ripening.

Preparation & Cooking Tips: Teardrop tomatoes are usually served whole. Their distinctive shape makes them a pleasant surprise in a salad. They are a nice counterbalance to a salad of arugula and endive. Or, as with cherry tomatoes, halve teardrop tomatoes, remove the pulp and stuff with flavored cream cheese or deviled egg.

Tomatillo

General Information: With the upsurge of interest in Southwestern cooking, tomatillos have become readily available. The lemon-herb taste of tomatillos (tohm-ah-TEE-ohs) provides the base for green sauces and salsas. Also known as Mexican green tomatoes, they are the size and shape of a small green tomato, except they are surrounded by parchment-like husks. Tomatillos are available year-round.

Selection & Storage: Pick firm, dry, evenly colored tomatillos whose husks show no signs of deterioration. Although tomatillos can turn yellow, they are generally used when they are firm and green. Refrigerate in a paper bag for up to 1 month.

Preparation & Cooking Tips: Remove husks and discard. Wash off the sticky residue, then cut out the core. Tomatillos can be eaten raw; however, the flavor of tomatillos is enhanced and they are less acidic when cooked. Cooking also softens their thick skin. Cooked tomatillos add body and acid to sauces, both fiery and fragrant.

NUTRITION FACTS

UNITED STATES	
Serving Size: 1 medium	
Calories	10
Protein	0 g
Fat	0 g
Carbohydrates	2 g
Fiber	1 g
Sodium	0 mg

CANADA		
Serving Size: per 1 medium		
Energy	10 cal	45 kJ
Protein		0.3 g
Fat		0.3 g
Carbohydrates		1.9 g
Dietary Fibre		0.6 g
Sodium		0.3 mg
Potassium		91 mg

NUTRITION FACTS

UNITED STATES	
NUTRITION FACTS NOT AVAILABLE	

CANADA	
NUTRITION FACTS NOT AVAILABLE	

Preparing and Cooking Globe Artichokes

To cook a whole artichoke, break off the stalk close to the base. Cut off the pointed top about one-third of the way down. Snip off the pointed end of each large outside leaf with scissors. Open up the leaves and rinse thoroughly. Bring a large pot of salted water to a boil and add the juice of 1 lemon and the prepared artichoke. Cover and simmer for 15 to 20 minutes or until a fork easily pierces the stalk.

Remove and drain well upside down. Open up the leaves and scrape out the fuzzy choke. Serve hot with clarified butter mixed with fresh dill, parsley or other herbs. Scrape the flesh from the base of the leaf with your teeth; discard leaf.

Other Vegetables

Alfalfa Sprouts

General Information: Alfalfa sprouts are tiny, silvery shoots of germinating alfalfa seeds. Mild and crunchy, alfalfa sprouts add flavor and texture to sandwiches and salads. Alfalfa sprouts are very low in calories, and are available year-round.

Selection & Storage: Look for fresh, tender, yet crisp sprouts with the buds attached. Soggy, limp sprouts could indicate old age. Avoid any that smell musty or have dark slime. Stores offer sprouts still in their growing trays or small plastic boxes. Refrigerate in the ventilated plastic box, or place in a plastic bag, for up to 2 days.

Preparation & Cooking Tips: Cut off any roots on the sprouts. The seed, or bean end, does not have to be removed. Rinse well and blot dry with paper towels. Enjoy them raw; alfalfa sprouts cannot stand up to heat. Add sprouts at the last moment as a garnish for hot soups or serve in a sandwich or salad. Use sparingly, as large amounts can be toxic.

NUTRITION FACTS

UNITED STATES	
Serving Size: 1 cup	
Calories	25
Protein	3 g
Fat	0.5 g
Carbohydrates	3 g
Fiber	2 g
Sodium	0 mg

CANADA		
Serving Size: per 50 g (375 mL/1½ cups)		
Energy	15 cal	60 kJ
Protein		2.0 g
Fat		0.4 g
Carbohydrates		1.9 g
Dietary Fibre		1.4 g
Sodium		3 mg
Potassium		40 mg

SOURCE: USDA

Other Vegetables

Anise

General Information: Also known as sweet anise or Florentine fennel, anise has a licorice-like aroma and flavor. Its seeds, often sold labeled as aniseed, and aniseed's flavor twin — star anise — are used for flavoring as well. Anise is available year-round.

Selection & Storage: Select fresh-looking, fragrant anise with no browning. Use soon after purchase. Revive wilted anise with a quick ice-water bath.

Preparation & Cooking Tips: Anise can enhance both sweet and salty dishes; use the leaves to flavor salads, soups, vegetables, fish and poultry. Prepare as you would celery, cutting off the stems and leaves, and removing the core and any strings. Use the stalks in relish trays, or chop for stews and soups.

Artichoke

General Information: Getting to the good part of an artichoke is an effort, but definitely worth the trouble. After the leaves are peeled away, the artichoke reveals an inedible, furry "choke." Under the choke is the best part of the artichoke: its heart. When artichokes are just picked, they have only 9 calories; but, as they are stored, the calories increase. They are available year-round.

Selection & Storage: Choose deep-green, heavy artichokes with leaves that squeak when pressed together. Refrigerate, unwashed, in a plastic bag for up to 4 days.

Preparation & Cooking Tips: Rinse thoroughly. With a sharp knife, cut off the stem near the base, then cut off the top quarter of the artichoke. Place 1 inch of water in a stainless steel pot with a tight lid. Place artichokes, stem-side up, in the water. Steam, covered, for 30 to 40 minutes. Test by sticking a toothpick in the stem; it's done when it feels similar to a boiled potato. Drain, stem-side up, and allow to cool. Serve with melted lemon butter or hollandaise sauce.

Bean Sprouts

General Information: Bean sprouts spring from mung beans. Unlike other sprouts, mung bean sprouts can stand up to heat. Bean sprouts are crunchy, faintly bittersweet and the color of pearls. Bean sprouts are sold fresh, by the pound; supermarkets usually offer them prepackaged. They are available year-round.

Selection & Storage: If possible, pick over the bean sprouts, selecting only those that are firm and white. Avoid bruised bean sprouts. Bean sprouts are best when used right away, but they can be kept a few days in a closed plastic bag in the refrigerator.

Preparation & Cooking Tips: Rinse bean sprouts well and look over carefully. Discard any bruised sprouts. Bean sprouts are featured in pad thai, a delicious dish of silky rice noodles, shrimp, scallions, coriander, lime juice and peanuts. They are also used in many Chinese dishes, such as pork lo mein, beef stir-fry and shredded chicken.

Beets

General Information: Nothing like the canned version, fresh beets have a rich, sweet earthiness that delights the palate. Beets are available year-round.

Selection & Storage: Choose beets that are no more than 2 inches in diameter. Look for dark color and unblemished skins with leaves that are deep green and fresh. Cut off the tops, leaving 1 to 2 inches of stem attached. Do not trim the roots. Refrigerate unwashed leaves and beets in separate plastic bags for up to 1 week.

Preparation & Cooking Tips: If the crown, or taproot, has been cut, the beet will bleed when cooked. Peel beets after cooking. Cover whole beets with cold water and cook for 30 minutes to 2 hours, depending on the age and size of the beets. Trim the tops and bottoms. The skin will pull off easily under cold running water. Beware of the beet juice, which is nearly impossible to remove from wood or plastic. Cooked beet greens also make a delicious, pungent dish.

NUTRITION FACTS

UNITED STATES — Serving Size: 1 bulb — Calories 73, Protein 3 g, Fat 0.4 g, Carbohydrates 17 g, Dietary Fiber 7 g, Sodium 122 mg. CANADA — Serving Size: per ½ bulb, 4 oz. (117) — Energy 35 cal, 000 kJ, Protein 1 g, Fat 0 g, Carbohydrates 22 g, Dietary Fibre 5 g, Sodium 60 mg, Potassium n/a

UNITED STATES — Serving Size: 1 medium — Calories 60, Protein 4 g, Fat 0 g, Carbohydrates 13 g, Fiber 7 g, Sodium 120 mg. CANADA — Serving Size: per 100 g (1 small) — Energy 47 cal, 200 kJ, Protein 3.3 g, Fat 0.2 g, Carbohydrates 11 g, Dietary Fibre 5.2 g, Sodium 94 mg, Potassium 370 mg

UNITED STATES — Serving Size: 1 cup — Calories 30, Protein 3 g, Fat 0 g, Carbohydrates 6 g, Fiber 2 g, Sodium 5 mg. CANADA — Serving Size: per 100 g (250 mL/1 cup) — Energy 30 cal, 130 kJ, Protein 3.0 g, Fat 0.2 g, Carbohydrates 5.9 g, Dietary Fibre 1.1 g, Sodium 6 mg, Potassium 149 mg

UNITED STATES — Serving Size: 1 medium — Calories 35, Protein 1 g, Fat 0 g, Carbohydrates 8 g, Fiber 2 g, Sodium 65 mg. CANADA — Serving Size: per 95 g (250 mL/1 cup) — Energy 36 cal, 150 kJ, Protein 1.2 g, Fat 0.1 g, Carbohydrates 8.2 g, Dietary Fibre 2.2 g, Sodium 59 mg, Potassium 309 mg

SOURCE: USDA

Other Vegetables

SOURCE: USDA

NUTRITION FACTS

Broccoli

UNITED STATES	
Serving Size: 1 medium stalk	
Calories	35
Protein	1 g
Fat	0 g
Carbohydrates	8 g
Fiber	2 g
Sodium	65 mg

CANADA		
Serving Size: per 95 g (250 mL/1 cup)		
Energy	27 cal	110 kJ
Protein		2.8 g
Fat		0.3 g
Carbohydrates		5.0 g
Dietary Fibre		2.3 g
Sodium		26 mg
Potassium		309 mg

General Information: Cup for cup, broccoli has as much vitamin C as an orange and almost as much calcium as milk. Broccoli is a member of the cruciferous family — recognized as a cancer fighter. The best news is that broccoli tastes great and is available year-round.

Selection & Storage: Choose tightly formed, deep-green heads with firm stalks. Some varieties are tinged with purple. Yellowing heads are past their prime. Refrigerate in a perforated plastic bag for no more than 4 days.

Preparation & Cooking Tips: Trim ends and peel the stalks. Always rinse broccoli in cold water before cooking. Cut the florets from the stalk in even sizes. To steam, place peeled and sliced stem-pieces in a steam rack. Put florets on top. Lower into a pot with 1 inch of boiling water. Cover and steam until crisp-tender, about 5 to 7 minutes. Broccoli is delicious stir-fried, sautéed or puréed. Try partially steamed broccoli sautéed with garlic and olives, or with ginger and sesame seeds.

Brussels Sprouts

UNITED STATES	
Serving Size: 1 cup	
Calories	40
Protein	3 g
Fat	0 g
Carbohydrates	8 g
Fiber	4 g
Sodium	20 mg

CANADA		
Serving Size: per 95 g (250 mL/1 cup)		
Energy	41 cal	170 kJ
Protein		3.2 g
Fat		0.3 g
Carbohydrates		8.5 g
Dietary Fibre		3.6 g
Sodium		24 mg
Potassium		370 mg

General Information: If purchased very fresh and cooked with care, Brussels sprouts have a delicate, nutty flavor. As a member of the cruciferous family, Brussels sprouts are thought to be cancer-fighting vegetables. They are available from late August through March.

Selection & Storage: Look for compact, tight heads that are bright green and firm. Buy evenly sized Brussels sprouts, the smaller, the better. Refrigerate in a perforated plastic bag for no more than 3 days.

Preparation & Cooking Tips: Rinse well. Trim the stems and cut an "X" in each. Remove any yellowed or withered leaves. Heat ½ inch of water to boiling in a large saucepan. Add sprouts. Boil, covered, for 8 to 10 minutes until crisp-tender. (Check water during cooking time; if it evaporates, add more boiling water.) Stick a fork in the bottom of a sprout; it's done when it feels like a baked potato. Do not overcook or the sprouts will be bitter. Drain, coat with butter, and season.

Carrots

UNITED STATES	
Serving Size: 1 medium, 7" long	
Calories	35
Protein	1 g
Fat	0 g
Carbohydrates	8 g
Fiber	2 g
Sodium	40 mg

CANADA		
Serving Size: per 80 g (1 med., 20cm or 8" long)		
Energy	35 cal	150 kJ
Protein		0.8 g
Fat		0.2 g
Carbohydrates		8.2 g
Dietary Fibre		1.9 g
Sodium		28 mg
Potassium		260 mg

General Information: Most carrots are eaten raw, but they respond well to innovation. Carrots take on a meltingly sweet flavor when cooked. And yes, they are low in calories. Carrots are available year-round.

Selection & Storage: Choose long, narrow carrots for the best taste. Avoid carrots that are bendable, have cracks or show withering. If buying carrots with greens attached, remove them before refrigerating the carrots in a plastic bag. Do not store carrots next to apples.

Preparation & Cooking Tips: Although carrots lose some of their vitamins when peeled, they taste better with skins removed. (Baby carrots can be brushed gently and served unpeeled.) Freshen limp carrots in a bowl of ice water. Carrots can be shredded, julienned or cut into "coins" and cooked any number of ways. Try them simmered, then dressed with butter, brown sugar and red wine vinegar. Or, purée them with a little orange juice and chicken broth. Also, add carrots to your stir-fries.

Cauliflower

UNITED STATES	
Serving Size: ⅙ medium head	
Calories	25
Protein	2 g
Fat	0 g
Carbohydrates	5 g
Fiber	2 g
Sodium	30 mg

CANADA		
Serving Size: per 100 g (250 mL/1 cup)		
Energy	24 cal	100 kJ
Protein		2.0 g
Fat		0.2 g
Carbohydrates		4.9 g
Dietary Fibre		1.8 g
Sodium		15 mg
Potassium		355 mg

General Information: Cauliflower is considered an anti-cancer vegetable. Most cauliflower is white, but there are green and purple varieties. Cauliflower can be substituted for broccoli in most recipes. It is available year-round.

Selection & Storage: Look for heads that are white, firm and heavy for their size with no speckling on the head or the leaves. Avoid cauliflowers with brown patches. Refrigerate, tightly wrapped, for no more than 5 days.

Preparation & Cooking Tips: Cauliflower is so versatile it can be eaten raw, blanched, steamed, boiled or fried. Peel off stem leaves. Turn cauliflower upside down. Cut the stem just above where the florets join together. Separate the florets into equal sizes. Cut if necessary. To reduce cauliflower's strong taste, cook it in milk. To keep the florets white, cook in water with a tablespoon of lemon juice or milk. Cooked cauliflower goes well with pepper, cumin, garlic, cheese, lemon, mustard or nutmeg.

Other Vegetables

Celery

General Information: Celery is a wonderful vegetable, capable of subtle nuances and a variety of textures. Most shoppers are familiar with Pascal celery, the tall, pale-green stalks with leaves. Another variety, golden celery, is grown under paper or a layer of soil to prevent the greening caused by chlorophyll. Celery is available year-round.

Selection & Storage: Buy stalks that are firm and unblemished with leaves that are green, not yellow. Refrigerate in a plastic bag for up to 2 weeks.

Preparation & Cooking Tips: Celery needs to be thoroughly cleaned. Pull ribs away from stalk and wash off dirt. If celery is tough, snap the rib near the top without breaking the strings and pull the piece towards the bottom. Do not discard leaves, but save for flavoring soups or pasta Bolognese. Raw celery goes very well with Stilton cheese. Kids like it with peanut butter or cream cheese packed in the groove. Braised or baked celery goes great with ham and roast beef.

Celery Root

General Information: Celery root, or celeriac, is an ugly, gnarled, delicious root. It is not the bulb or base of regular celery. Celery root has a distinctive taste, a cross between strong celery and parsley with a nutty twist. Celery roots can range in size from an apple to a small cantaloupe. It is available in winter.

Selection & Storage: Select small, 1-pound celery roots (larger ones can be woody or hollow). Test the bottom; if it's soft, don't buy it. Try to find a root with a minimum of gnarls for easier peeling. Trim off stems. Refrigerate, wrapped in plastic, for up to 1 week.

Preparation & Cooking Tips: Scrub with a brush. Cut off the top and bottom. Peel with a very sharp knife. Celery root will discolor, so drop pieces into acidulated water. Celery root slices are often blanched before being grated for salads. Celery root is good with a strong mustard mayonnaise, seafood, potato purées, poultry stuffings or braised with meat stews.

Corn

General Information: Purists claim the only way to cook corn-on-the-cob is to have the water boiling before the corn is picked; that's when the corn is at its sweetest — the sugar starts turning to starch the instant it is picked. Corn is best from May through September.

Selection & Storage: Choose corn with husks that are tightly wrapped, grass-green and slightly damp. The cornsilk can be dry, but not rotting, and stem ends moist, not yellowed. Do not store corn.

Preparation & Cooking Tips: Shuck the corn (remove the husks and the corn silk), right before cooking. To boil corn, drop shucked ears in a large pot of rapidly boiling water. Cook for 3 to 5 minutes and serve immediately. Before roasting or grilling the corn in its husk, the corn silk must be removed. Pull the husks down, but not off the stem. Remove silks, rewrap husks and tie at the top. If grilling, soak husked corn in water 10 minutes, then roast for 15 minutes.

Green Asparagus

General Information: Asparagus is the herald of spring. Its tender stalks poke up from the ground during the first warm and wet days of the season. The best asparagus comes to market from early March to June.

Selection & Storage: Buy firm, bright-green stalks with tight, purple-tinted buds. If the spears are khaki-green, they are past their prime. Use as soon as possible after purchase. To store, trim the ends. Stand stalks upright in 1 inch of water in a tall container. Cover the tops with a plastic bag and refrigerate for no more than a few days.

Preparation & Cooking Tips: Gently snap each asparagus stalk at the bottom; it should break at the very spot where the woodiness begins. Discard woody ends. Soak in cold water. Thicker stalks require peeling. To cook, lay spears in 1 inch of water in a wide, non-aluminum pan. Bring to a gentle boil. Thin spears will take 3 to 5 minutes; medium, 5 to 8; and thick, 10 to 12 minutes. Cook to crisp-tender. Stick with a fork to test. Serve immediately.

NUTRITION FACTS

UNITED STATES
Serving Size: 2 medium stalks
- Calories 13
- Protein.............0.5 g
- Fat ....0 g
- Carbohydrates.............3 g
- Fiber...............1 g
- Sodium..............70 mg

CANADA
Serving Size: per 80 g (2 stalks)
- Energy............13 cal....50 kJ
- Protein.............0.6 g
- Fat ....0.1 g
- Carbohydrates ....2.9 g
- Dietary Fibre ....1.2 g
- Sodium ....70 mg
- Potassium ....230 mg

UNITED STATES
Serving Size: ½ cup
- Calories 30
- Protein.............1 g
- Fat ....0 g
- Carbohydrates.............7 g
- Fiber...............1 g
- Sodium ....80 mg

CANADA
Serving Size: per 80 g (125 mL/½ cup)
- Energy............30 cal....130 kJ
- Protein.............1.2 g
- Fat ....0.2 g
- Carbohydrates ....7.4 g
- Dietary Fibre ....1.4 g
- Sodium ....80 mg
- Potassium ....240 mg

UNITED STATES
Serving Size: 1 medium
- Calories 80
- Protein.............3 g
- Fat ....1 g
- Carbohydrates.............18 g
- Fiber...............3 g
- Sodium ....0 mg

CANADA
Serving Size: per 140 g (1 med., 15 cm or 6")
- Energy............86 cal....360 kJ
- Protein.............3.2 g
- Fat ....1.2 g
- Carbohydrates ....19 g
- Dietary Fibre ....3.2 g
- Sodium ....15 mg
- Potassium ....270 mg

UNITED STATES
Serving Size: 5 spears
- Calories 25
- Protein.............2 g
- Fat ....0 g
- Carbohydrates.............4 g
- Fiber...............2 g
- Sodium ....0 mg

CANADA
Serving Size: per 50 g (375mL/1½ cup)
- Energy............15 cal....60 kJ
- Protein.............2.0 g
- Fat ....0.4 g
- Carbohydrates ....1.9 g
- Dietary Fibre ....1.4 g
- Sodium ....3 mg
- Potassium ....40 mg

SOURCE: USDA

Other Vegetables

Okra

General Information: Finger-sized, okra has ridged skin and tapered ends. When cooked, okra releases a substance that thickens any liquid. Okra is picked when immature. Mature okra is used for making rope and coarse paper. Okra is available year-round, but is most plentiful in summer.

Selection & Storage: Look for small okra (under 4 inches), that is bright green and firm. Larger ones will be tough, as will pale-green okra. If the okra is flabby or rubbery, it will be tough and chewy when cooked. Use okra the day of purchase, as it does not store well.

Preparation & Cooking Tips: Rinse and dry. If it is to be cooked whole, cut off cap, but don't open seed pouch. For recipes calling for sliced okra, cut off the caps first. Okra is a key ingredient in gumbo, and goes well with lemon, tomatoes and vinegar. Add slices of okra to soups in the last 10 minutes of cooking. (1 cup of slices will thicken 3 cups of liquid.) Okra can be dipped in cornmeal batter and deep-fried to crunchy perfection.

Parsnip

General Information: The parsnip is a wonderful root vegetable. When young, the parsnip has a sweet, nutty flavor that can be used to the clever cook's advantage. Parsnips look like thick, white carrots. They are available most of the year, but are best in the colder months. (They sweeten after the first frost.)

Selection & Storage: Look for parsnips that are firm, crisp and without cracks. Buy smaller parsnips if possible. Older, larger parsnips can be aggressive in taste. Refrigerate in a plastic bag for up to 2 weeks.

Preparation & Cooking Tips: Trim off the root ends and the tops. Peel with a vegetable peeler. Split large parsnips in half and remove the woody core. Cook parsnip wedges with roast beef, adding during the last hour of cooking. Or, add slices or strips to soups and stews in the last 30 minutes of cooking. Parsnips are wonderful when puréed with mashed potatoes or baked apples. They are also good roasted with brown sugar, butter and nutmeg.

Rutabaga

General Information: With the look of a large turnip, rutabagas have firmer, yellow flesh and a stronger, sweeter flavor. They are a good source of vitamin C and are available year-round.

Selection & Storage: Choose firm, solid rutabagas free from scars and bruises. The sweeter flavor of smaller rutabagas, about 4 inches in diameter, makes for better eating. Refrigerate for up to 2 weeks

Preparation & Cooking Tips: Rutabagas can be eaten raw, but it's best to blanch them beforehand. Trim the top and bottom of the rutabaga and cut in half, then peel with a vegetable peeler. Rutabagas can be baked, roasted, boiled, braised, microwaved, steamed and stir-fried. They are a delicious complement to pork, duck, ham and spicy dishes.

Seaphire™

General Information: New to consumers, and also known as sea asparagus or samphire, this plant grows in salt water, imparting it with a salty flavor and crisp, crunchy texture. It is high in vitamin A, and a good source of calcium and iron. Seaphire™ is available year-round.

Selection & Storage: Seaphire™ is hand-picked and packaged. Look for crisp, firm, emerald-green stalks with no signs of wilting or browning. Refrigerate (do not freeze) for up to 2 weeks.

Preparation & Cooking Tips: Seaphire™ can be eaten raw or cooked; rinse before using. It is also delicious added to salads, stir-fries and vegetable dishes.

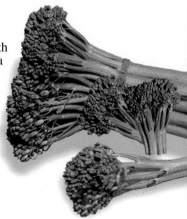

NUTRITION FACTS

UNITED STATES
Serving Size: 1 cup, sliced
Calories 40
Protein ....2 g
Fat ....0 g
Carbohydrates ....8 g
Fiber ....3 g
Sodium ....10 mg

CANADA
Serving Size: per 100 g (250 mL/1 cup)
Energy ....38 cal .....160 kJ
Protein ....2.0 g
Fat ....0.1 g
Carbohydrates ....7.6 g
Dietary Fibre ....3.2 g
Sodium ....8 mg
Potassium ....303 mg

UNITED STATES
Serving Size: 1 medium
Calories 80
Protein ....1 g
Fat ....0 g
Carbohydrates ....18 g
Fiber ....5 g
Sodium ....10 mg

CANADA
Serving Size: per 85 g (1 med, 16.5 cm or 6½" long)
Energy ....64 cal .....270 kJ
Protein ....1.0 g
Fat ....0.3 g
Carbohydrates ....15 g
Dietary Fibre ....4.2 g
Sodium ....9 mg
Potassium ....319 mg

UNITED STATES
Serving Size: 1 cup, cubed
Calories 50
Protein ....1.6 g
Fat ....0.3 g
Carbohydrates ....11 g
Fiber ....3.5 g
Sodium ....28 mg

CANADA
Serving Size: per 75 g (125 mL/½ cup)
Energy ....27 cal .....110 kJ
Protein ....0.9 g
Fat ....0.2 g
Carbohydrates ....6.0 g
Dietary Fibre ....1.8 g
Sodium ....15 mg
Potassium ....249 mg

UNITED STATES
Serving Size: 3 ounces
Calories 30
Protein ....1 g
Fat ....0 g
Carbohydrates ....6 g
Fiber ....3 g
Sodium ....1350 mg

CANADA
Serving Size: 3 ounces
Energy ....30 cal .....120 kJ
Protein ....1 g
Fat ....0 g
Carbohydrates ....6 g
Dietary Fibre ....3 g
Sodium ....1350 mg
Potassium ....199 mg

SOURCE: USDA

Other Vegetables

Turnip

General Information: People who claim they don't like the taste of turnips probably never ate a young one. Small turnips are delicious with a mild, sweet flavor. Fresh turnips are available year-round, with the peak season from October through February.

Selection & Storage: Look for turnips no larger than an egg. If the leaves are attached, check the freshness. If they are bright-green and healthy, the turnip should be as well. Choose turnips that are heavy for their size; light ones will be woody when cooked. Turnips keep for several weeks in a cool, dark place (50°F to 55°F).

Preparation & Cooking Tips: Trim tops and bottoms. Baby turnips can be cooked unpeeled. Peel and quarter larger turnips. Add turnip chunks in the last hour of cooking roast pork or boil the turnips and purée with mashed potatoes and carrots. Slice turnips thinly and cook in apple juice and butter. The turnips will become lightly caramelized. Serve as a side dish for a winter meal.

White Asparagus

General Information: White asparagus is creamy-white and thick-stemmed. The white asparagus stalk is grown underground so it can't produce chlorophyll and turn green. Consequently, the white variety is milder and more delicate than the green. It is available year-round.

Selection & Storage: Look for straight and firm stalks with tight buds. To store, trim the ends. Stand stalks upright in an inch of water in a tall container. Cover the tops with a plastic bag and refrigerate for no more than 2 days.

Preparation & Cooking Tips: Prepare asparagus right before cooking, as it tends to dry out quickly. White asparagus requires peeling. With a sharp knife, start at the bud and peel down the stem, almost to the bottom. Bunch stalks together and trim to equal size. Tie with a string into serving-size bundles. Lay bundles in a flat, non-aluminum pan with water to cover. Bring to a gentle boil and cook for 10 to 15 minutes to crisp-tender. Stick with a fork to test. Drain and blot with a cloth towel. Serve immediately.

NUTRITION FACTS

UNITED STATES
Serving Size: 1 cup, cubed

Calories	36
Protein	1 g
Fat	0 g
Carbohydrates	8 g
Fiber	2 g
Sodium	88 mg

CANADA
Serving Size: per 95 g (175 mL/¾ cup)

Energy	26 cal .... 110 kJ
Protein	0.9 g
Fat	0.1 g
Carbohydrates	5.9 g
Dietary Fibre	1.7 g
Sodium	64 mg
Potassium	180 mg

UNITED STATES

NUTRITION FACTS
NOT AVAILABLE

CANADA

NUTRITION FACTS
NOT AVAILABLE

SOURCE: USDA

Vegetable handling and preparation

Always wash and scrub raw vegetables before eating or cooking. Salad leaves should be rinsed with cold water to remove any grit or insects, as well as chemical residues. It is just as important to dry the salad leaves well so that the dressing is not be diluted and the leaves stay fresh and crisp.

Some dense raw vegetables, such as potatoes and onions, can be stored at cool room temperature. Refrigerate other raw vegetables for optimum taste and freshness. After cooking, all vegetables must be refrigerated or frozen within two hours.

In countless recipes, vegetables and other ingredients are chopped to varying degrees of fineness. For most chopping, a large chef's knife should be used. You can also use a food processor, but take care not to over-process the vegetables to a pulp. To julienne vegetables, cut into matchsticks. For matchsticks, vegetables should be peeled and cut across into pieces about 2 inches long. Lay each piece of vegetable flat and cut it into slices ⅛" thick or less.

Arugula

General Information: Arugula goes by many names: rocket, roquette and rugula. Arugula has a distinct, peppery bite. It is available year-round.

Selection & Storage: The younger (and smaller) the arugula leaf, the less pungent its bite. Look for emerald-green leaves 2 to 4 inches in length. Avoid if the leaves are yellowing or limp. Arugula is sold in bunches with the roots still attached. Arugula is highly perishable; immediately wrap the roots in a damp paper towel. Enclose in a plastic bag and refrigerate for no more than 2 days.

Preparation & Cooking Tips: Arugula requires thorough washing. To prepare, chop off the roots and any thick stems. Dunk leaves up and down in a sink full of cold water. Let stand for 1 minute. Swirl the leaves around, wait 1 minute and then remove. Arugula is a lively addition to salad greens. It can be used to spice up pasta. Drizzle young leaves with virgin olive oil. Add salt and parmesan cheese. Arugula goes well with fresh pears, too.

Baby Dill

General Information: Dill's feathery, fern-like leaves are aromatic and tasty in sauces, dips and soups. The dill seed is more spirited and is found in breads and pickles. The distinctive flavor of fresh dill leaves is muted in its dried form. Dill leaves have a wonderful affinity for salmon and other fishes. Fresh dill is available year-round.

Selection & Storage: Dill will not look crisp even when fresh. Look for bunches with deep-green leaves with no sign of rot. Refrigerate, wrapped, for a few days. Chopped or whole leaves can be frozen with water in ice cube trays. Once frozen, store cubes in a plastic bag in the freezer.

Preparation & Cooking Tips: Rinse the dill and dry with paper towels. Chop off thick stems. With scissors, mince the dill to desired size. Dill is great in potato salads, borscht, carrots, fish, egg salad and savory breads. Dill will lose its flavor when heated, so add fresh dill near the end of the cooking time. Add fresh chopped dill as a garnish.

Basil

General Information: Most people know basil as the key ingredient in pesto sauce, but it is so much more. Basil is available in a wide variety of flavors, from lemon basil to the purplish opal basil. Basil has a pungent flavor that has been described as a cross between licorice and cloves. Basil is usually available year-round.

Selection & Storage: Choose leaves that are fresh, unspotted and fragrant. Wrap leaves in slightly damp paper towels and place in a plastic bag or put stems in a glass of water (change the water every few days), then cover with a plastic bag and secure. Refrigerate.

Preparation & Cooking Tips: Wash and remove leaves from main stems. If a recipe calls for 1 teaspoon of dried basil, double the amount for fresh basil. Throw a handful of basil leaves in an ordinary salad and your taste buds will rejoice. Sprinkle sliced tomatoes and slices of mozzarella with basil, oil and vinegar for an appetizer. Put the mixture on French bread, then broil for a tasty bruschetta.

Bay Leaf

General Information: Bay leaves are used to flavor stews, soups, vegetables and meats. There are two main varieties of bay leaves: Turkish and Californian. The Turkish variety has a more subtle flavor. Fresh bay leaves are superior to dried bay leaves, which have just a fraction of the flavor of the fresh.

Selection & Storage: Select deep-green leaves that are free of brown spots. Store in a plastic bag in the refrigerator for up to 3 days.

Preparation & Cooking Tips: Leaving bay leaves in a dish too long can turn the food bitter. Always remove bay leaves before serving. Never crush a bay leaf before adding to the food; it's too difficult to retrieve. Bay leaves may be inserted between meat chunks in quick-cooking kabobs. To make a standard herb bouquet, tuck sprigs of thyme, parsley and a bay leaf into a piece of cheesecloth. Tie together and place in the dish as it cooks.

Herbs

Chervil

General Information: Chervil has a taste reminiscent of licorice or anise. A member of the carrot family, chervil is as fundamental to French cooking as parsley. Chervil is one of the four *fines herbs* that French chefs use to flavor their savory soups and sauces. (The other *fines herbs* are chives, parsley and tarragon.) Chervil is said to intensify the flavor of accompanying herbs.

Selection & Storage: Chervil, like many herbs, is sold by the bunch. Look for feathery, delicate light-green leaves with a heady aroma. It can be stored in the refrigerator in a plastic bag for a day or two. Chervil's fragile nature prevents it from being dried or frozen for later use.

Preparation & Cooking Tips: Wash chervil thoroughly, then dry on paper towels. Chop chervil finely and add to soups, stews, vegetables, and meat or fish dishes. Whole sprigs may be used for garnish. Chervil's sweet, anise-like flavor is strongest when raw, so add it to hot dishes just before serving.

Chives

General Information: Related to the onion and leek, the delicate, hollow stalks resemble grass and taste like mild onion. Chives produce a pretty lavender flower that is also edible. Chives are an ingredient in the *fines herbs,* which the French add to savory dishes. They are available year-round.

Selection & Storage: Choose chives with a uniform green color and no sign of browning or wilting. Chives can be kept in a plastic bag in the refrigerator for up to 1 week. They are best, however, when used immediately.

Preparation & Cooking Tips: Rinse chives and dry on a paper towel. Snip with scissors to desired length. Do not chop chives or they will become bruised. Cooking will diminish their flavor, so add to a dish at the last moment. If using as a garnish, add just before serving, because cut chives can turn bitter. Make a quick chip dip with low-fat cottage cheese, low-fat mayonnaise and chopped chives. Chives are a good complement to potatoes, carrots and green beans.

Cilantro

General Information: Cilantro is very much an acquired taste. Those who find cilantro palatable will soon find it is nearly addictive. Cilantro is a key ingredient in spicy Thai, Caribbean and Latin American dishes. It is available year-round.

Selection & Storage: Look for fresh, leafy bunches. Try to buy cilantro with the roots still attached. At home, place the cilantro in a sturdy glass with water covering the roots. Wrap the leaves loosely in a plastic bag and place in the refrigerator. Change the water every few days and the cilantro will last nearly 2 weeks. For cilantro without roots, follow the same procedure, but store for only 1 week. Cilantro does not freeze well.

Preparation & Cooking Tips: Do not wash cilantro until ready for use. Cut off roots and thick stems. Wash leaves in a sink of cold water. Remove and spin dry. Chopped in generous amounts and simmered with tomatillos and hot peppers, cilantro makes a pungent sauce.

Cinnamon

General Information: What Americans know as cinnamon is, in fact, cassia. True cinnamon (Ceylon) is less sweet than cassia. For some reason, only spicy-sweet cassia cinnamon is widely available in North America. Cinnamon comes from the inner layer bark of a tropical evergreen tree. The most prized cinnamon is the thin shoot in the middle of the tree. The bark is harvested during the rainy season when it is softer. As the bark dries, it begins to curl, naturally creating "quills" or sticks. Powdered cinnamon is made from ground sticks.

Selection & Storage: Keep in an airtight container in a cool, dark place.

Preparation & Cooking Tips: The sweet, nutty flavor of cinnamon is distinctive. Cinnamon sticks are often used in warmed winter drinks or as a flavoring for iced tea. They are also found in chutneys and pickled foods. Cinnamon can make a lively surprise in savory dishes and stews. Remove cinnamon sticks before serving.

NUTRITION FACTS

UNITED STATES

NUTRITION FACTS NOT AVAILABLE

CANADA
Serving Size: 1 tablespoon
Energy.........4.4 cal.....18.8 kJ
Protein.....................0.4 g
Fat ....0 g
Carbohydrates ....0.9 g
Dietary Fibre ....0.2 g
Sodium ....1.5 mg
Potassium ....90 mg

UNITED STATES
Serving Size: 1 tablespoon, chopped
Calories 0.9
Protein ....0 g
Fat ....0 g
Carbohydrates ....0.1 g
Dietary Fiber ....5 g
Sodium ....0 mg

CANADA
Serving Size: 1 tbsp., chopped, raw
Energy ....6 cal.....30 kJ
Protein.....................0.7 g
Fat ....0.2 g
Carbohydrates ....1 g
Dietary Fibre ....0.8 g
Sodium ....2 mg
Potassium ....63 mg

UNITED STATES
Serving Size: 1 cup, raw
Calories 11
Protein.....................0.9 g
Fat ....0.2 g
Carbohydrates....................2 g
Dietary Fiber ....1.3 g
Sodium ....25 mg

CANADA
Serving Size: per 4 g (15 mL/1 tbsp)
Energy ....1 cal.....0 kJ
Protein.....................0.1 g
Fat ....0.0 g
Carbohydrates ....0.1 g
Dietary Fibre ....0.2 g
Sodium ....1 mg
Potassium ....24 mg

UNITED STATES
Serving Size: 1 teaspoon
Calories 6
Protein............................0 g
Fat ....0 g
Carbohydrates....................2 g
Dietary Fiber ....1 g
Sodium ....1 mg

CANADA
Serving Size: per 2 g (.5 mL/1 tsp)
Energy...........5 cal.....20.9 kJ
Protein.....................0.8 g
Fat ....0.0 g
Carbohydrates ....1.6 g
Dietary Fibre....................n/a
Sodium ....0.5 mg
Potassium ....10 mg

SOURCE: USDA

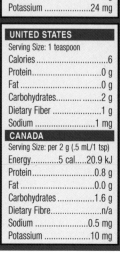

Herbs

Herbs & Spices

NUTRITION FACTS

UNITED STATES
Serving Size: 1 cup sprigs
Calories 4
Protein..........................0.3 g
Fat ....0.1 g
Carbohydrates ....0.6 g
Fiber..............................0.2 g
Sodium ....5 mg

CANADA
Serving Size: 5 sprigs
Energy...........0.4 cal.....1.8 kJ
Protein.............................0 g
Fat ....0 g
Carbohydrates ....0 g
Dietary Fibre ....0 g
Sodium ....0.6 mg
Potassium ....7.3 mg

UNITED STATES
Serving Size: 1 cup, sliced
Calories 36
Protein...............................1 g
Fat ....0 g
Carbohydrates ....9 g
Fiber..............................n/a
Sodium ....61 mg

CANADA
Serving Size: ½ bulb=117 g
Energy...........36 cal.....350 kJ
Protein..........................1.4 g
Fat ....0.2 g
Carbohydrates ....8.5 g
Dietary Fibre ....3 g
Sodium ....60 mg
Potassium ....484 mg

UNITED STATES
Serving Size: 1 clove
Calories 0
Protein.............................0 g
Fat ....0 g
Carbohydrates ....1 g
Dietary Fiber ....0 g
Sodium ....1 mg

CANADA
Serving Size: per 4 g (1 clove)
Energy ....6 cal.....30 kJ
Protein..........................0.3 g
Fat ....0.0 g
Carbohydrates ....1.3 g
Dietary Fibre ....0.1 g
Sodium ....1 mg
Potassium ....16 mg

UNITED STATES
Serving Size: 1 tablespoon
Calories 0
Protein.............................0 g
Fat ....0 g
Carbohydrates ....1 g
Dietary Fiber ....0 g
Sodium ....0 mg

CANADA
Serving Size: 4 g (0.6 cm x 2.5 cm)
Energy ....3 cal.....10 kJ
Protein..........................0.1 g
Fat ....0.0 g
Carbohydrates ....0.7 g
Dietary Fibre ....0.1 g
Sodium ....0.6 mg
Potassium ....18 mg

SOURCE: USDA

Dill

General Information: Aromatic dill has been used as a flavoring for centuries. Both the leaves (dillweed) and the seeds (dillseed) are used.

Selection & Storage: Dill wilts almost immediately after picking, so don't be concerned when buying fresh dill that looks a bit droopy. Place fresh dill stems in a container of water, or wrap the leaves in damp paper towels and refrigerate for no more than 2 days, or chop the leaves, place in an ice cube tray filled with water, tightly seal and freeze.

Preparation & Cooking Tips: Chop dill and add to salad dressings, eggs, stews and seafood. Dill leaves lose their flavor quickly, so add in the last few minutes of cooking time. Dill is also a delicious flavor complement to tomatoes, cabbage, beets and cucumbers.

Fennel

General Information: The flavor of fennel is sweeter and more delicate than anise. When cooked, fennel's flavor becomes even more mellow. The fennel bulb, stalks and flowery greens are all edible. Fennel seeds, used in flavoring sausages, come from a non-bulbous fennel. Look for fennel from late fall to early spring.

Selection & Storage: Choose clean, crisp, pearly bulbs with no sign of browning. Check for cracks. The attached greenery should be soft, fragrant and green. Fennel does not store well. Wrap it tightly in plastic and keep in the refrigerator for up to 4 days.

Preparation & Cooking Tips: Slice off the tough bottom of the bulb. Cut off the stalks; if cooking them, peel. Pull off layers of the bulb and discard the hard core. If eating raw, remove the strings from the outer layers of bulb. Cut or slice as desired. Fennel is great raw in salads. It can also be braised, boiled, sautéed, baked, broiled or grilled (try it in kabobs). Puréed, cooked fennel is a delight.

Garlic

General Information: Garlic is a most remarkable bulb. It can be roasted to a nutty sweetness or minced to a pungent wake-up call. American garlic has white skin. Mexican and Italian garlic have mauve-colored skins and are milder. Garlic is available year-round.

Selection & Storage: Pick heads that are firm. Do not buy garlic that has green growth. Also, avoid any garlic that appears musty. Squeeze garlic heads, if any of the cloves yield, the garlic is past its prime. Store in a cool, dark bin.

Preparation & Cooking Tips: Remove cloves from the head. Press the flat of a knife onto clove to loosen skin. To roast garlic, break up a head of garlic into cloves. Do not peel, but slice off the wide end of each clove. Place garlic on a double layer of foil. Drizzle with olive oil and seal tightly. Bake in a 350°F oven for 15 minutes. Slip tender cloves from their skins and mash, then spread on toasted French bread or blend in mashed potatoes.

Gingerroot

General Information: Fresh ginger tastes decidedly different than powdered ginger. The beige, knobby root has a bite, a sweetness and woodsy aroma all its own. Powdered ginger and gingerroot should not be used interchangeably. Gingerroot has a tan skin with white- to creamy-yellow flesh. The texture is coarse and can be stringy. Gingerroot is one of the first spices to be traded to the West. Available year-round.

Selection & Storage: Look for robust roots with a spicy fragrance. Any sign of cracking or withering indicates old age. Unpeeled ginger, tightly wrapped, can be kept in the refrigerator for 3 weeks. Peeled ginger can be placed in a jar of sherry and refrigerated for 3 months.

Preparation & Cooking Tips: Cut off as much ginger as needed. Gently peel the thin beige skin from the root. The flesh beneath the skin is the most flavorful. Slice the ginger into "coins." Slices will lend an indirect flavor. Minced gingerroot will give a more pungent flavor.

Herbs

Herbs & Spices

Horseradish Root

General Information: The spiky green leaves of the horseradish root can be used in salads, but the plant's main attraction is its root. Large, white and fiercely spicy, when freshly peeled and grated, horseradish root releases an aroma so pungent that it provokes tears. Its strength fades quickly after grating, so use it immediately or preserve it in vinegar. It is available year-round.

Selection & Storage: Look for roots that are unbruised and firm. Grate the root as needed and keep in a closed bottle of salted vinegar. Cut away the hard inner portion of the root, then cut the remaining root into chunks and preserve; or wrap the roots tightly and keep in the freezer; defrosting is not necessary before grating.

Preparation & Cooking Tips: Horseradish is not generally cooked, but slices can be included in a strong stew. Shredded, it makes a nice "nest" for seafood or cold roast beef. Use it to add zip to cold or hot meals. Add to ketchup with lemon to make the traditional seafood cocktail sauce.

Italian Parsley

General Information: Italian parsley, with its flat leaves, looks more like cilantro than the classic curly leaf parsley. The taste of Italian parsley is similar but more pronounced than that of its curly-leafed cousin. Italian parsley is medium-green with multi-pointed leaves about ½ inch wide. Parsley is a natural breath-freshener and is often used to balance garlic in a dish.

Selection & Storage: Look for bunches of fresh leaves with no sign of wilting. Slice stems on an angle. Place in a glass of water and wrap in a plastic bag. Refrigerate. Change water every few days.

Preparation & Cooking Tips: Remove thick stems and chop parsley leaves to desired size. Parsley, when combined with garlic and grated lemon peel, makes the Italian garnish *gremolata,* which is served atop the dish osso buco. When combined with shallots or garlic, parsley is the basis of the French mixture *persillade,* which is added to savory dishes just before serving.

Lemon Grass

General Information: A member of the grass family, lemon grass has a bulbous base. Several narrow, pale yellowish-green stalks grow from the bulb. Inside the stalk is citral, an oil also found in the skin of lemons. A cornerstone of Thai cooking, lemon grass can be used raw or cooked, and is available year-round.

Selection & Storage: Lemon grass is sold by the stalk or in a bunch. Look for full, fresh lemon grass with an aroma like a cross between fresh-mown hay and lemon. If the base is browning, do not buy. The greener the stalk, the fresher it is. Wrap each stalk in foil and refrigerate for up to 2 weeks; or freeze; it may lose a bit of flavor, but it will cut more easily, as freezing softens the tough fibers.

Preparation & Cooking Tips: Many recipes call for "bruising" the outer leaves before adding to hot liquid. Pound them with a mallet to release fragrant oils. Remove before serving. The inner pale stalks are edible if finely sliced. Lemon grass is inedible unless peeled.

Marjoram

General Information: Marjoram is a member of the mint family and closely resembles oregano in flavor. The leaves are oval, 1 inch long and pale green. Native to the Mediterranean region, marjoram is commonly used in French and Italian cuisine, and is also featured in Scandinavian, German and Austrian dishes. Fresh marjoram is available year-round.

Selection & Storage: Select marjoram that appears fresh and unwilted. Wrap leaves in slightly damp paper towels and place in a plastic bag, or put stems in a glass of water (change the water every few days). Cover with a plastic bag, secure and refrigerate. To freeze, chop fresh marjoram, mix with oil, then freeze in an airtight container.

Preparation & Cooking Tips: Rinse the leaves and pat dry. Snip the leaves from the stem, chop and add to salads, eggs, butter sauces, dressing, soups, beans or pastas. A sprig can be used in meat stocks or with green vegetables. It is outstanding with lamb and non-oily fish.

NUTRITION FACTS

UNITED STATES
Serving Size: 1 tablespoon
Calories 0
Protein.........................0 g
Fat ....0 g
Carbohydrates............ ....1 g
Fiber...........................0 g
Sodium ....0 mg
CANADA
Serving Size: per 5 g (5 mL/1 tsp.)
Energy ....4 cal.....20 kJ
Protein.........................0.2 g
Fat ....0.0 g
Carbohydrates ....1.0 g
Dietary Fibre ....1.6 g
Sodium ....0 mg
Potassium ....28 mg

UNITED STATES

NUTRITION FACTS
NOT AVAILABLE

CANADA
Serving Size: per 4 g (15 mL/1 tbsp.)
Energy ....1 cal.....0 kJ
Protein.........................0.1 g
Fat ....0.0 g
Carbohydrates ....0.3 g
Dietary Fibre ....2 g
Sodium ....2 mg
Potassium ....21 mg

UNITED STATES

NUTRITION FACTS
NOT AVAILABLE

CANADA
Serving Size: 1 tablespoon
Energy.........4.7 cal.....19.8 kJ
Protein............................0 g
Fat ....0 g
Carbohydrates ....1.2 g
Dietary Fibre.....................na
Sodium ....0 mg
Potassium ....34.7 mg

UNITED STATES

NUTRITION FACTS
NOT AVAILABLE

CANADA
Serving Size: 1 tablespoon
Energy.........4.6 cal.....19.3 kJ
Protein.........................0.2 g
Fat ....0.1 g
Carbohydrates ....1 g
Dietary Fibre ....0.6 g
Sodium ....0.4 mg
Potassium ....25.8 mg

SOURCE: USDA

NUTRITION FACTS

UNITED STATES

NUTRITION FACTS
NOT AVAILABLE

CANADA
Serving Size: 2 leaves
Energy............2.2 cal....9.3 kJ
Protein...........................0.1 g
Fat ....0 g
Carbohydrates ....0.4 g
Dietary Fibre ....0.2 g
Sodium ....0.9 mg
Potassium ....18.2 mg

UNITED STATES

NUTRITION FACTS
NOT AVAILABLE

CANADA
Serving Size: 1 tablespoon
Energy.......13.7 cal.....57.6 kJ
Protein...........................0.4 g
Fat ....0.1 g
Carbohydrates ....2.8 g
Dietary Fibre ....1.9 g
Sodium ....0.6 mg
Potassium ....75 mg

UNITED STATES

NUTRITION FACTS
NOT AVAILABLE

CANADA
Serving Size: 10 sprigs, raw
Energy............3.6 cal.....15 kJ
Protein...........................0.2 g
Fat ....0 g
Carbohydrates ....0.6 g
Dietary Fibre ....0.3 g
Sodium ....5.6 mg
Potassium ....55.4 mg

UNITED STATES

NUTRITION FACTS
NOT AVAILABLE

CANADA

NUTRITION FACTS
NOT AVAILABLE

SOURCE: USDA

Mint

General Information: Although there are 25 varieties of mint, the two most commonly used mints are peppermint and spearmint. Peppermint, the more pungent of the two, has bright-green leaves with purplish stems. Spearmint has either true green leaves or grayish-green leaves.

Selection & Storage: Choose fresh mint with evenly colored leaves. Store mint in a glass of water, stems down. Cover leaves with a plastic bag and secure bag to glass; refrigerate. Change the water every few days, and mint will stay fresh for at least 1 week.

Preparation & Cooking Tips: Wash, dry, and snip off the leaves. Use leaves whole or chopped. Mint is great with vegetables such as peas, new potatoes and carrots. Or, add a handful of mint leaves to salad greens. A good lamb marinade combines mint, raspberry vinegar, soy sauce and garlic. Use mint in teas, soups, candies and desserts, or use mint in yogurt dip or dressing. A great garnish, mint complements the flavors of a fruit salad.

Oregano

General Information: Strong and spicy, oregano is a natural in tomato dishes and sauces. There are two varieties of oregano: Mediterranean and Mexican. Mediterranean oregano is the milder, while Mexican oregano is used in highly spiced dishes. Both are available year-round.

Selection & Storage: Look for fresh leaves with no brown spots. Oregano will keep for a few days in a plastic bag in the refrigerator; or tie the stems together and hang upside down in a well-ventilated area to dry. Keep dried oregano in an airtight container. To freeze, place chopped fresh oregano in water in an ice cube tray. Store frozen cubes in a plastic bag in the freezer.

Preparation & Cooking Tips: Wash oregano and pat dry. Snip leaves from the stems, chop and add to pastas, dressings, sauces, poultry, seafood or any tomato dish. To impart a subtle oregano flavor to a dish, use the oregano as a brush. Tie the stems together, dip in oil and baste meats or potatoes.

Parsley

General Information: There are two varieties of parsley: curly and flat-leaf (or Italian). Parsley is much more than a garnish. Parsley is one of the four *fines herbs* that French chefs use to flavor their savory soups and sauces. It is available year-round.

Selection & Storage: Choose parsley with bright-green, curly leaves. Thoroughly wash and shake off excess moisture. Wrap in paper towels, then a plastic bag. Refrigerate for up to 1 week; or, put stems in a glass of water (change the water every few days). Cover with a plastic bag, secure, and refrigerate; or, freeze, tightly wrapped in foil.

Preparation & Cooking Tips: Wilted parsley can be revived by cutting off ½ inch of the stems and placing in a glass of cold water. Refrigerate for 1 hour. Parsley, when combined with garlic and grated lemon peel, makes the Italian garnish *gremolata,* which is served atop the dish osso buco. When combined with shallots or garlic, parsley is the basis of the French mixture *persillade.*

Parsley Root

General Information: Parsley root comes from a variety of parsley that is grown for its root, although the leaves are edible. Parsley root, with its creamy white skin, looks like a small parsnip. It is often double-rooted and tastes like a combination of carrots and celery. It is particularly good in combination with other vegetables. Parsley root is available year-round.

Selection & Storage: Buy parsley roots with the greens attached with creamy white and unblemished roots and fresh, not limp, leaves. Buy parsley roots of the same size, preferably small to medium. Wrap parsley roots and their greens in a plastic bag and refrigerate for up to 1 week.

Preparation & Cooking Tips: Trim greens, wash, dry and reserve for other use. Scrub the roots with a vegetable brush. Peel roots. Parsley roots are delicious when puréed, creamed or steamed. They perk up mashed potatoes wonderfully. Use one part parsley roots to three parts potatoes.

Rhubarb

General Information: Most people know of rhubarb as a pie ingredient (in fact, its nickname is pieplant). Rhubarb's red stalks are charmingly tart. (Never eat the leaves or rhizomes of the rhubarb plant.) There are 2 varieties of rhubarb, hothouse and field grown. Hothouse rhubarb is available all year long and has pink to pale-red stalks and yellow-green leaves. Field-grown rhubarb stalks are cherry red and have a more pronounced flavor. Field-grown rhubarb is at its peak from April to June.

Selection & Storage: Rhubarb is sold ripe. Choose firm stalks that are fresh and crisp. Most rhubarb is sold leafless. If the leaves are still attached, remove. Refrigerate, unwashed, in a plastic bag for 1 week.

Preparation & Cooking Tips: If the rhubarb is overly mature, it may be stringy and need to have the fibrous strings removed. Peel them like celery stalks. Rhubarb may be stewed, baked in pies, preserved in jellies or made into a tart sauce. Use 1 cup of sugar for every 2 cups of rhubarb.

Rosemary

General Information: Rosemary grows wild on the sea cliffs of the Mediterranean, taking in the sun and salty air. With its silvery green, spiky leaves, rosemary has a pungent aroma. The flavor hints at lemon and pine.

Selection & Storage: Look for sprigs that are fresh and show no signs of drying out. The leaves will feel velvety. In a plastic bag in the refrigerator, rosemary will last about a week. Rosemary is easily dried. Tie sprigs together and hang upside down in a well-ventilated area out of the sun. When fully dry (leaves will be hard); snip off leaves and store in an airtight container.

Preparation & Cooking Tips: Rinse rosemary and pat dry. Chop to desired size. Whole sprigs may be used in soups, stews or other dishes. Remove sprigs before serving. Sprigs can be placed in the cavities of chicken or fish for a lovely rosemary flavor. Rosemary is a delicious bread seasoning, and is fabulous paired with lamb. Rosemary should be used in moderation or it will overwhelm the dish.

Sage

General Information: With narrow, oval, gray-green leaves, sage has the pungent flavor of musty mint. It is often used in Thanksgiving stuffing, but it can do so much more. The Italians fry sage leaves in butter to flavor pastas. Sage is available year-round.

Selection & Storage: Look for soft, silvery green leaves with no brown spots. It should have a heady aroma. Refrigerate, unwashed, in a paper towel for up to 4 days.

Preparation & Cooking Tips: Sage is a natural partner with pork, poultry, and polenta. You can make a sage-infused (flavored) oil easily. Reserve a few leaves from a cup of fresh sage for garnish. In a saucepan over moderate heat, cook the sage in 2 cups of olive oil. Heat until the herbs start to sizzle, but do not let oil smoke. Remove from heat. When cool, discard cooked sage. Place the reserved sage in a pretty bottle. Add the oil, making sure to cover the sage (if sage is not covered by oil, it will mold). Cork.

Savory

General Information: Savory has bigger leaves than thyme, and is similar in flavor, though a touch more bitter. There are many varieties of savory, but the two most commonly used are summer savory and winter savory. Summer savory is sweeter and used more often in cooking. Winter savory has a peppery flavor. Winter savory is a small, shrubby perennial, whereas summer savory is an annual with lilac flowers.

Selection & Storage: Look for fresh leaves that are shiny on the upper surface with no brown spots. Refrigerate in a plastic bag for 3 to 4 days; or chop finely and mix with water. Freeze in an ice cube tray and then store in a plastic bag.

Preparation & Cooking Tips: Rinse sprigs, then dry with paper towels. Snip leaves from stem. Leaves can be used whole or chopped. Savory goes well with beans, pork, poultry and veal, as well as hearty vegetables such as cabbage. Use in herb butter, marinades and stuffings.

NUTRITION FACTS

UNITED STATES
Serving Size: 1 cup
Calories	25
Protein	1 g
Fat	0 g
Carbohydrates	6 g
Dietary Fiber	2 g
Sodium	0 mg

CANADA
Serving Size: per 125 g (250 mL/1 cup)
Energy	26 cal.....110 kJ
Protein	1.1 g
Fat	0.3 g
Carbohydrates	5.7 g
Dietary Fibre	2.3 g
Sodium	5 mg
Potassium	360 mg

UNITED STATES

NUTRITION FACTS
NOT AVAILABLE

CANADA
Serving Size: per 1 g (5 mL/1 tsp.)
Energy	2.2 cal.....9.3 kJ
Protein	0 g
Fat	0.1 g
Carbohydrates	0.3 g
Dietary Fibre	0.2 g
Sodium	0.4 mg
Potassium	11.3 mg

UNITED STATES

NUTRITION FACTS
NOT AVAILABLE

CANADA
Serving Size: 1 tablespoon
Energy	6.2 cal.....26.3 kJ
Protein	0.2 g
Fat	0.2 g
Carbohydrates	1.2 g
Dietary Fibre	0.8 g
Sodium	0.2 mg
Potassium	21.4 mg

UNITED STATES

NUTRITION FACTS
NOT AVAILABLE

CANADA

NUTRITION FACTS
NOT AVAILABLE

SOURCE: USDA

Sorrel

General Information: Sorrel is a tart and tasty member of the buckwheat family. Sorrel leaves are shaped like spinach, range in color from pale to dark green, and are from 2 to 12 inches in length. As sorrel matures, it becomes more acidic. English sorrel has pale-green, large, arrow-shaped leaves. French sorrel has a lemony flavor. Both are available year-round.

Selection & Storage: Look for bunches with firm, green leaves and stems with no spots or signs of wilting. Refrigerate, unwashed, in a plastic bag in the crisper section for 2 days.

Preparation & Cooking Tips: Wash and drain thoroughly. Add a few leaves to a green salad; it's too sour to eat a whole salad of sorrel leaves. Cooked sorrel can be used in soups or stews. As sorrel's color fades when boiled, try mixing it with greens of a brighter shade. To eat it like cooked spinach, plunge the sorrel into salted, boiling water and remove almost immediately.

Tarragon

General Information: Many a cook has discovered how fresh tarragon can enrich an egg, chicken or shrimp dish. It is available in the summer and early fall.

Selection & Storage: Look for deep-green tarragon sprigs with long, narrow, pointed leaves. Sniff for a peppery scent with anise undertones. Tarragon will keep only a few days, wrapped and in the refrigerator.

Preparation & Cooking Tips: Wash tarragon sprigs and dry with paper towels. Remove thick stems. Use caution when seasoning with tarragon: although its flavor is subtle, the herb is assertive and can easily overwhelm other ingredients. For tarragon vinegar, bruise tarragon sprigs with a mallet. Place in a heat-proof canning jar. Bring red- or white-wine vinegar to a boil and pour into jar. Seal the bottle and let sit for 2 weeks, shaking occasionally. Strain vinegar through cheesecloth. Add a fresh sprig of tarragon to a sterilized, pretty bottle. Pour in vinegar. Cork the bottle and store in cool, dry place.

Thyme

General Information: Thyme is one of the most commonly used culinary herbs. It is a perennial bush with gray-green leaves. Thyme, with its fragrant minty, lightly lemon aroma, is used in everything from chewing gum to cough syrup. Fresh thyme is available during the summer months.

Selection & Storage: Thyme is sold in bunches of sprigs. Look for fragrant, gray-green and fresh-looking leaves. There are many varieties of the herb, but garden thyme, with its sharp, peppery taste and haunting aroma, is the one most cooks use. Wrap thyme in a barely damp paper towel. Place in a plastic bag and refrigerate for up to 5 days.

Preparation & Cooking Tips: Young shoots of thyme are used as a garnish and as flavoring in soup and gravy. It is featured in many tomato, onion and corn dishes. Thyme can be rubbed over roasts or birds (or placed in the bird's cavity) to season the meat. Thyme is robust and can easily dominate a dish rather than enhance it, so use sparingly.

NUTRITION FACTS

UNITED STATES

NUTRITION FACTS NOT AVAILABLE

CANADA

NUTRITION FACTS NOT AVAILABLE

UNITED STATES

Serving Size: 1 tablespoon, ground
Calories 14
Protein..............................1 g
Fat ....0.3 g
Carbohydrates...........2.41 g
Dietary Fiber ....0.4 g
Sodium ....3 mg

CANADA

Serving Size: 1 tablespoon
Energy.......11.8 cal....49.7 kJ
Protein..........................0.3 g
Fat ....0.3 g
Carbohydrates ....2.7 g
Dietary Fibre ....1.9 g
Sodium ....2.3 mg
Potassium ....35 mg

UNITED STATES

Serving Size: 1 teaspoon
Calories 1
Protein.............................0 g
Fat ....0 g
Carbohydrates.................1 g
Dietary Fiber ....0 g
Sodium ....0 mg

CANADA

Serving Size: 1 g (5 mL/1 teaspoon)
Energy............0.8 cal....3.3 kJ
Protein..........................0.0 g
Fat ....0.0 g
Carbohydrates ....0.1 g
Dietary Fibre ....0.1 g
Sodium ....0.0 mg
Potassium ....4.8 mg

SOURCE: USDA

Preparing Delicate Herbs

To chop fresh herbs: Hold the leaves or sprigs together in a bunch and chop coarsely with knife or kitchen shears. Continue chopping to desired fineness.

To store fresh herbs: Herbs lose their aroma and flavor quickly. To keep fresh for several days, trim the ends off the stems and place in a tall glass of cold water with a pinch of sugar. Store in a cool place in the refrigerator. Change water and trim stems as necessary. To revive wilted sprigs, moisten with a fine mist of water and chill briefly.

The Spice of Life

Cinnamon is one of the oldest and most flavorful spices. The inner skin of fragrant tree bark from cinnamon and cassia trees can be harvested after 20 to 30 years of growth. The trees continue to grow and produce cinnamon for many years. For cinnamon sticks, the upper branches are carefully cut and the inner bark removed, which naturally curl into quills. Use cinnamon sticks to flavor and stir hot beverages such as mulled wine or apple cider.

Cassia cinnamon, commonly marketed on America, is native to Southeast Asia, southern China and northern Vietnam. It has a strong, spicy sweet flavor. Ceylon cinnamon is known as old-fashioned cinnamon – less sweet with a complex citrus flavor. Powdered cinnamon is made from crushed sticks.

For cinnamon butter to spread on muffins, waffles or toast, just mix 4 ounces of softened, unsalted butter with 1 to 2 tablespoons of sugar and ½ teaspoon cinnamon.

The strength of the flavor of spices depends upon the essential oil content – the higher the level, the stronger the flavor.

Arrowroot

General Information: Arrowroot is commonly available ground into a powder and used as a thickening agent. Arrowroot grows in Bermuda, the Caribbean islands, Brazil, Southeast Asia, Australia and South Africa. It is also known as goo and Chinese potato.

Selection & Storage: Fresh arrowroot looks like an onion, with brown roots coming from both ends. Store for up to 2 weeks in a cool, dark place (50°F to 55°F).

Preparation & Cooking Tips: To use as a thickening agent, add 1 teaspoon of arrowroot powder to a quarter cup of cold liquid. Mix well and add to dish; or use as a glaze over a fruit tart. Arrowroot has several advantages over other thickening agents. Most thickeners leave sauces white or cloudy, but arrowroot becomes transparent, giving the dish a silky quality. Arrowroot has twice the thickening power of flour and, unlike cornstarch, arrowroot is tasteless. It is also easier to digest than wheat flour.

Bamboo Shoots

General Information: There are two types of bamboo shoots, winter and spring. Winter shoots are smaller and more tender, while spring roots tend to be more fibrous. Bamboo shoots look like cylindrical spikes of overlaid brown to green leaves that come to a point. Their flavor is slightly acidic with a good crunch. Fresh bamboo shoots are available in winter and spring.

Selection & Storage: Look for small bamboo shoots without blemishes (spring ones will be larger). Refrigerate unpeeled bamboo shoots for 1 week; refrigerate peeled and parboiled bamboo shoots stored in a container of water for up to 5 days.

Preparation & Cooking Tips: The tightly wound, fibrous leaves must be removed to get to the pale, buff-colored core. Use a sharp knife and shave the shoot as if it were a pencil being sharpened. Cut off bases of the shoots and discard. Cook for 5 minutes to remove the poisonous hydrocyanic acid. Drain and cook again in fresh water for 5 minutes.

Boniato

General Information: Boniato is what people in the Caribbean call a sweet potato. Unlike our sweet potato, the boniato's flesh is creamy yellow with a subtle taste of roasted chestnuts. Its flesh is drier and fluffier than our sweet potato. Boniato is an irregularly shaped tuber with patchy, purplish skin. Good in flans and muffins, boniatos are also delicious baked, boiled, fried, steamed, roasted or puréed. They are available from April to January.

Selection & Storage: Look for hard, firm tubers free of mold, soft spots or holes. The skin will look patchy, but avoid those with wrinkled or wet places. Store in a loosely sealed paper bag at room temperature for 2 to 3 days.

Preparation & Cooking Tips: To boil or steam, peel boniatos. Use a sharp knife and drop boniatos immediately into water so the skin will not discolor. Be sure water covers them while cooking. Baked boniatos are delicious, including the crisp skin. Serve boniatos when done, as they tend to get starchy if they sit too long.

Breadfruit

General Information: Breadfruit looks like a melon with bumpy green scales. Breadfruit is eaten as a vegetable. Its taste varies with its state of ripeness. When all green, it is like a raw potato. Cooked when partially ripe, breadfruit has the consistency of a sticky plantain. When fully ripe, it can be made into a custard-like dish. Breadfruit is never eaten raw, and is sporadically available.

Selection & Storage: Breadfruit is kept in drums of water. Pick a breadfruit with even-sized scales that feels dense, not spongy. When breadfruit ripens, the peel gets brown speckles. Breadfruit does not store well, so buy them at the desired ripeness and use immediately.

Preparation & Cooking Tips: Cut a hard breadfruit into quarters, lengthwise. Remove the dark core and discard. Pare the skin off and put cut pieces into water for boiling. Breadfruit can be roasted in the peel for 1 hour in a 375°F oven. This will yield a nutty-flavored side dish with a dry, firm texture. Serve with spicy coconut sauce.

NUTRITION FACTS

UNITED STATES
Serving Size: 1 tablespoon, ground
Calories 29
Protein.............................0 g
Fat ....0 g
Carbohydrates....................7 g
Dietary Fiber ....0 g
Sodium ....0 mg

CANADA
Serving Size: per 1 root
Energy.............21 cal....89 kJ
Protein...........................1.3 g
Fat ....0.0 g
Carbohydrates ....4.4 g
Dietary Fibre ....0.4 g
Sodium ....8.5 mg
Potassium ....149 mg

UNITED STATES
Serving Size: ½ cup
Calories 20
Protein.............................2 g
Fat ....0 g
Carbohydrates....................4 g
Dietary Fiber ....4 g
Sodium ....0 mg

CANADA
Serving Size: per ¼ cup, dry
Energy.............22 cal....90 kJ
Protein...........................2.1 g
Fat ....0.2 g
Carbohydrates ....4.2 g
Dietary Fibre ....2.0 g
Sodium ....03 mg
Potassium ....426 mg

UNITED STATES
Serving Size: 1 medium
Calories 117
Protein.............................2 g
Fat ....0 g
Carbohydrates..................28 g
Dietary Fiber ....3 g
Sodium ....11 mg

CANADA

NUTRITION FACTS
NOT AVAILABLE

UNITED STATES
Serving Size: ½ cup
Calories 110
Protein.............................1 g
Fat ....0 g
Carbohydrates..................30 g
Dietary Fiber ....5 g
Sodium ....0 mg

CANADA
Serving Size: per ¼ small fruit
Energy...........98 cal....413 kJ
Protein...........................1.0 g
Fat ....0.2 g
Carbohydrates ....26 g
Dietary Fibre ....4.7 g
Sodium ....1.9 mg
Potassium ....470 mg

SOURCE: USDA

Cactus Leaves/Nopales

General Information: Cactus leaves are fleshy oval leaves of the prickly pear cactus. The texture of cactus leaves is similar to okra. Tender but crunchy, cactus leaves taste like a combination of green pepper, green beans and asparagus with a lemon twist. Cactus leaves, or nopales (no-PAH-les), as they are called in Mexico, are available year-round. They are plentiful in the spring.

Selection & Storage: Look for medium-green, crisp cactus leaves that are small to medium in size with no sign of wrinkling. If purchased very fresh and wrapped in plastic, they will last 2 weeks in the refrigerator.

Preparation & Cooking Tips: Most cactus leaves are sold with the prickers removed. Peel off the "eyes" and any stray prickers with a vegetable peeler. Steam over boiling water for 3 minutes. Slice cooked cactus leaves and add to scrambled eggs; or dice cooked cactus leaves and place between two tortillas with grated cheese. Pan-fry and slice for an appetizer.

Calabaza

General Information: Calabaza (kah-lah-BAH-sah) is a large squash familiar to those in the Caribbean and Latin America. It is known as the West Indian pumpkin. Skin color can vary from green to tan to sunset-orange. The round calabaza ranges from the size of a cantaloupe to that of a watermelon. Its flesh is carrot-orange, sweet, succulent and fine grained. It can be substituted in recipes calling for butternut or hubbard squash.

Selection & Storage: If buying a whole calabaza, check for a firmly attached stem; avoid skin blemishes, dents or soft spots. When buying chunks of calabaza, choose the least fibrous, most finely grained flesh. Stored in a cool, dark place (50°F to 55°F), a whole calabaza will last 6 weeks. Refrigerate cut calabaza, tightly wrapped, and use within 1 week.

Preparation & Cooking Tips: Cleave whole calabazas with a sharp knife. Cut into 3-inch wedges. Remove seeds and fibers, then peel the skin. Cut into desired size.

Cardoon

General Information: The cardoon, is a thistle, like the globe artichoke. Unlike the artichoke, the stalks of the cardoon not the flower, are edible. It grows in bunches like celery, and tastes like artichoke hearts and bitter celery. It is available from midwinter to early spring.

Selection & Storage: Look for supple, firm stalks with a silvery gray-green color. The tops will be discolored. This is a result of removing the thistle tops and does not affect the taste. Wrap cardoon bottoms in a damp paper towel. Surround with a paper bag and refrigerate for up to 2 weeks.

Preparation & Cooking Tips: Cardoon needs to be pre-cooked to rid it of bitterness. Cut trimmed stalks in half crosswise. Drop into a large pot of boiling, salted water. Boil until tender, 15 to 30 minutes. Keep testing. Drain and cool in running water. Place in a bowl of water and individually cut off strings with a paring knife. Cut to recipe size. Cardoon can be dressed with a vinaigrette, lemon butter or cheese sauce.

Cherimoya

General Information: Also known as custard apple or sherbert fruit, this large tropical fruit looks like an oversized green pinecone. The cherimoya has juicy, creamy white flesh and large, black seeds. Its custard-like texture tastes like a combination of pineapple, papaya, mango and vanilla custard, thus making the cherimoya a wonderful dessert fruit. Cherimoyas are available November through May.

Selection & Storage: Choose fruit that is yellow-green and firm, heavy for its size and without blemishes; surface scars are normal. Avoid any that are dark or splotched. Ripen at room temperature for a few days until just softened; then refrigerate, tightly wrapped, up to 4 days.

Preparation & Cooking Tips: Cherimoyas should be served well-chilled. The easiest way to eat this seed-filled fruit is to spoon it from the shell; simply halve, remove the seeds and scoop out the flesh with a spoon.

NUTRITION FACTS

Cactus Leaves/Nopales

UNITED STATES	
Serving Size: 1 piece	
Calories	12
Protein	0 g
Fat	0 g
Carbohydrates	3 g
Dietary Fiber	1 g
Sodium	2 mg

CANADA	
Serving Size: 1 cup, sliced	
Energy	13 cal.....57 kJ
Protein	1.1 g
Fat	0.1 g
Carbohydrates	2.9 g
Dietary Fibre	1.9 g
Sodium	18.9 mg
Potassium	274 mg

Calabaza

UNITED STATES	
Serving Size: 1 cup	
Calories	49
Protein	0 g
Fat	0 g
Carbohydrates	11 g
Dietary Fiber	1 g
Sodium	7 mg

CANADA	
NUTRITION FACTS NOT AVAILABLE	

Cardoon

UNITED STATES	
Serving Size: ½ cup	
Calories	36
Protein	1 g
Fat	0 g
Carbohydrates	9 g
Dietary Fiber	n/a
Sodium	303 mg

CANADA	
Serving Size: 75g	
Energy	15 cal.....63 kJ
Protein	0.5 g
Fat	0 g
Carbohydrates	3.7 g
Dietary Fibre	n/a
Sodium	127.5 mg
Potassium	300 mg

Cherimoya

UNITED STATES	
Serving Size: ½ fruit	
Calories	257
Protein	0.4 g
Fat	1 g
Carbohydrates	66 g
Dietary Fiber	7 g
Sodium	0 mg

CANADA	
Serving Size: per ⅙ medium	
Energy	85 cal.....350 kJ
Protein	1.2 g
Fat	0.4 g
Carbohydrates	22 g
Dietary Fibre	2.4 g
Sodium	n/a
Potassium	n/a

SOURCE: USDA

Feijoa

General Information: The feijoa (fay-JOH-ah or fay-YOH-ah) is often mistakenly called the pineapple guava. Feijoas have an exotic aroma for such a small, bumpy, egg-shaped fruit. One whiff holds the scent of pineapple, Concord grapes, quince and mint. The flesh is tart, creamy and granular, like a Seckel pear. When ripe, the center is jelly-like with tiny seeds. Feijoas are available from spring to early summer, and again from fall to early winter.

Selection & Storage: Unripened feijoas can be bitter. When ripe, they feel like soft pears when lightly pressed. The skin ranges from lime green to olive green. To speed ripening, place in a paper bag with an apple. Refrigerate ripe feijoas for 1 or 2 days; or purée the raw fruit (skin removed) and refrigerate for 1 week or freeze for months.

Preparation & Cooking Tips: Peel the thin, bitter skin with a vegetable peeler. Feijoas are good raw or cooked, but tend to dominate a dish.

Gai Choy/Chinese Mustard

General Information: Gai choy, or gaai choy, is also known as Chinese mustard cabbage. It is not the same thing as cabbage, but it is similar in appearance, nutritional value and use. Young and fresh gai choy is tender and can be eaten in its entirety. When more mature, gai choy is used by Cantonese cooks in soups; or it is preserved with chilies or pickled in brine or sugar and eaten throughout the year. It can be shredded and preserved like sauerkraut.

Selection & Storage: Select gai choy with firm, broad leaves with no sign of yellowing, and pale-green stalks with no holes – a sign of old age. Avoid limp or tired-looking gai choy. Refrigerate, unwashed, in a loosely wrapped plastic bag up to 5 days.

Preparation & Cooking Tips: Cut the greens into pieces before washing. Fill the sink with cold water. Rinse the leaves. Remove and drain the sink. Refill and wash again. Fresh gai choy can be stir-fried with ginger and salt, or add it to soups.

Gai Lon/Chinese Broccoli

General Information: Gai lon, or gaai laan, is also known as Chinese broccoli or Chinese kale. Whatever it is called, gai lon is a highly nutritious, green, leafy plant with smooth, round stems and small, white flowers. It looks like Swiss chard. The firm stem is tender, delicate and full of flavor that is earthy and slightly bitter. The white flowers and smaller leaves are also eaten. Gai lon is rich in vitamins A and C.

Selection & Storage: Look for stems that are fresh and deep olive green. Choose bunches with flowers that are mostly in the bud stage, rather than blooming. Refrigerate in a plastic bag for only a few days.

Preparation & Cooking Tips: Remove large leaves. If the stems seem tough, peel the outer skin. Prepare by blanching in boiling, salted water and then dressing with thick, brown oyster sauce. Gai lon also works well in stir-fries with beef, poultry and pork, or with fish and noodles, and in soups.

Galangal

General Information: Galangal (guh-LANG-gul) is a member of the ginger family with a fiery, pungent and distinctive flavor. Galangal comes in two varieties: lesser galangal and greater galangal. As with ginger, the edible part of galangal is its rhizome, or underground stem. Galangal is potent, tasting of ginger, pepper and sour lemon. (Lesser galangal is the more potent of the two.) When very fresh, galangal is ivory white, with very little separation between skin and flesh.

Selection & Storage: The roots must be firm. If they appear wrinkled or shriveled, do not buy. Refrigerate, uncut and unwrapped, for 3 weeks; or peel the root, place it in a jar of sherry and refrigerate for several months. Galangal can also be frozen, tightly wrapped in foil.

Preparation & Cooking Tips: Slices of galangal are used to flavor soups and stews (remove before serving); or it is pounded with lemon grass, chilies, shallots and garlic into a paste.

NUTRITION FACTS

UNITED STATES
Serving Size: 1 medium
Calories 25
Protein.........................1 g
Fat ....0 g
Carbohydrates...................5 g
Dietary Fiber ....2 g
Sodium..........................2 mg

CANADA
Serving Size: per ¾ cup
Energy..........49 cal.....200 kJ
Protein......................1.2 g
Fat ....0.8 g
Carbohydrates ....11 g
Dietary Fibre.....................n/a
Sodium........................25 mg
Potassium ....565 mg

UNITED STATES

NUTRITION FACTS
NOT AVAILABLE

CANADA

NOT AVAILABLE

UNITED STATES
Serving Size: 1 cup, cooked
Calories 19
Protein.............................1 g
Fat ....1 g
Carbohydrates ....3 g
Dietary Fiber ....2 g
Sodium..........................6 mg

CANADA
Serving Size: per 1 cup
Energy.............19 cal.....80 kJ
Protein......................1.0 g
Fat ....0.6 g
Carbohydrates ....3.3 g
Dietary Fibre ....2.2 g
Sodium ....6.1 mg
Potassium ....229 mg

UNITED STATES

NUTRITION FACTS
NOT AVAILABLE

CANADA

NUTRITION FACTS
NOT AVAILABLE

SOURCE: USDA

Ethnic

Gil Choy/Chinese Chives

General Information: Gil choy is often known as Chinese chives. There are two varieties: yellow chives and flowering chives. Yellow chives are mildly onion-flavored. Their color comes from being grown out of direct sunlight. The flavor of flowering chives is more garlicky. Both are available in spring and early summer.

Selection & Storage: Select gil choy that is fresh looking, not wilted. Flowering chives will be stiff and aromatic. Yellow chives are limp, but do not buy those with brown edges. Wash, dry, then place between layers of paper towels. Put in a plastic bag and place in the lower part of the refrigerator. Yellow chives will last only 1 day. Flowering chives will last for 2 days

Preparation & Cooking Tips: Chop off the tough ends of flowering chives. Trim away any decaying parts of yellow chives. Gil choy is often stir-fried or cooked whole and served as a side dish to accompany noodle soup. Gil choy is also good in omelets, risotto and fish dishes.

NUTRITION FACTS	
UNITED STATES	
NUTRITION FACTS NOT AVAILABLE	
CANADA	
NUTRITION FACTS NOT AVAILABLE	

Gobo Root/Burdock Cabbage

General Information: Gobo root is a native of Siberia. Inside its scruffy exterior is a grayish-white flesh with a sweet, earthy flavor and a crisply tender texture. Gobo root is also called burdock. The taproot of the gobo, or burdock, can grow to 2 feet in length and is very narrow. It is available year-round.

Selection & Storage: Choose firm, not flabby, mud-crusted gobo roots that are no more than 1 inch in diameter and about 18 inches in length. Wrap gobo roots in wet paper towels, then in a plastic bag. Keep the toweling damp and the gobo will stay fresh for 1 week.

Preparation & Cooking Tips: Scrub off the mud. Peel each piece right before using or it will discolor. Soak peeled pieces in salted water for 10 minutes to reduce aftertaste. Shredded gobo root can be used in stir-fries. Gobo root should be thought of as a flavoring ingredient, rather than a star of its own dish. Cook it with grains or stews.

UNITED STATES	
Serving Size: 1 cup (118 g)	
Calories	85
Protein	2 g
Fat	0 g
Carbohydrates	20 g
Dietary Fiber	4 g
Sodium	6 mg
CANADA	
Serving Size: per 1 root (156 g)	
Energy	112 cal.....469 kJ
Protein	2.3 g
Fat	0.2 g
Carbohydrates	27 g
Dietary Fibre	5.1 g
Sodium	7.8 mg
Potassium	480 mg

Jicama

General Information: The jicama (HEE-ka-mah) is a tuberous root that resembles a large, beige turnip. Its crunchy, juicy texture resembles that of waterchestnuts, but the flavor is sweet and nutty. It is available year-round, and at its peak from fall to spring.

Selection & Storage: Jicama can assume all sorts of shapes and vary from 1/2 pound to 6 pounds. Look for unblemished jicamas, though the patchy skin is a characteristic. Scrape the skin with a fingernail to check that the flesh is creamy and juicy; avoid those with dry flesh. Store, uncut, in a cool dark place for 2 to 3 weeks. Once cut, wrap tightly and use within 1 week.

Preparation & Cooking Tips: Halve or quarter, then remove the thin skin. Jicama will not discolor, so it can be prepared well in advance. Great in salads or stir-fries, jicama is also good with dips. Sprinkle jicama slices with lime juice and some cayenne pepper for a good appetizer. Jicama will not lose its crunchiness when cooked.

UNITED STATES	
Serving Size: 3 ounces	
Calories	35
Protein	1 g
Fat	0 g
Carbohydrates	7 g
Dietary Fiber	2 g
Sodium	5 mg
CANADA	
Serving Size: per 1 cup	
Energy	51 cal.....210 kJ
Protein	1.8 g
Fat	0.3 g
Carbohydrates	11 g
Dietary Fibre	6.1 g
Sodium	8 mg
Potassium	219 mg

Khan Choy/Chinese Celery

General Information: Khan choy is also known as Chinese celery. It is distinctly different from Western celery. Khan choy stalks are thin, hollow and very crisp. Compared to Western celery, Khan choy seems spindly and frail. As with European celery, Khan choy's meager crown of head leaves looks more like the stems and leaves of celeriac. But appearances are deceiving. Both the stems and leaves of Khan choy have an intense, herbal flavor.

Selection & Storage: Khan choy varies in color from white to dark green. Choose crisp and strong Khan choy with no yellowing leaves or faded stems. Refrigerate in the crisper section, wrapped in a plastic bag, for several days.

Preparation & Cooking Tips: Rinse well. With a sharp knife, cut off the base to free the ribs. Steam or stir-fry the leaves and stems. Khan choy is also delicious added to soups and braised dishes.

UNITED STATES	
NUTRITION FACTS NOT AVAILABLE	
CANADA	
NUTRITION FACTS NOT AVAILABLE	

SOURCE: USDA

Kiwano/Horned Melon

General Information: Kiwanos look like something out of science fiction. Three to 5 inches long, kiwanos have bright-yellow skin – and horns, which explains why the kiwano is called the horned melon. Inside, the kiwano has a bright lime-green, jelly-like center which is stuffed with edible seeds. The taste of the horned melon is pleasant: a combination of banana, melon, cucumber and lime. They are available from late February to June.

Selection & Storage: Look for kiwanos with some yellow or orange color, and firm, unblemished skin. Never refrigerate kiwanos, as cold destroys their subtropical flesh. Keep in a cool, dry place until ripe. When the kiwano turns orangish-yellow, it is ripe. Do not keep kiwanos with bananas or apples, unless you want to speed ripening.

Preparation & Cooking Tips: Slice in half lengthwise. Scoop out the green jelly and seeds. Taste to see if sugar needs to be added. The shell is inedible.

Lo Bok

General Information: The Korean lo bok radish is very similar in flavor and texture to the Japanese daikon radish. Some varieties of lo bok have a green crown, but most are whitish. Lo bok is available year-round, but will be at its most flavorful and mild in the fall and winter. Spring and summer radishes will be hotter and yet weaker in flavor.

Selection & Storage: Look for firm and plump lo bok. Be sure there is no mold or cracks. If the greens are attached, look to see that they are not yellowed. Lo bok does not store well. It quickly loses moisture and becomes tasteless and limp. Remove green tops, wrap tightly in plastic and store in the refrigerator. For eating raw, it will only keep 2 days. For soup use, it will keep 1 week.

Preparation & Cooking Tips: Wash well. Trim the root tips and peel. Eaten raw, lo bok can be quite pungent. Shred it and mix with other vegetables or use as a condiment for other Korean dishes. Lo bok is often used in the garlicky condiment kimchee.

Malanga

General Information: Malanga is as popular in the tropics as the potato is in North America. With its similarity in size and shape to the taro root, the two are often confused. Malanga has an unusual flavor. Some have likened it to black walnuts; others think it has an earthy flavor. The texture of cooked malanga is surprisingly smooth, like cooked black beans combined with boiled new potatoes. Malanga comes in three basic shapes: curved, yam-like or shaped like a club. It is available year-round.

Selection & Storage: Look for light-colored, firm malanga with no soft spots or evidence of mold. Store at room temperature for only a few days.

Preparation & Cooking Tips: Scrub skin with a brush. Trim the ends and peel. Cut out any discolored areas. Do not serve raw. Malanga can be boiled in 3-inch chunks for about 20 minutes until crisp-tender. Drain and serve with spicy sausages or garlic sauce. Malanga is good in soups, or as chips and fritters. Do not over cook.

Mamey Sapote

General Information: Mamey sapote (sah-PO-tay) has become increasingly popular in America, especially with the Cuban-American population. Mamey sapote is a large, football-shaped fruit that grows on an ornamental evergreen tree. The brown skin has a rough texture that is part peach fuzz and part sandpaper. The flesh of the mamey sapote is either creamy pink or salmon-orange. In the middle of the mamey sapote sits a large, avocado-like pit. Mamey sapotes have a wonderful flavor that has been described as a combination of sweet potato, avocado and honey. Some say there is also a hint of marzipan. They are available from January through September.

Selection & Storage: Choose firm, unblemished mamey sapotes. Even though the skin is rough, it bruises easily. Mamey sapotes are ripe when squeezably soft. Store at room temperature. They will ripen in about 3 days.

Preparation & Cooking Tips: Peel and pit, then enjoy as is, or drizzle with lime juice or blend into a shake.

NUTRITION FACTS

UNITED STATES
Serving Size: 3.5 ounces
Calories 24
Protein.............................1 g
Fat ....0 g
Carbohydrates..................0 g
Dietary Fiber ....1 g
Sodium ....1 mg

CANADA

NUTRITION FACTS
NOT AVAILABLE

UNITED STATES
Serving Size: 1 medium
Calories 57
Protein.............................2 g
Fat ....2 g
Carbohydrates...........12 g
Dietary Fiber ....6 g
Sodium ....81 mg

CANADA
Serving Size: per 1 medium (7" long)
Energy..........60 cal.....253 kJ
Protein...........................2.0 g
Fat ....0.3 g
Carbohydrates ....13 g
Dietary Fibre ....5.4 g
Sodium ....70.9 mg
Potassium ....767 mg

UNITED STATES
Serving Size: ½ cup, baked
Calories 74
Protein.............................2 g
Fat ....1 g
Carbohydrates..................17 g
Dietary Fiber ....1 g
Sodium ....4 mg

CANADA

NUTRITION FACTS
NOT AVAILABLE

UNITED STATES

NUTRITION FACTS
NOT AVAILABLE

CANADA

NUTRITION FACTS
NOT AVAILABLE

SOURCE: USDA

Piloncillo/Panela

General Information: Piloncillo is the Mexican name for raw or crude sugar. No sugar is truly raw or unrefined, but piloncillo is "less refined" sugar. When sugar cane is processed, it separates into sugar crystals and a sticky mass of molasses. The crystals go on to further refinement. The brown molasses substance is poured into molds, left to harden, and then used as a sweetener. In India, it is formed into cakes and called jaggery. In Colombia, it is called panda. And in Mexico, it is formed into 3-inch cones called Piloncillo or panela.

Selection & Storage: Piloncillo comes prepackaged. Store in a cool, dark place.

Preparation & Cooking Tips: Piloncillo is used mostly in Mexican desserts, or in flavoring dishes such as cooked squash. To use, grate the cone of sugar on the fine side of a grater, or pulverize it in a food processor. Placing small amounts of Piloncillo in warm liquid also works. The closest taste equivalent of Piloncillo is dark brown sugar.

NUTRITION FACTS

UNITED STATES	
Serving Size: 1 teaspoon	
Calories	15
Protein	0 g
Fat	0 g
Carbohydrates	4 g
Dietary Fiber	na
Sodium	0 mg

CANADA
NUTRITION FACTS NOT AVAILABLE

Pomegranate

General Information: The pomegranate is a berry with delicious seeds. Each seed is encased in a delicious, sweet-tart scarlet pulp. Separating the seeds are tough, white membranes. Beware of pomegranate's red juice; it stains permanently. Pomegranates are available in November and December.

Selection & Storage: Choose deeply colored, large pomegranates. Press the crown end. If powdery clouds appear, do not buy, as it is past its prime. Pomegranates keep very well. Refrigerate, whole, for up to 3 months.

Preparation & Cooking Tips: Cut pomegranate in half and eat the kernels with a spoon; or don rubber gloves to extract seeds. Cut out the blossom end and some of the white pith. Do not pierce into the red. Score the leathery skin and break apart with your hands, not a knife, following the cut lines. Bend the rind and pull out the seeds. The seeds are most often used by scattering them in a salad or fruit compote.

UNITED STATES	
Serving Size: 1 medium	
Calories	100
Protein	1 g
Fat	0 g
Carbohydrates	26 g
Dietary Fiber	1 g
Sodium	0 mg

CANADA	
Serving Size: per 155 g (1 medium)	
Energy	105 cal.....440 kJ
Protein	1.5 g
Fat	3.5 g
Carbohydrates	27 g
Dietary Fibre	0.9 g
Sodium	5 mg
Potassium	401 mg

Prickly/Cactus Pear

General Information: Prickly pears, also known as cactus pears, come from the nopales and opuntia cacti. They are actually berries, not pears, and are packed with edible, crunchy seeds. The prickly skin is either medium green or dark magenta. The flesh is brilliant fuschia, crimson or orange. Some varieties are mild and taste of watermelon; others are more tart. They are generally available from summer through early spring.

Selection & Storage: Choose prickly pears that are deeply colored, not faded, and tender, but not squishy. Avoid those with mold. Let ripen to a soft consistency at room temperature, then refrigerate for up to 1 week.

Preparation & Cooking Tips: Most prickly pears have had their prickers removed, but there are always unseen prickers lurking. To peel, hold the pear with a fork, cut off both ends, then cut an incision lengthwise. Slide knife under the skin and peel skin off. Always serve prickly pear chilled. It can be used in salads or tropical drinks.

UNITED STATES	
Serving Size: 1 medium	
Calories	45
Protein	1 g
Fat	0.5 g
Carbohydrates	10 g
Dietary Fiber	4 g
Sodium	5 mg

CANADA	
Serving Size: per 100 g (1 medium)	
Energy	42 cal.....180 kJ
Protein	0.8 g
Fat	0.5 g
Carbohydrates	10 g
Dietary Fibre	3.7 g
Sodium	5 mg
Potassium	226 mg

Pummelo

General Information: Pummelos (pom-UH-loh), or pomelos, are thought to be the ancestors of grapefruit. They are one of the largest citrus fruits, ranging in size from a cantaloupe to a watermelon. Pummelos are slightly pear-shaped. Their thick skin is soft and varies in color from yellow to tan to pink. Their flesh varies dramatically from tart to juicy sweet but they are never bitter. Pummelos are available from mid-January to mid-February.

Selection & Storage: Look for pummelos that are heavy for their size and unblemished, with a sweetly fragrant aroma. Refrigerate for up to 1 week.

Preparation & Cooking Tips: Pummelos can be used in the same manner as grapefruit. The skin is particularly good when candied. Remove all skin and pith from the pummelo before eating. Cut thick slabs of skin off the top and bottom. Score the sides and peel pith and skin. Serve with sugar or in fruit salad.

UNITED STATES	
Serving Size: 1 cup	
Calories	70
Protein	1 g
Fat	0 g
Carbohydrates	18 g
Dietary Fiber	2 g
Sodium	0 mg

CANADA	
Serving Size: per 200 g (250 mL/1cup)	
Energy	76 cal.....320 kJ
Protein	1.5 g
Fat	0.1 g
Carbohydrates	19 g
Dietary Fibre	na
Sodium	2 mg
Potassium	434 mg

SOURCE: USDA

NUTRITION FACTS

UNITED STATES
Serving Size: 2 medium
Calories 100
Protein...............................1 g
Fat ....0 g
Carbohydrates..............28 g
Dietary Fiber ....3 g
Sodium ....5 mg

CANADA
Serving Size: per 1 large
Energy...........63 cal.....260 kJ
Protein............................0.4 g
Fat ....0.1 g
Carbohydrates ....17 g
Dietary Fibre ....1.9 g
Sodium ....4 mg
Potassium ....217 mg

UNITED STATES
Serving Size: 1 cup
Calories 110
Protein...............................4 g
Fat ....0 g
Carbohydrates..............25 g
Dietary Fiber ....4 g
Sodium ....25 mg

CANADA
Serving Size: per ½ cup, dry
Energy...........58 cal.....240 kJ
Protein............................2.3 g
Fat ....0.1 g
Carbohydrates ....13 g
Dietary Fibre ....2.3 g
Sodium ....14 mg
Potassium ....267 mg

UNITED STATES
Serving Size: per ½ medium
Calories 150
Protein...............................2 g
Fat ....0.5 g
Carbohydrates..............38 g
Dietary Fiber ....3 g
Sodium ....10 mg

CANADA
Serving Size: per ¼ cup, dry
Energy...........47 cal.....620 kJ
Protein............................2.3 g
Fat ....0.7 g
Carbohydrates ....37 g
Dietary Fibre ....3 g
Sodium ....11 mg
Potassium ....378 mg

UNITED STATES
Serving Size: 1 cup, raw
Calories 9
Protein...............................1 g
Fat ....0 g
Carbohydrates.................2 g
Dietary Fiber ....1 g
Sodium ....46 mg

CANADA
Serving Size: per ½ cup
Energy...........10 cal.....40 kJ
Protein............................1.1 g
Fat ....0.2 g
Carbohydrates ....1.6 g
Dietary Fibre ....0.8 g
Sodium ....49 mg
Potassium ....189 mg

SOURCE: USDA

Quince

General Information: Quinces have a potent, wild, tropical, musky aroma. Shaped like a fat pear or a golden delicious apple, the skin of a quince can be smooth or woolly. Most consider them too tart to be eaten raw. The hard, ivory flesh softens and turns pale orange when cooked. Its flavor also improves admirably when cooked, becoming a rich apple-pear flavor. Quinces have a high pectin content, which makes them a good choice for jams and jellies. They are mostly available in the fall.

Selection & Storage: Select large, fragrant, smooth quinces. Store at room temperature it they'll be used right away. For longer storage, wrap each quince in plastic and refrigerate for a few weeks. Do not allow them to touch each other.

Preparation & Cooking Tips: Peel the quince. Carefully core; the center is hard. Poach, bake or braise. In many cuisines, quinces are paired with meat in stews. Cooked quince can be puréed like applesauce.

Salsify

General Information: Salsify is nicknamed the oyster plant, as some say it has a subtle but definite oyster taste. Others find it tastes like an artichoke heart. There are two commonly available varieties of salsify: the white and the black. White salsify is shaped like a parsnip and is generally 1 foot long and 2½ inches in diameter. Salsify is available from late fall through early spring.

Selection & Storage: White salsify is sold in bunches, usually with leaves attached. Black salsify is sold leafless. Look for medium-sized roots that are not limp (large roots are too fibrous). Wrap tightly in plastic and store in the refrigerator for 1 to 2 weeks.

Preparation & Cooking Tips: Wear rubber gloves when working with salsify. Its rusty-brown juice will stain and possibly cause skin irritation. Peeled salsify will discolor unless it is kept in acidulated water. Braise, boil, steam or purée for soups and chowders.

Sapote

General Information: There are at least ten varieties of sapote (sah-PO-tay) available in the United States. One, also known as sapodilla, is brown, round or egg-shaped and tastes like a pear injected with maple syrup. Black sapote, also known as black persimmon, has green skin and brown flesh that tastes like chocolate pudding. Mamey sapote looks like a football, has salmon flesh and a sweet potato, avocado and honey flavor. White sapote, a member of the citrus family, is the size of an orange or a slightly flattened grapefruit. Its thin skin varies from bright green to yellow. The flesh of a white sapote is marvelously creamy and smooth and is described as orange sherbet, or a blend of mango, coconut, caramel and vanilla. One variety or another of sapote is available January through September.

Selection & Storage: Store at room temperature until soft as a plum.

Preparation & Cooking Tips: Halve, remove seeds and scoop out flesh.

Shanghai Bok Choy

General Information: Shanghai bok choy is a fancy name for baby bok choy. For a green, it is undeniably cute, with its white stalks and deep-green leaves. Shanghai bok choy is milder and sweeter than the mature bok choy. A member of the cabbage family, it has a light, fresh mustard flavor and requires little cooking. It is available year-round.

Selection & Storage: Look for firm, unblemished leaves. Wrap Shanghai bok choy tightly in paper towels and refrigerate in the vegetable crisper for up to 1 week.

Preparation & Cooking Tips: Figure on ¼ to ⅓ pound of Shanghai bok choy per person. Cut as directed by recipe and then wash pieces in two changes of cold water. Shanghai bok choy is good raw in salads. Bok choy's flavor is enhanced by heat. It cooks up quickly to the crisp-tender stage. Braise it whole or split. Shanghai bok choy is delicious in stir-fries and with seared seafood, chicken, beef or pork; or add slivered leaves to soups.

Sin Qua/Chinese Okra

General Information: Sin qua is a giant of the vegetable world. Left to its own devices, it can grow as long as 9 feet! Sin qua, otherwise known as Chinese okra, is best eaten when small, about 1 to 2 feet, as it can become bitter when mature. Its flesh is fibrous and spongy. When cooked, sin qua's flavor is said to be a combination of zucchini and cucumber. Very absorbent, sin qua takes of the flavors of whatever sauce it is in. Sin qua is available year-round.

Selection & Storage: Look for sin qua that is 12 to 18 inches long with firm texture and no sign of mold. Refrigerate in the vegetable crisper for up to 1 week.

Preparation & Cooking Tips: Rinse well. With a vegetable peeler or paring knife, slice off the sharp edges of the vegetable's 10 ridges. If the sin qua is very fresh, it can be sliced very thinly and added to salads. To cook, cut the slices at least ½ inch thick. Sin qua is very good stir-fried with shrimp, in tempura batter or cooked in oyster sauce.

Sunchoke

General Information: Sunchokes, often called Jerusalem artichokes, are the roots of a plant in the sunflower family. Their taste resembles that of an artichoke heart, but the vegetable has nothing to do with the city of Jerusalem. Sunchokes look like bulbous ginger roots with many stubby outcroppings. The ivory flesh has the consistency of water chestnuts and tastes of artichokes and salsify. They are available all year-round.

Selection & Storage: Look for firm sunchokes that are evenly beige. Some say the lumpier ones are more flavorful than the smooth ones. Avoid any with green sprouts or blotches. Refrigerate in a plastic bag for up to 1 week.

Preparation & Cooking Tips: Sunchokes must be scrubbed thoroughly. If peeled before cooking, drop the sunchokes into acidulated water. Sunchokes may be peeled after cooking. The simplest way to serve sunchokes is to steam them for 8 to 15 minutes.

Tabouleh

General Information: Tabouleh (tuh-BOO-luh), which has almost as many spellings as ingredients, is a Middle Eastern dish. Tabouleh is a combination of bulghur wheat, tomatoes, cucumber, parsley, mint, green onions, olive oil and lemon juice. Tabouleh is available, freshly prepared, in the deli section of the supermarket.

Selection & Storage: Tabouleh is sold by weight or container size. After purchase, refrigerate for 3 days.

Preparation & Cooking Tips: To make tabouleh at home, combine 1 cup bulghur wheat with 1 cup cold water, ½ cup fresh lemon juice and ⅓ cup olive oil. Mix well and let stand for 30 minutes at room temperature. Fluff the mixture with a fork. Add 1 cup each of chopped fresh mint and fresh parsley and another ⅓ cup olive oil. Toss again. Add 4 chopped, ripe tomatoes and 1 peeled and chopped cucumber. Toss again and allow to stand 30 minutes. Serves 6.

Tamarinds

General Information: Tamarinds, also called Indian dates, are the bean-shaped, dark-brown pods of the evergreen tamarind tree. They taste like a combination of apricots, dates and lemons. Tamarinds are the "secret" ingredient in Worcestershire sauce. Tamarind pods are about 5 inches long, bumpy and brittle. Crack open a pod to reveal a dark, date-like pulp surrounding small seeds. Sour-sweet tamarinds are used to flavor chutneys and curries. Tamarinds are available year-round.

Selection & Storage: Select unbroken pods with no sign of damage. Refrigerate in a bag for up to 1 month.

Preparation & Cooking Tips: Remove the pod's brittle shell; then remove the seeds. The pulp can be eaten raw or used to make a syrup, curry or chutney. With concentrated tamarinds or a dried block of tamarinds, sift through the pulp to remove the seeds. Follow the instructions on the package.

NUTRITION FACTS

UNITED STATES
Serving Size: 1 medium, cooked
Calories 49
Protein...............................3 g
Fat ....0 g
Carbohydrates ....11 g
Dietary Fiber ....5 g
Sodium ....361 mg

CANADA

NUTRITION FACTS
NOT AVAILABLE

UNITED STATES
Serving Size: 3 ounces
Calories 76
Protein...............................2 g
Fat ....0 g
Carbohydrates.................17 g
Dietary Fiber ....1 g
Sodium ....6 mg

CANADA
Serving Size: per ¾ cup
Energy...........84 cal.....350 kJ
Protein...........................2.2 g
Fat ....0.0 g
Carbohydrates ....19 g
Dietary Fibre ....1.8 g
Sodium ....4 mg
Potassium ....472 mg

UNITED STATES
Serving Size: ½ cup
Calories 152
Protein...............................3 g
Fat ....9 g
Carbohydrates.................17 g
Dietary Fiber ....5 g
Sodium ....265 mg

CANADA

NUTRITION FACTS
NOT AVAILABLE

UNITED STATES
Serving Size: 1 cup
Calories 290
Protein...............................3 g
Fat ....0.5 g
Carbohydrates.................75 g
Dietary Fiber ....6 g
Sodium ....35 mg

CANADA
Serving Size: per ¾ cup
Energy.........215 cal.....900 kJ
Protein...........................2.5 g
Fat ....0.5 g
Carbohydrates ....56 g
Dietary Fibre ....4.6 g
Sodium ....25 mg
Potassium ....565 mg

SOURCE: USDA

NUTRITION FACTS

UNITED STATES	
Serving Size: 1 cup	
Calories	110
Protein	2 g
Fat	0 g
Carbohydrates	28 g
Dietary Fiber	4 g
Sodium	10 mg

CANADA
NUTRITION FACTS NOT AVAILABLE

Taro Root

General Information: The taste of taro root has been likened to a combination of artichoke heart and boiled chestnuts. There are two varieties: dasheen has shaggy brown skin, circled with distinct rings and is about the size of a turnip; the other variety, eddo, is a smaller cormel that attaches to a larger taro root. Both are available year-round.

Selection & Storage: Choose full, firm taro roots with no sign of shriveling at either end. Check for signs of molding. Store in a single layer in a cool, well-ventilated place for a few days. Do not refrigerate.

Preparation & Cooking Tips: Wear rubber gloves; taro roots have an irritating juice. Never eat taro raw. Slice the ends off of the roots. Peel and remove discolored spots. Put in cold water at once. Taro's flavor intensifies during cooking, but the root dries out. Serve baked taro with lots of gravy or meat juices. Taro root's flesh, which can vary from white to yellow to pale pink, turns mauve-gray or violet when cooked.

UNITED STATES	
Serving Size: .55 g	
Calories	2
Protein	0 g
Fat	0 g
Carbohydrates	0.5 g
Dietary Fiber	0 g
Sodium	0 mg

CANADA	
Serving Size: 2g	
Energy	7 cal.....29 kJ
Protein	0.2 g
Fat	0.2 g
Carbohydrates	1.3 g
Dietary Fibre	n/a
Sodium	0.8 mg
Potassium	50.5 mg

Turmeric

General Information: Turmeric is the root of a tropical plant that is related to ginger. Turmeric's flavor is bitter, pungent and aromatic. The skin of turmeric is light brown, but the flesh is a brilliant reddish-orange. Turmeric is boiled or steamed and then dried. It is then ground to a powder, which is the most commonly available form of turmeric.

Selection & Storage: Look for fresh turmeric roots with stubby "fingers" jutting out from the sides. These yield the best-quality turmeric. Look for robust roots with a spicy fragrance. Refrigerate unpeeled turmeric, tightly wrapped, for 3 weeks.

Preparation & Cooking Tips: Don't confuse turmeric with the more expensive saffron. Adding turmeric to a dish will produce a color similar to saffron's warm yellow, but the taste is decidedly different. Use grated turmeric in fish dishes or in rice dishes that can benefit from its pungency and color.

UNITED STATES
NUTRITION FACTS NOT AVAILABLE

CANADA
NUTRITION FACTS NOT AVAILABLE

Yu Choy/Chinese Flowering Cabbage

General Information: Yu choy, or Chinese flowering cabbage, is also known as yow chow sum and choy sum. Yu choy looks much the same as broccoli raab, with narrow stems, dark-green leaves and small yellow flowers. The flowers are edible. Yu choy is milder and sweeter than broccoli raab, and is available year-round.

Selection & Storage: Buy firm stalks with fresh leaves free of brown spots. If the stalks look old or fibrous, do not purchase. Refrigerate, loosely wrapped in a plastic bag, for up to 1 week.

Preparation & Cooking Tips: Yu choy tends to be gritty and needs to be thoroughly washed. Trim the bottoms and then cut into desired size. Then, wash with two changes of water. Yu choy is delicious in salads with other greens. When steamed, it is crisp, yet tender, with a delicate flavor. The mustardy flavor of yu choy pairs well with pasta. It is also good cooked in a bit of olive oil with garlic.

UNITED STATES	
Serving Size: 1 cup, cooked	
Calories	267
Protein	4 g
Fat	14 g
Carbohydrates	33 g
Dietary Fiber	1 g
Sodium	450 mg

CANADA	
Serving Size: per ½ cup	
Energy	120 cal.....500 kJ
Protein	3.1 g
Fat	0.4 g
Carbohydrates	27 g
Dietary Fibre	1.6 g
Sodium	8 mg
Potassium	764 mg

Yuca

General Information: Yuca (YOO-kah) is a prime crop of tropical and subtropical countries. Also known as manioc or cassava, yuca has two main varieties: bitter and sweet. Bitter yuca is poisonous unless cooked. Sweet yuca is dense, softly fibrous, and starchy. It is sweetly chewy. Yuca roots have a brown, bark-like peel and are about 8 to 12 inches long. When yuca is dried and ground, it becomes tapioca. Fresh yuca is available year-round.

Selection & Storage: Sniff yuca for a clean and fresh aroma with no hint of ammonia or sourness. Choose roots that are completely covered with its bark-like skin. Avoid those with cracks, sliminess or mold. Once cut, discard any that have grayish-blue fibers or any darkness near the skin. Do not refrigerate, but keep cool. Yuca will last only a few days.

Preparation & Cooking Tips: To peel, cut into 3-inch sections. Cut an incision down the side. Place a paring knife under the underskin and peel. Remove the central fibrous cord after cooking.

SOURCE: USDA

The Melting Pot

America has become a melting pot in ethnic diversity, enhancing traditional choices for produce. Your favorite supermarket carries many exciting produce selections that add color and tempting flavors to traditional dinner fare.

Foods that seemed strange may soon become common in our culinary vocabulary.

As Americans enlarge their repertoire of fruits and vegetable to meet the 5 per day recommendation, the avant-garde in the kitchen are acquiring unfamiliar ingredients from all over the world to expand the variety of fresh produce served at home.

Take your family on an around world food tour. Specialty produce enhances meals and snacks, reflecting the melting pot of diverse taste and culture called America.

Acidulated water

Used to prevent cut fruits and vegetables from discoloring, acidulated water is simply water with lemon or lime juice added. A good rule of thumb is 1 quart of cold water with 2 or 3 tablespoons of juice added ($\frac{1}{2}$ cup of dry white wine may be used in place of the juice). To prevent browning of produce, simply dip pieces of fruit or vegetables in the water.

Ambrosia

The food of the Greek and Roman gods. A dessert made of oranges and coconut mixed with whipped cream or yogurt.

Antipasto

Typical Italian hors d'oeuvres served hot or cold.

Au gratin

French term describing a dish topped with cheese or bread crumbs and browned.

Bain marie

A French term referring to a pan half filled with hot water kept just below the boiling point in which a container of food is cooked.

Baste

Brushing or spooning a sauce or marinade during roasting to keep moist.

Blanch

Immerse whole or cut vegetables or fruit into boiling water for a few minutes, then plunge in cold water, which stops the cooking process and keeps their colors bright. Also called parboiling.

Bouquet garni

A bundle of herbs tied together or bagged in cheesecloth and added to a dish for flavor; often removed before serving. The classic bouquet garni includes 3 stalks of parsley, 1 stalk of thyme and 1 bay leaf, but may also include chervil, marjoram, lemon, thyme, savory, tarragon, chives or orange zest.

Braise

This method is best for long-cooking vegetables such as carrots, potatoes and eggplant. Slowly cook vegetables in a small amount of liquid (which may then be used as a delicious sauce) in a heavy sauté pan or Dutch oven until vegetables are tender.

Canape

A French word describing an appetizer consisting of toast or cracker topped with a spread.

Clarify

To clarify butter, heat until butter separates. The clear yellow layer on top is the clarified butter. The milky layer below can be discarded or used in soups.

Compote

Sweetened stewed fruit, cooked to keep the fruit as whole as possible.

Coulis

A pourable, liquid puree made of fruit and used as a sauce.

Crudités

Raw vegetables used as hors d'oeuvres, often served with dips.

Crystallize
The term describes the sugar coating of fruits.

Dice
Cut fruits or vegetables into cubes. As a noun, the resulting chunks of fruit or vegetables.

Farinaceous foods
Foods with a high starch content, including rice and potatoes.

Fines herbes
A classic French combination of herbs, mixing equal amounts of parsley, sage, tarragon, thyme, basil, celery seed, chervil, chives, marjoram, mint and sweet savory to flavor soups, sauces, egg dishes, entrées and more.

Flambe
A dish that with alcohol added and set aflame. The alcohol burns off, but the flavor remains.

Flesh
The "meat" of the fruit or vegetable.

Florentine
Indicates a dish has spinach in the recipe.

Freezer burn
Dried out and discolored patches on food caused by exposure to air when frozen and dehydration.

Glaze
Brush the surface with a beaten egg, milk or honey to moisten or give a glossy appearance.

Gremolata
A flavorful blend of parsley, lemon zest and garlic, used as a refreshing garnish for osso bucco and other dishes.

Grill
Many fruits and vegetables can be grilled, either directly upon the grill, in a grilling basket, on skewers or wrapped in foil. Keep fruits and vegetables about 4 to 6 inches from the heat source; avoid excessively high heat or flames. A little oil may be used to prevent drying.

Hull
Removing leafy parts from soft fruits such as strawberries or blackberries.

Infuse
Extracting the flavors of spices or herbs by soaking them in liquid heated in a covered pan.

Julienne
To cut into very small slices lengthwise.

Macerate
Much like marinating, to macerate a food (usually a fruit) means to soak it in a liquid until it is infused with the liquid's flavor. Spirits, such as brandy, rum or liqueur, are often used.

Marinate
Soaking food in a seasoned liquid – often a blend of oil, wine, vinegar and herbs – to add flavor or to tenderize.

Non-reactive pan
A pan that does not contain aluminum, which can discolor some fruits and vegetables such as okra, during the cooking process.

Parboil
Partly cooking food in water or stock.

Pare
Peeling or trimming food, usually vegetables.

Pectin
A substance found naturally in fruits and vegetables. It is an essential ingredient in jams and jellies.

Piquant
A French term referring to a sharp, pungent, possibly sour, flavor.

Pit
As a verb, to pit means to remove the pit from the fruit or vegetable before preparing or eating.

Pith
The whitish strands and pulpy material between the outer peel and membrane of citrus fruits. Some recipes call for pith to be removed.

Plump
To soak dried fruit in liquid until some of the liquid is absorbed. To plump dried fruits such as raisins or currants, cover them in a bowl with boiling water and let stand for 5 minutes before draining.

Poach
To cook in simmering liquid until tender. Apples and pears cook beautifully by this process. Using a large, heavy pot, bring liquid to a boil. Stand fruit or vegetables upright in the mixture, reduce heat and cook slowly until just tender.

Pulp
The juicy insides of a number of fruits and vegetables, particularly citrus fruits and tomatoes.

Purée
Food processed in a food processor or blender until mashed and smooth.

Ramekin
A small, straight-sided ovenproof dish.

Reduce
Thickening a liquid mixture, such as soup or sauce by boiling, uncovered, to reduce excess liquid.

Refresh

Immerse cooked fresh vegetables in cold water to prevent further cooking and revive limp vegetables.

Roux

Equal parts of oil and flour cooked together and added to sauces to thicken.

Sauté

Slice, dice, shred or strip vegetables, then cook in a heavy pan with a little oil or butter over high heat until vegetables are shiny. Then cover and cook at a lower temperature until vegetables are crisp-tender.

Scald

Plunging fruits into boiling water to facilitate the peeling of skins.

Seed

Seed means to remove the seeds from a fruit or vegetable before preparing or eating.

Steam

Bring an inch or so of water to boil in a saucepan or steamer. Place fruit or vegetables in a steamer basket or colander and cover. Steam until crisp-tender.

Stir-fry

Borrowed from the Orient, this method of fast-cooking requires that all ingredients be prepared beforehand and then cooked together in a small amount of oil over high heat while stirring rapidly and constantly.

Sweat

Cooking vegetables in oil over low heat in covered pan until tender. It draws out the juices and flavor.

Zest

Outer, colored part of citrus peel, containing strong flavor. Grated and used to flavor many salads, desserts and sauces.